LANDSCAPE TRAINING MANUAL FOR IRRIGATION TECHNICIANS

IRRIGATION

TRAINING MANUAL SPONSOR

By purchasing this manual you may now access more than 20 training videos and e-learning modules at www.landscapetechnician.net.

You must first *register* on the website. On the home page (top right) you will see login fields. Click on the *Enter Registration Code* link just below those fields. Follow the registration page instructions to *create your account*.

Your Unique Registration Code Is:

DND-9CR-AQW

Only one registration per person is required even if multiple titles were purchased.

Revised (2nd) Edition, November 2011

© 2011 by the Professional Landcare Network (PLANET).
© 2003 by the Associated Landscape Contractors of America. © renewed 2006 by the Professional Landcare Network.
All rights reserved.
This publication is protected by copyright. No part of this book may be reproduced in any form or by any electronic or mechanical means, including information storage and retrieval systems, without permission in writing from the publisher. For more information regarding permission(s), write to: Professional Landcare Network, 950 Herndon Parkway, Suite 450, Herndon, VA 20170; Attention: Communications Manager.

Landcarenetwork.org
(800) 395-2522

Printed in the United States of America.
ISBN 13: 978-0-9840219-1-8
ISBN 10: 0-9840219-1-4

Table of Contents

LANDSCAPE TRAINING MANUAL FOR IRRIGATION TECHNICIANS

Acknowledgements
Introduction

Chapters
1. First Aid & Safety 1
2. Landscape Plan Reading & Calculations 17
3. Irrigation Plan Reading 35
4. Irrigation Concepts 45
5. Irrigation System Components & Maintenance 59
6. Wiring & Electrical Troubleshooting 83
7. Landscape Equipment Safety & Maintenance 101
8. Water Management & Auditing 123
9. Plants & Planting 143
10. Turf Installation 169

Appendices
Work Orders & Communication 180
Field Circuit Test Worksheet 182
Irrigation Drawings 183
Material Safety Data Sheet (MSDS) .186
Snow & Ice Management. 188
Resources 193
Glossary 195

Acknowledgements

AND SPECIAL RECOGNITION

We wish to recognize and express appreciation to the individuals listed below for providing technical and other relevant input on this project.

James Andersen, Timberline Landscaping, Inc., Colorado Springs, CO
Jeff Benway*, Exteriors & Illuminations, Englewood, CO
John Bertsch, The L.L. Johnson Distributing Company, Denver, CO
Wendy Booth, Ivy Street Design Group, Inc., Denver, CO
Bill Cary, Pickens Technical College, Aurora, CO
Whitney Cranshaw, Colorado State University, Fort Collins, CO
Aaron Cruz, Timberline Landscaping, Inc., Colorado Springs, CO
Gary Cyprian, Timberline Landscaping, Inc., Colorado Springs, CO
Kevin Davis*, Gardeners' Guild, Richmond, CA
Tim Emick*, Timberline Landscaping, Inc., Colorado Springs, CO
Braulio Enriquez, The Brickman Group, Nashville, TN
Jim Fridgen*, Swingle Lawn, Tree and Landscape Care, Denver, CO
Tim Gibbons*, All Phase Landscape, Aurora, CO
Elias Godinez*, Pacific Landscape Management, Hillsboro, OR
Kelly Gouge, Swingle Lawn, Tree and Landscape Care, Denver, CO
Robert Graham, All Phase Landscape, Aurora, CO
Joel Hafner*, Fine Earth Landscape, Poolesville, MD
Stacy Hageman, The L.L. Johnson Distributing Company, Denver, CO
Fred Hesser*, Aurora Public Schools, Aurora, CO
Tim LaPointe*, All Phase Landscape, Aurora, CO
Anne Larson, Certified Landscape Professional, Gardening Examiner, Des Moines, IA
Daniel Levine*, ValleyCrest Landscape Maintenance, Parker, CO
Bobby McNary, Timberline Landscaping, Inc., Colorado Springs, CO
Jesus "Chuy" Medrano*, CoCal Landscape Services, Inc., Denver, CO
Salvador Mendoza, The Brickman Group, Cincinnati, OH
Ricardo Muñoz, Schultz Industries, Inc., Golden, CO
Jose Nuñez-Gonzalez, Schultz Industries, Inc., Golden, CO
Jeff Oxley*, Schultz Industries, Inc., Golden, CO
Chuck Perry, The L.L. Johnson Distributing Company, Denver CO
Steve Schreck, Timberline Landscaping, Inc. Colorado Springs, CO
Sol Sinclair-Tucker, Timberline Landscaping, Inc., Colorado Springs, CO
Mary Small, Colorado State University Extension, Jefferson County, Golden, CO
Michael Smith, Control Tech USA, Inc., Parker, CO
Tim Stanford*, Aurora Public Schools, Aurora, CO
Bancroft "Skip" Titter, Denver, CO
John van Roessel*, JVR Landscape, Calgary, Alberta
Bob von Bernuth, Irrigation Association, Arlington, VA
Arvid Vikse*, Exteriors & Illuminations, Englewood, CO
Barry Wagner*, Outdoor Craftsmen, Erie, CO
Thia Walker, Colorado State University, Fort Collins, CO
Richard Wilbert*, SiteSource, Thornton, CO

Special recognition

This manual would not have been possible without the financial and intellectual support of Hunter Industries. We are grateful to the Hunter team for providing subject expertise, ongoing technical advice and numerous illustrations and photographs.

We also wish to thank the following individuals for their tireless efforts to research, write and review material for this manual and the videos. The joint Associated Landscape Contractors of Colorado (ALCC) and Professional Landcare Network (PLANET) task force members who served as the subject matter experts charged with developing content outlines, directing the work of the technical writer and assisting with video production were:

- Cable Baker*, RCB Gardens, BC, who served as the metric consultant to the project
- Brian Benedict*, Pacific Landscape Management, OR
- Tim Caldwell*, The Savanna Group, IL
- Lyle Fair*, All Phase Landscape, CO
- David Iribarne*, City of Petaluma, CA
- Matthew Owens*, Potomac Garden Center, MD
- Eric Schultz*, Schultz Industries, Inc., CO
- Lisa Somnis*, Timberline Landscaping, Inc., CO
- Clifford Ruth*, North Carolina Cooperative Extension, NC
- Jim Stanhouse*, Signature Landscapes, NV, who provided formulas and calculations for sample problems
- Lynda Wightman, Hunter Industries, Missoula, MT and Phil Robisch, Hunter Industries, San Marcos, CA, who provided technical input and numerous photos and other graphic elements
- Tano Delgado*, All Phase Landscape, who translated the videos into Spanish and provided the Spanish voiceover content
- Members of PLANET's International Certification Council who provided the Occupational Analysis on which this curriculum is based.

These individual professionals from throughout North America shared their professional expertise because they are committed to increasing knowledge and improving training in the green industry.

The editorial and production team whose combined skills brought this project to fruition: Lyn Dean, the project manager and technical writer; Karen Meyer, who provided the design and layout of the manuals and the video portal; Helene de Rosier, head of the translation team; Kass Larson, who built the website and video portal; Jennifer Sullivan, the editor; Godot Communications team, that provided cinematography, editing and production of the videos; Kristen Fefes, Becky Garber and Megan Kelley from Associated Landscape Contractors of Colorado (ALCC); and Sabeena Hickman, Shaine Anderson, Karen Barnett, Zane Castle, Cecilia Riek and Sheri Jackson from Professional Landcare Network (PLANET).

The combined effort of everyone who contributed to this project is certainly testimony to the fact that the final outcome is far greater than the sum of the individual parts. Because there were so many people who assisted with this project, we may have failed to recognize all of the contributors and reviewers. We appreciate the active participation of everyone who has shared their expertise and participated in reviewing the content of this manual.

Photo credits

Numerous individuals provided photos and illustrations to enhance the beauty and learning effectiveness of this training manual by helping the words and concepts come alive. Photos and illustrations are individually credited throughout, with the exception of those provided by ALCC, ALCC Excellence in Landscape Awards program and Shutterstock. We wish to provide special thanks to Bugwood.org and to those who provide images to Bugwood, for allowing us to use several photos. We also want to express our thanks to all those unnamed persons who provide images to Shutterstock.

Disclaimer: Every effort was taken to credit correctly each photo and we deeply apologize for any error that may have occurred.

About the manuals and videos

This manual is one of a three-part set developed to train landscape technicians in fundamental aspects of landscape installation, maintenance and irrigation. For quality technical training in landscape installation and irrigation, please refer to the Landscape Training Manual for Installation Technicians and the Landscape Training Manual for Irrigation Technicians. The manuals are accompanied by several related videos that can be viewed from the internet.

Within the body of the manuals, supplemental videos are indicated with a video icon. The access code for the videos was provided with this book.

*The above noted individuals are Landscape Industry Certified

Introduction

LANDSCAPE TRAINING MANUAL FOR IRRIGATION TECHNICIANS

Perhaps in no other area in the green industry are things changing faster than in irrigation contracting and management. In the last 10 years, technology has revolutionized the way irrigation systems are designed, installed and maintained. As a result, irrigation contractors have adapted their work quickly and effectively to use new tools and technology to help conserve water resources and protect water quality – an area that is seeing increasing government regulations and attention.

Recent years have brought improvements in the mechanics and quality of irrigation system components that are more durable, more precise and more efficient than ever before. In addition, high tech innovations have provided a wide range of water management options such as off-site computerized scheduling and on-site controllers that utilize satellite or weather based information.

Yet, amidst these changes and improvements, the properties of water and how it must be managed remain unchanged. Core concepts involving hydraulics, gravity loss and friction loss, as well as certain calculations, are constants for irrigation professionals. Without a solid understanding of these key concepts, the innovative systems and technologies could not be adopted for the greatest benefits.

Irrigation technicians who want to excel at their jobs now need two kinds of knowledge: first, those unchanging principles dealing with the nature of water, and second, how to install and maintain irrigation designs properly and teach customers of all kinds to use their systems effectively.

This manual and supplemental web-based videos were developed to help irrigation technicians in this process. They were written and developed by practicing irrigation specialists who deal with the concepts and installations every day. This manual offers high quality employee training and is also a study guide for testing under the Landscape Industry Certified Exterior Technician program in the United States and Canada. Every attempt has been made to give the reader up-to-date information about skills and techniques commonly used in irrigation work.

Chapter 1

First Aid & Safety

What You Will Learn

After reading this chapter, you will be able to:

- Explain the importance of prevention and describe preventive measures that can reduce the chances of accidents or injuries on the job for at least eight situations.

- Discuss the importance of preparation and name at least five daily preparation measures that will aid in the event of a medical emergency.

- Name at least 10 possible emergency situations you could encounter on the job.

- Describe possible symptoms of medical conditions and what actions to take and to avoid for at least 10 medical emergency situations that could occur.

- Find training in first aid, CPR (cardiopulmonary resuscitation), and use of an AED (automated external defibrillator).

Chapter 1

Preview

Prevention
- Barricades
- Product use
- Clothing and PPE
- Driving safely and vehicle safety
- Electricity
- Footwear
- Lifting
- Training

Preparation
- Communications
- Emergency contacts
- First-aid kit
- First aid and CPR training
- Known allergies

Situations and Responses
- Multiple health and related issues

Manual sponsored by **Hunter Industries**

Overview

If a medical emergency occurs on the job, the injured or sick person needs to get immediate help. However, the care given to the victim before emergency medical personnel arrive can make the difference between a full or partial recovery, or even life and death. This chapter details how to be prepared to assess and deal with an emergency situation until medical help is available.

Three important sections are covered in this chapter:

1. **Prevention** — Steps to prevent accidents and medical emergencies from occurring.
2. **Preparation** — Ways to be prepared for emergencies.
3. **Situations and Responses** — How to identify different emergency medical situations, and how to help or respond appropriately until medical professionals arrive.

Prevention

Prevention is the best way to minimize the risks of being injured. Many accidents are easily preventable when you identify potential hazards. The table that follows lists several situations that may be encountered on the job in the landscape industry, as well as some preventive measures that can reduce the number and severity of mishaps.

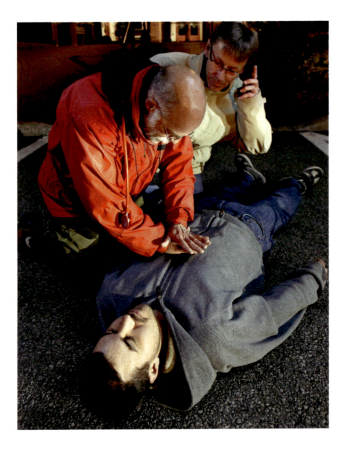

IMPORTANT!

Familiarity with this information does not qualify you to give emergency medical care. However, proper training in first aid, CPR (cardiopulmonary resuscitation), and AED (automated external defibrillator) may qualify you to perform certain procedures during an emergency.

This information is intended to provide an introduction to topics about which people working in the landscape industry should know. The Red Cross, St. John's Ambulance (Canada) and other resources can provide more comprehensive information, as well as qualified instruction in first aid and safety.

Preventive Measures

Situation	Preventive Measures
Barricading/Securing Work Area	If hazards such as holes, trenches, falling limbs, etc., are present in your work area, set up barricades to keep people well away from the danger areas.
Product Use	Before working with pesticides, fertilizers or other products, read the label and material safety data sheets (MSDS) carefully! Remember, the "label is the law." Take proper precautions by wearing protective clothing and equipment and using other safety devices (such as a respirator), as recommended on the label for pesticides and other products. Also see the next section, *"Clothing and Personal Protective Equipment."* Most states require specific training and/or certification or licensure for those who use and apply products. In Canada, ensure that you have the applicable provincial pesticide applicator's license.
Clothing and Personal Protective Equipment (PPE)	Wear clothing and safety equipment appropriate for the job being performed. A task analysis or job site analysis completed prior to beginning work helps determine the potential hazards and the PPE required. Protective gear might include gloves, hardhat, goggles or safety glasses, earplugs, safety vests, etc. When working with pesticides or other products, a respirator may be necessary. Pesticide labels include information on the proper protective equipment to use/wear. Be sure to read the label. See also Product Use above.
Driving Safely and Vehicle Safety	Before backing up a vehicle, always look in all directions. Use a spotter whenever one is available. When driving a vehicle with a trailer in tow, use special care. The recommended maximum speed for a truck hauling a trailer is 55 mph (90 km/hr). When operating a tractor designed for one person, do not allow a passenger to ride along. Special care must be taken when transporting products in a vehicle. Hazardous materials (hazmat) training is required in most areas when transporting products. Additional training, licensing or permits may be required by employers and employees when transporting specific products and/or when transporting large volumes of products, or other liquid cargo, including water. Also, be aware of and up-to-date on local and state/provincial regulations for transporting products across state/provincial borders. *Note: If talking on the phone when driving, always use a hands-free device. This is the law in many states and provinces. The best safety precaution is to avoid talking on the phone while driving and never text while driving!*

Landscape Irrigation

Preventive Measures

Situation	Preventive Measures
Electricity	If a power line is down, immediately contact the electric company and ensure that no one enters the surrounding area until the site is secured by the service provider. Before working on any electrical equipment, ensure that the electricity has been turned off and remains off while working. If working on a controller or wiring, make sure the electricity is turned off and disconnected from the power source.

Mountain High Tree, Lawn & Landscape Company

Footwear	Wear proper, safety-approved work boots while performing landscape work. In the United States, the Occupational Safety and Health Administration (OSHA) designates standards for footwear. In Canada, work boots must be labeled with the Canadian Standards Association (CSA) green triangle.
Lifting	Face the object being lifted to avoid twisting your back. Bend at the knees with a straight back when lifting. Lift with your legs. Do not strain to lift a heavy object. If the object is too heavy, get help. Take extra care when carrying something over an uneven or slippery surface.

Swingle Lawn, Tree & Landscape Care

Tools and Equipment	Ensure that all tools and equipment are properly maintained and functioning correctly. All guards should be in place and guards should not be altered or removed. When transporting tools and equipment, be sure the correct safety procedures are followed for securing them in the vehicle or trailer.

Jocelyn Chilvers Design

Training	All personnel must receive proper training in the tasks they will perform. Make sure that there is a documentation process in place that tracks when each individual received training and also when updated training or certification is required. Only those who have had adequate instruction and supervision are allowed to operate trenchers, mowers, chainsaws, or any other power equipment. Some power equipment requires certification (for example, forklifts).

Preventive Measures

Situation	Preventive Measures
Training (cont'd)	Hazmat (hazardous materials) training is a requirement in most areas. In Canada, the equivalent training requirement is through WHMIS (Workplace Hazardous Materials Information System).
Utility Locates and Trench Shoring	Before digging or trenching, check for underground utility lines by calling the utility. In 2007, the Common Ground Alliance (CGA) launched 811 as the U.S. national "call before you dig" number. Calling 811 will connect you directly to the local one-call number. In Canada, each province has its own "one-call" number to call before digging.  Be cautious as even this information has its limitations and can be incorrect. The one-call services will typically only locate public utility lines, not private lines such as 110 power to parking lot lights, signage or sprinkler controllers. Keep in mind that it is always the contractor's responsibility to call the utility notification service, pot-hole marks by hand-digging to determine the depth of lines, stay 18" away from marks with machinery, and to make sure marks remain visible. It is common to call for re-marking several times during a project.  Typically, during landscape construction projects, trench shoring becomes necessary to prevent collapse of soil, which can cause injury or death to workers. Specific training and certification are available and required in most areas for any excavation where a worker's head or shoulders will be below the native soil level. Various shoring systems are available and shoring design must meet federally regulated standards.
Weather	*Hot weather* — Drink lots of water before being thirsty — at least 16 ounces (500 ml) every hour. Wear lightweight clothing and a hat. Apply sunscreen. Schedule frequent rest periods in the shade and drink water. Use good judgment. If someone collapses from heat stress, help by responding as indicated below under Heat Cramps and Heat Exhaustion, but also use it as a sign to be sure all workers are sufficiently hydrated. *Cold weather* — Dress warmly and stay dry. Choose materials that hold body heat — wool is a better choice than cotton. If the temperature is likely to change, dress in layers. Remove clothing during the day as temperatures warm and add layers as the temperatures cool. Keep waterproof clothing handy in case it rains or snows while working. Hypothermia danger increases with wind, time of exposure and wetness. *Lightning storm* — If possible, get indoors or into a vehicle. If you cannot get indoors, go to a low spot and crouch down. Do not seek shelter under a tree.

Landscape Irrigation

Preparation

Although preventive measures, such as those outlined above, can reduce the likelihood of injury or accidents, emergency situations may still occur. When someone is in need of urgent care, and time is critical, the resources should be readily available. Be prepared! The following table lists several ways to be prepared for emergencies.

Preparation Measures

Category	Preparation Measures
Communications Emergency Contacts	*Cellular phones* — Be sure to have a charged and functioning cellular phone on hand. Some landscape contractors require all vehicles to have a mobile charger for all communication devices. *Two-way radios* — Since cellular phones do not operate in all locations, be sure to have two-way radios on hand as well for communication during emergencies. Keep a list of emergency phone numbers on hand. While 911 should be your first call in an emergency, other important phone numbers include: • Poison control center • Electric company • Other utilities
Level One or Two First Aid Kit	Keep a first aid kit handy and make sure it is fully stocked. Ensure that the kit has disposable latex and non-latex gloves. Wear them to prevent contact with blood and fluids, and potential exposure to blood-transmitted diseases.
First Aid/CPR/AED Training	Training in first aid, CPR (cardiopulmonary resuscitation) and AED (automated external defibrillator) can make a difference between life and death in emergency situations. This training is available from the Red Cross and a variety of other sources. To find a course in your area visit www.redcross.org and in Canada, www.redcross.ca.
Known Allergies	Be sure to know whether anyone on the work crew has allergies. If someone with severe allergies carries specific medication or an anaphylaxis kit, be sure to know where it is and how to use it. Anaphylaxis is a rapid and severe allergic reaction that can be life threatening if not treated immediately. Be sure that the medications are not expired, since many booster shots have a shelf life of only one year, after which time they may not be effective.

Emergency Situations & Effective Responses

Even when reasonable precautions are taken, medical emergencies may still arise. If an injury or other medical emergency occurs, it is important to stay calm and think clearly before acting.

GET HELP—Call 911 immediately

When possible, have one person call for help while the most qualified individual attends to the injured or sick person. Below is a list of emergency medical situations (in alphabetical order) that may occur. For each situation, there is a list of:

- What to Look For — Descriptions of common symptoms to help identify the cause of the problem
- DOs — Actions to take while waiting for emergency medical personnel to arrive
- DON'Ts — Actions to avoid

Keep first-aid kits in vehicles and in the shop.

Note: Recommended actions to take during emergencies are updated over time. Be sure to keep up to date on training.

Complete paperwork

When the emergency has passed, remember to complete appropriate paperwork, such as company accident reports related to insurance and workers compensation claims.

Allergic Reactions

Some people experience allergic reactions when exposed to substances that most people tolerate without a problem. These substances can include venom from spiders, bee stings, certain foods, pollen or medications. Some allergic reactions can be severe or even life threatening.

What to look for

- Hives
- Wheezing or labored breathing
- Swollen eyes, face or tongue
- Weakness or dizziness
- Cramps or abdominal pain
- Nausea or vomiting

Do

- Ensure victim has an open airway and is breathing.
- If the victim carries emergency allergy medication, help him/her take it.
- If the reaction is from a bee sting, try to remove the stinger. Scrape it away but don't squeeze it (don't use tweezers). Squeezing could release more venom.
- If a bee sting does NOT cause a visible allergic reaction, remove stinger and treat with alcohol.

Don't

- Don't place a pillow under the victim's head if he is having difficulty breathing.
- Don't squeeze the wound area of a bee sting to remove the stinger.

Amputation

If a body part becomes severed due to an accident, it can sometimes be re-attached by physicians at a trauma center.

What to look for

- Body part that has been cut off
- Bleeding

Do

- Control bleeding at the amputated site using firm, direct pressure with clean, dry dressing or cloth. Elevate the injured area over the heart level, or if lying, elevate the feet.
- Gently rinse the severed body part with water only.
- Wrap the severed body part in gauze or a clean cloth or towel. Place it in a plastic bag. Keep cool and dry but do not allow to freeze. If possible, put the wrapped part in water with a small amount of ice.
- Call 911 or transport person to a hospital as quickly as possible.

Don't

- Don't place the severed body part directly on ice.

Bleeding

The loss of a small amount of blood is usually not serious. However, losing two or more pints of blood (one or more litres) can be life threatening. Be cautious when exposed to another person's blood. There is a risk of infection from blood-borne pathogens. Consider seeking medical attention if direct contact with another person's blood occurs.

What to look for

All sources of bleeding

Do

First: Apply direct pressure to the wound using a sterile dressing or clean cloth.
If you do not believe a bone is broken: Elevate the wounded area above the level of the heart.
If bleeding continues: Apply pressure to a pressure point. There are 26 pressure points located along main arteries. This will not be effective unless a pressure point is located. In either case, continue direct pressure to the wound.
If bleeding still does not stop: As a last resort, apply a tourniquet. Since this can cut off the blood supply to tissues that need it, apply a tourniquet only in a life-threatening situation.

Don't

- Don't move the person unless he/she is in immediate danger.
- Don't try to clean a large wound.
- Don't remove a dressing if it becomes blood soaked. Put a new one on top.
- Don't remove any object stuck in the wound as it may cause more severe bleeding.

Burns Caused by Heat

Burns are classified by their degree of severity. While minor burns are not serious, severe burns can be life threatening and/or cause permanent disfigurement.

1st-degree burns Least severe. Only the top layer of skin, the epidermis, is injured. Sunburn is considered a 1st-degree burn.

2nd-degree burns Injures the first layer of skin and the one below it, the dermis. Hot liquids can cause 2nd-degree burns.

3rd-degree burns Most severe. Destroys all skin layers. Muscle and bone can also be damaged. Fire and prolonged contact with hot objects are among the most common causes of 3rd-degree burns.

What to look for

1st-degree burns:
- Pain
- Red skin
- Slight swelling

2nd-degree burns:
- Pain (can be severe)
- Red or mottled skin
- Blisters
- Swelling
- Wetness

3rd-degree burns:
- White or charred skin
- Little or no pain

Do

1st-degree burns:
- Submerge the burned area (1st and 2nd-degree burns only) in cold water or hold under cold running water.
- Apply cloth or towels soaked in cool water.

2nd-degree burns:
- Submerge the burned area in cold water (1st and 2nd-degree burns only).
- Apply cloth or towels soaked in cool water.
- Gently blot the burn dry and apply a sterile dressing or clean cloth.
- If arms or legs are burned, elevate them.

3rd-degree burns:
- Cover the burned area with a thick sterile dressing or clean cloth.
- If arms or legs are burned, elevate them.
- Call 911

Don't

2nd-degree burns:
- Don't break blisters.

3rd-degree burns:
- Don't apply ice or water to severe burns.
- Don't put ointments, creams or other substances on severe burns.
- Don't remove charred clothing that is sticking to burns.

Landscape Irrigation

Chemical Burns/Chemicals in Eyes

Some products can cause serious burns to the skin or eyes. Quick action will often reduce injury from chemical contact. A Material Safety Data Sheet (MSDS) is required under the OSHA Hazard Communication Standard in the U.S. and WHMIS (Workplace Hazardous Materials Information System) in Canada. The MSDS provides detailed information prepared by the manufacturer of a hazardous product. It describes the physical and chemical properties of the product, as well as information such as toxicity, procedures for spills and leaks, and storage guidelines.

The MSDS also indicates the potential health and physical hazards of a chemical and describes how to respond effectively to exposure situations. Refer to the sample MSDS in the Appendix.

What to look for

- Red, irritated skin
- Rash
- Blisters
- Pain

Do

- Have the MSDS immediately available.
- If possible, identify the chemical involved. Save the packaging from the product that caused the burn.
- Call 911 and a poison control center.
- Wash the product off of skin as quickly as possible with a shower or hose. Flush with lots of water for 20 minutes.
- If a product gets in the eye, flush the eye with water for 20 minutes. Tilt the head sideways, hold the eyelid open, then flush from the inner corner (by the nose) outward.
- If the person has contacted dry lime, brush it away before flushing with water.

Don't

- Don't rub if a product is in an eye.
- Don't apply ointments to a product burn.

Wear safety glasses to protect eyes.

Electrical Injury

Contact with electrical current is potentially fatal as it can stop the heart and damage internal organs. The degree of injury depends on the strength of the current and how long the victim is exposed to it.

CAUTION: Keep people and equipment the proper distance from power lines to avoid arcing. Arcing is bright luminous discharge of current that is formed when a strong current jumps a gap in a circuit. Arcing can cause burns and in some cases explosions.

What to look for

- Charred skin
- Blisters
- Irregular or no heartbeat
- Rapid or no breathing
- Rapid or no pulse
- Muscular pain
- Fatigue
- Headache

Do

- If the victim is in contact with electrical current, turn off the electricity at the source.
- If the victim is in contact with electrical current and it cannot be turned off, use a dry rake handle, broomstick, rope or other non-conductive object to separate the victim from the current.
- Monitor victim for pulse and breathing.
- Treat electrical burns as severe 3rd-degree burns (see Burns on page 9).

Don't

- Don't approach the victim until you are sure the area is secure.
- Don't touch someone who is in contact with electrical current.
- Don't move a victim of electrical injury unless he or she is in immediate danger.

Eye Injury — Dust and Small Particles

Wear the eye protection appropriate for the tasks. Make sure the eye protection fits properly, stays in place and is in good condition. If dust or small particles get in the eye, which can happen even when wearing eye protection, use the following guidelines.

What to look for

- Eye redness that may be corneal abrasion
- Eye scratches/ lacerations

Do

- Use eyewash to flush the eye with generous amounts of liquid.
- Cover for protection if needed, even to prevent rubbing.
- Seek medical attention if a particle doesn't wash out or if redness or pain persists.

Don't

- Don't rub the eye as that can cause additional scratching or embed a particle more deeply, causing further damage.

Fractured Bones

A fracture is when a bone cracks or breaks. Bone fractures are often obvious, but not always. If you are not sure of the severity of the injury, assume there is a fracture.

What to look for

- Sound or feel of bone snapping
- Bone piercing through the skin
- Pain
- Swelling
- Deformed appearance of limb

Do

- If the bone has pierced skin, cover with a clean dressing.
- Immobilize the injured area. For an injured arm or leg, use a splint or sling to secure the limb in the position in which it was found.
- Seek medical attention right away.

Don't

- Don't move the victim until the injured area is immobilized.
- Don't apply pressure and get pressure off of affected area.

Frostbite

Frostbite is when the skin freezes from prolonged exposure to cold temperatures. Fingers, toes, ears, nose and cheeks are most often affected. Risk of frostbite is higher in conditions of cold temperature with high wind speed and if clothing or skin is wet. See also "hypothermia" on page 14.

What to look for

Mild frostbite:
- Redness
- Burning
- Coldness
- Numbness

Severe frostbite:
- Swelling
- Blisters
- Gray or blotchy white skin
- Blackened skin

Do

- Rewarm the frostbitten area by placing in warm (not hot) water for at least 30 minutes.
- If warm water is not available, gently wrap the frostbitten area in wool or warm blankets.
- Drink warm, decaffeinated beverages (caffeine can restrict circulation).

Don't

- Don't rewarm the frostbitten area too quickly.
- Don't rub the frostbitten area.
- Don't break blisters.
- Don't walk if feet are frostbitten.
- Don't warm the frostbitten area with dry heat from a heating pad, heat lamp, campfire, hair dryer, radiator or other source.
- Don't drink caffeinated beverages, such as coffee or tea.
- Don't have alcohol or tobacco.

Heart Attack

Fatalities from heart attacks can often be avoided if the victim receives prompt medical attention. An automated external defibrillator (AED) can check a person's heart rhythm, advise whether a shock is needed, and tell rescuers what steps to take. AEDs are becoming more common and may be located in sports arenas, office buildings and shopping malls. Some states and provinces require notification of local emergency communications (emergency medical services or EMS) of the location and type of AED. Keep your First Aid/CPR/AED certification current.

What to look for

- Discomfort or pressure in chest
- Shortness of breath
- Irregular heartbeat
- Sweating
- Jaw pain
- Heartburn or indigestion
- Arm pain (usually in left arm)
- Upper back pain
- Nausea
- Anxiety

Do

- Tell someone else what is going on and call or ask someone to call 911.
- If victim uses heart medicine (nitroglycerin), place a tablet under the tongue.
- Position the victim in a half-sitting position with the legs up and bent at the knees.
- Put a pillow or rolled towel under the knees. Support the back.
- Loosen any clothing around the victim's neck, chest and waist.
- Monitor for breathing and pulse.
- If trained in CPR, be prepared to begin chest compressions.

Don't

- Don't wait to see if pain goes away.
- Don't allow victim to eat or drink anything.
- Don't allow victim to lie down if breathing is difficult.

Heat Cramps and Heat Exhaustion

Heat illness occurs when the body's core temperature rises above safe levels. Heat-related illnesses should be treated immediately and aggressively, as consequences can be severe or even life threatening.

What to look for

Heat cramps:
- Muscle cramps, usually in the legs or abdomen

Heat exhaustion:
- Cool, pale, moist skin
- Dilated (enlarged) pupils
- Heavy perspiration
- Extreme thirst
- Headache
- Nausea, vomiting
- Weakness or dizziness

Do

- Seek medical attention.
- Move to a cooler place.
- Lie the victim down with legs elevated.
- Cool down with water, wet towels, a cold compress, a fan, etc.
- Drink water, sports drink or salt water (1 teaspoon salt to 1 quart water; 5 ml salt to 1 litre).

Don't

- Don't drink beverages containing alcohol or caffeine.
- Don't drink more fluids if victim is vomiting.

Heatstroke

As with other heat-related illnesses described above, heatstroke should be treated immediately and aggressively, as consequences can be severe or even life threatening.

What to look for

- Dry, hot, red skin
- Dilated (enlarged) pupils
- Rapid pulse
- Rapid breathing
- Weakness
- Muscle spasms
- Seizures
- Unconsciousness

Do

- Lower the body temperature rapidly by immersing in cold water, applying cold packs or any other method available.
- Call 911.

Don't

- Don't eat or drink anything.

Hypothermia

Hypothermia occurs when the body's internal temperature drops below 95° F (35° C). Hypothermia danger increases with wind, time of exposure, and wetness. Be aware that hypothermia can occur even when land temperatures are above freezing and when water temperatures are near but below body temperature.

What to look for

- Shivering
- Clumsiness
- Confusion
- Slurred speech
- Muscle stiffness
- Irregular heartbeat

Do

- Move to a warm, dry location and rewarm.
- Replace wet clothes with dry clothes or blankets.
- If victim can swallow easily, offer warm, sweetened beverages.
- Seek medical attention.

Don't

- Don't rewarm with dry heat from a heating pad, heat lamp, campfire, hair dryer, radiator or other source.
- Don't drink caffeinated beverages such as coffee or tea.
- Don't have alcohol or tobacco.

Impaled Objects

Impaled objects have pierced some part of the body and remain in place. In most cases, it should be left in place to prevent further damage.

What to look for

- An object that has pierced the body

Do

- If object is in an eye, place pads around eye then place a cup or cover over the object to secure it. Cover the other eye to reduce eye movement.
- If the object has penetrated the cheek and is in the mouth, DO remove it. This will prevent choking if a piece breaks off. Place packs between teeth and cheek wall. Secure object with padding if it hasn't penetrated cheek.
- Seek medical attention.

Don't

- Don't remove the object unless it has penetrated the cheek (see the "DO" column to the left).

Nosebleed

Nosebleeds not resulting from injury are usually not serious.

What to look for

- Blood running from the nose

Do

- Sit up and pinch nostrils shut.
- If bleeding cannot be stopped, get medical assistance.

Don't

- Don't tip head back. Blood can drain into the back of throat and cause choking.

Snakebite

Bites from poisonous snakes are potentially deadly, though fatalities are preventable if antivenom is given within four hours. Poisonous snakes include pit vipers (rattlesnakes, cottonmouths and copperheads) and coral snakes.

What to look for

- Pain and/or swelling
- Discoloration
- Dizziness
- Droopy eyelids
- Slurred speech
- Drowsiness
- Drooling and/or nausea
- Sweating
- Difficulty breathing
- Shock
- Delirium

Do

- Lie still.
- Place the bitten area lower than the heart.
- Seek medical attention.

Don't

- Don't cut into a snakebite.
- Don't apply a tourniquet.
- Don't apply a cold compress.

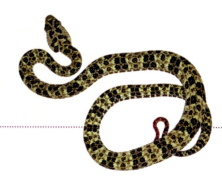

Spinal Cord Damage

Injury to the spinal cord can result in loss of movement below the site of the injury. If someone is found unconscious and you are not sure if spinal cord damage has occurred, assume that it has.

What to look for

- Pain in head, neck, back or abdomen
- Numbness or tingling in arms or legs
- Paralysis
- Loss of bladder control
- Anyone found lying down unconscious

Do

- Keep the victim still.
- Call 911.
- Monitor for breathing and pulse.

Don't

- Don't move the injured person unless there is a life-threatening danger.
- Don't twist the head, neck or back.

Summary

A recurring theme throughout the chapters in all of the *Landscape Training Manuals* is the importance of prevention. Prevention includes assessing potential hazards and taking appropriate precautions to safeguard yourself and others, as well as to protect property (landscape and buildings) and equipment from damage.

Although prevention is a key factor, accidents and injuries may still occur. Preparation addresses readiness to respond to an accident or injury. This means having the appropriate training and tools available to respond, including first aid/CPR/AED training, charged cellular phones, a properly stocked first-aid kit, awareness of AED devices at the work site, etc.

Several common emergency situations have been described. For each, characteristics are listed to help identify what to look for. General guidelines about how to respond are given (actions to take and actions to be avoided) that can help someone who becomes hurt or incapacitated.

Appropriate training is important both for accident prevention and best response during emergency situations when accidents or medical situations occur.

Appropriate responses to emergency situations can help save lives.

Chapter 2

Landscape Plan Reading & Calculations

What You Will Learn

After reading this chapter, you will be able to:

- Identify the common elements of landscape plans and describe the purpose of each.
- State the purpose of the drawing scale and identify two common methods to indicate the scale.
- Describe what the architect's, engineer's and metric measuring scales are used for and describe the differences between the three scales.
- Describe how to take measurements from landscape drawings using an architect's scale.
- Give examples of landscape applications for making linear, area and volume calculations.
- Demonstrate understanding of "order of operations" when doing mathematical calculations.
- Use various formulas to correctly calculate and estimate quantities of landscape materials.
- Estimate or measure areas of turf, native grass, beds to be maintained and/or linear feet of edging to be managed.
- Calculate plant spacing.
- Use the 3-step method for solving for an unknown quantity.
- Use the tables and formulas in an Appendix as resources in the future.

Chapter 2

Preview

Common Elements of Landscape Plans
- Title block
- North arrow
- Legend
- Specifications
- Drawing scale

Estimating from Landscape Plans
- Scales for measuring plans
- Architect's, engineer's and metric scales
- How to use a scale

Useful Calculations for Landscape Work
- Reminders for mathematical calculations
- Linear, area and volume calculations
- Solving for an unknown
- Calculating plant spacing

Test Your Knowledge — Sample Problems
- Answers to sample problems

Manual sponsored by Hunter Industries

Landscape Irrigation

Overview

A landscape plan provides a lot of valuable information. It may show the original landscape layout or proposed changes to a current landscape, including plant locations or relocations, materials to be used and location of items like private electric or gas lines, domestic water supply lines, sewer lines, sprinkler lines, irrigation mainlines, isolation valves and backflow preventers, or relevant and existing fixtures, drainage, and/or topography on the site.

Reading and interpreting landscape plans enables you to:
- Understand the overall intentions of the landscape designer, i.e., what the final result will be.
- Identify the types and locations of materials that are specified by the design in the landscape plan.
- Estimate the quantity of materials needed to complete construction according to the design.
- Understand and estimate the maintenance needs according to the design.
- Avoid damaging private site utilities that a utility location service may not locate as part of their service.

This chapter describes the most common elements of landscape plans and how to estimate, calculate and measure installation materials or areas to be maintained.

Common Elements of Landscape Plans

There are several different types of landscape plans, including grading plans, planting plans, irrigation plans, etc. Though each type of plan has its unique drawing conventions, there are some elements that are common to nearly all landscape plans, such as, title block, specifications, north arrow, drawing scale and legend.

Title block

A title block is a collection of information about the landscape project and the drawing. It is typically contained in a box or rectangle along the bottom or side of a drawing on each page of a plan. Some or all of the following information is placed in the title block:

- Project name
- Client's name
- Sheet number
- Date
- Project location
- Designer's name
- Consultant's name
- Sheet title
- Drawing scale (sometimes)
- Landscape architect's seal (in some cases)

North arrow

A north arrow is a graphic symbol on the plan with an arrow or indicator that points north. The arrow's purpose is to orient a plan to the site so there is no confusion as to where the various aspects of construction or maintenance are to take place. North arrows are drawn many different ways. See one example below.

Shown below: Generic Title Block and to the right, a North arrow

Professional Landcare Network | Page 18

Legend

Landscape designers use symbols on the plan to represent various different elements in the landscape. These elements can include physical objects, such as plants, pipes, sprinklers, etc., or imaginary objects, such as property boundaries and contour lines. A drawing legend shows the symbols used on a plan and indicates what they represent.

Specifications

Specifications are a list of instructions and requirements that the landscape contractor must follow when implementing a design. Specifications are intended to ensure that landscape construction is carried out to a satisfactory level of quality.

Specifications often include guidelines for:
- Product selection
- Excavation
- Planting techniques
- Grading and drainage
- Maintenance requirements
- Site preparation
- Mulching
- Cleanup
- Soil preparation

Drawing scale

Landscape plans are created to scale. This means there is a direct relationship between the distances on the drawing and the actual distances on the site. The drawing scale specifies this relationship.

For example, if a landscape plan has a drawing scale of 1" = 20', a walkway measured to be 1" long on the plan is actually 20' long on the site represented by the plan. In metric units, if a landscape plan has a drawing scale of 1:100, a walkway measured to be 1 cm long on the plan is actually 100 cm or 1 metre long on the site represented by the plan.

Scale: 1" = 30'

The drawing scale is often shown with a scale bar like the one above. Scale bars are marked off in inches or fractions of an inch and labeled with the actual distance that each increment represents. Metric drawing scales use metric units. For example, the scale may read: 1cm = 15m.

There are several ways the drawing scale may be shown on a landscape plan. They include:

Equivalence
Example: "one inch equals fifty feet"

This means 1" measured on the plan represents a distance of 50' on the site.

Ratio
Example: 1:600

A ratio shows the relationship between a measured distance on the plan and the actual distance on the site using the same units of measure. In this example, 1" measured on the plan equals 600" (50') on the site. Metric scales always show ratios.

Estimating from Landscape Plans

In landscape construction, estimating refers to the process of calculating — with reasonable accuracy — quantities of materials and con-struction or maintenance costs associated with a project.

Quantity estimates are based on measurements taken either on-site or read directly from a landscape plan. Once these measurements are totaled and quantified as square feet (yards or metres) of wood mulch, linear metres (or yards) of metal edging, or number of deciduous trees (2" caliper), costs can be assigned to materials, labor, equipment and sub-contractors to arrive at a cost estimate for an entire project.

Landscape Irrigation

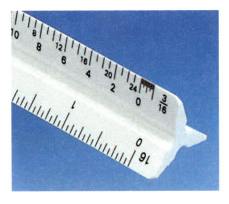
Architect's Scale

Engineer's Scale

Metric Scale

Scales for measuring plans

To estimate quantities from a landscape plan, you must be able to take accurate measurements from a drawing. This is greatly simplified by using a measuring device called a measuring scale, which should not be confused with a drawing scale described in the previous section. The most commonly used scales are approximately 12" (30 cm) long and look somewhat similar to a common ruler, but with a triangular profile. Each face of the scale is marked in two or more increments corresponding to a different drawing scale. The three most common scales are the architect's scale, engineer's scale and the metric scale. When using the correct measuring scale properly, distances on a plan can be read directly as distances on the site. (See *"How to read a scale"* on page 21).

Each is discussed below, followed by instructions on how to read a scale.

Architect's scale

Architect's scales are used to measure distances on plans drawn in architectural units. In architectural units, distances are read in feet, inches and fractions of an inch. Architectural units are often used in landscape plans for residential properties.

Architect's scales are marked in increments corresponding to the most commonly used architectural drawing scales ranging from 1/16" = 1' (one sixteenth of an inch equals one foot) to 3" = 1' (three inches equals one foot).

Engineer's scale

Engineer's scales are used to measure distances on plans drawn in decimal units. In decimal units, distances are read in feet and tenths of a foot. Decimal units are typically used in landscape plans for commercial properties.

Engineering scales are marked in divisions ranging from 10 units per inch to 60 units per inch. Each face of the engineer's scale can be used to read several different drawing scales. For example, the face marked in 20 units per inch can be used to read plans drawn at 1" = 2' (each mark equals 0.1'), 1" = 20' (each mark equals 1') or 1" = 200' (each mark equals 10'). With an engineer's scale, you can easily measure distances on plans with scales ranging from 1" = 1' to 1" = 600'.

Metric scale

Metric scales are used to measure distances on plans drawn in metric units of either metres or millimetres. Commonly used scales are 1:50, 1:75 and 1:100 for smaller projects.

Each face of the metric scale can be used to read several drawing scales. For example, the face marked 1:100 can be used for plans drawn to that scale, with each unit on the scale indicating one metre on the site. It can also be used for a 1:1000 drawing, with each unit on the scale indicating ten metres on the site.

Landscape Plan Reading & Calculations

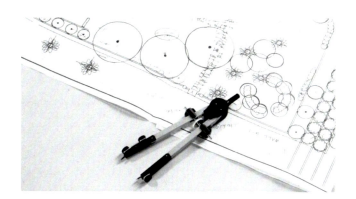

Scaled drawings provide the basis for measurements.

Verify plan scale

Regardless of the scale you are using — engineer's, architect's or metric — be sure to use the correct scale, the one that matches the plan. Also, be sure that the plan was not enlarged or reduced, because this will cause the measurements to be incorrect. To verify whether the plan has been enlarged or reduced, use your scale ruler to measure the drawing scale on the plan.

Example
The plan scale states 1 inch equals 20 feet (1:20).
- When the measuring scale is placed on the plan's printed scale, the drawing scale, 1 inch equals 40 feet.
    - o This means that the plan has been reduced by half, causing the scale to double.
- Use the one inch equals 40 feet side of the measuring scale to obtain accurate measurements of the site.

How to use a scale

To use a scale, flip to find the face that matches the scale of the drawing you are working with.
1. Measure between two points on the drawing, as you would with a common ruler.
2. Read the distance from the scale. This is the actual distance. There is no need to perform calculations or conversions.

Read the top line of numbers on the scale from left to right and the bottom measurements from right to left (⅛" scale is read from left to right and the ¼" scale is read from right to left). Refer to the photos of the scale rulers on the previous page and to the example below explaining how to read scale.

How to read an architect's scale

Often, the ruler will have two scales on it with the marks alternating one and then the other, odd to even. In the examples below, the ⅛" scale numbers are in **bold**, the ¼" scale numbers are *italic*.

Determine the scale to be used on your plan.
Example: ⅛" = 1 foot (or ¼" = 1 foot).

Select the corresponding scale on the ruler. Each side will have four scales on it, so make sure you have the correct one. The scale will have several short marks to the left (or right) of a zero which represent divisions of a foot. Long marks to the right (or left) of a zero represent feet.

On the ⅛", the divisions are two inches each. On the ¼" scale, the divisions are one inch each. Confirm the readings illustrated below as 12' 6" and 7' 9".

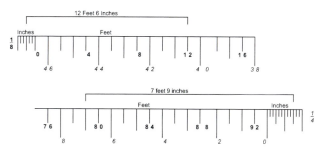

Architect's scale (Note: The architect's scale, as shown above, is not to scale. Its purpose is to illustrate how to read a scale.)

Scales are intended to be used as follows:

Line up the zero mark with the beginning of the section you want to measure. The nearest mark the line passes is the foot measurement. Then slide the ruler to the right (or left) and count the number of inches.

Useful Calculations for Landscape Work

In landscape construction, some knowledge of basic algebra and geometry is extremely useful and has many applications. Using a few simple formulas, you can calculate a lot of important quantities, such as:

- The number of ground cover plants needed in a planting bed
- The amount of concrete required for a patio
- The quantity of sod needed to cover a lawn area
- The linear feet of trimming or edging that needs to be maintained
- The area of turf to be mowed
- The amount of mulch or rock required

The following sections explain how to estimate quantities of materials or square feet of area to be maintained using formulas to calculate perimeters, areas and volumes.

Note: For all calculations, be sure all numerical measures are converted to common units before making calculations. For example, yards, feet, inches and fractions of feet must be converted to a common unit. Similarly, metres and decimal equivalents of metres (centimetres) must be converted to one common unit. Several tables showing common conversions are given in the Weights and Measures Conversions *Appendix* of this manual.

{
U.S. and Imperial Units
Occasionally, you may see the term "imperial" when referring to units of measurement. Imperial refers to a system of measurement that is based on old English measures. The U.S. system of measurement was founded on imperial units and some U.S. units are identical to imperial units. Most of the rest of world has adopted metric units.

U.S. distance measures, such as inches, feet and yards, and U.S. weight measures, pounds and ounces, are identical to imperial measures. Therefore, sometimes these units will be called U.S./imperial units or imperial units, usually when being compared to metric units.
}

Length Conversions — U.S. / Imperial

Unit	Abbreviation or Symbol	Equivalents	Metric Equivalents
inch	in or "	0.083 foot	2.54 centimetres
foot	ft or '	12 inches 0.333 yard	30.48 centimetres
yard	yd	3 feet 36 inches	0.9144 metre
rod	rd	5.5 yards 16.5 feet	5.029 metres
mile	mi	5280 feet 1760 yards 320 rods	1.609 kilometres

Length Conversions — Metric

Unit	Abbreviation or Symbol	Equivalents	Imperial Equivalents
millimetre	mm	0.1 centimetre 0.001 metre	0.039 inch
centimetre	cm	10 millimetres 0.01 metre	0.39 inch
metre	m	1000 millimetres 100 centimetres	1.0936 yards
kilometre	km	1000 metres	0.6214 mile

Reminders for mathematical calculations

Order of operations
The following is the order to follow when doing calculations. Following correct order for each calculation helps avoid errors, which could be costly.
1. First, calculate the value of the operations in brackets (parentheses). When there are brackets within brackets, do the operations in the inner brackets first, moving from left to right.
2. Next, calculate the value of the exponents. (See more about exponents below).
3. Then, multiply and divide from left to right in the order the operations occur.
4. Finally, add and subtract from left to right in the order the operations occur.

How mathematical operations are expressed
Be alert to different methods of expressing mathematical operations. Multiplication and division can be expressed different ways.

Multiplication and division
Multiplication can be written several different ways, such as with an asterisk (*), an "x" or brackets (parentheses). The following examples are three ways that "8 times 3" can be represented.
  8 * 3; 8 x 3; (8) (3) or 8 (3)

If multiplying using a symbol, no sign is needed. For example, 2w (where w = width) means "2 times w."

A fraction bar is also a division symbol, so:
  $1/3$ is $1 \div 3$

Dividing a fraction is the way to convert it to a decimal equivalent.

Example:
If a measurement is 2 inches, how many feet is it?
  2"/12"/ft = 0.167 feet

Exponents
The power that a number is raised to is equivalent to the number of times you multiply that number by itself. Some examples are:
  $2^3 = 2 \times 2 \times 2 = 8$
  $3^2 = 3 \times 3 = 9$
  $5^2 = 5 \times 5 = 25$

π (pi)
If π (pi) is in the calculation, always use the value 3.14. Pi is the ratio of a circle's circumference to its diameter. It is used in all calculations involving circles, as shown in the sections that follow.

Decimal Equivalents: Inches in Decimal Feet

Inches	Feet
1.0	0.083
2.0	0.167
3.0	0.250
4.0	0.333
5.0	0.417
6.0	0.500
7.0	0.583
8.0	0.667
9.0	0.750
10.0	0.833
11.0	0.917

Decimal Equivalents: Minutes in Decimal Hours

Minutes	Hours
5	0.08
10	0.17
15	0.25
20	0.33
25	0.42
30	0.50
35	0.58
40	0.67
45	0.75
50	0.83
55	0.92

Linear calculations
Linear dimensions refer to the distance along an edge or the combined distances along several edges. The total distance around a closed shape, such as a square or rectangle, is called the perimeter. The distance around a circle is called the circumference. In landscape irrigation and construction, linear calculations have many applications, such as determining the quantity of edging or trimming needed around a planting bed, or estimating the length of piping needed for an irrigation system.

Landscape Irrigation

For most shapes, finding the perimeter means adding up the length of all the sides. To make calculations on a circular perimeter, the radius must be known or measured (and is equal to half the diameter) as well as the value pi (π), which is 3.14. Circumference (C) = $2\pi r$. Common shapes and the formulas used to calculate the perimeter (the value P) are given in this section. Sample problems are given below.

Example calculations — Linear

Rectangle

length (l) = 70

width (w) = 20

Rectangle Perimeter = 2l + 2w
 P = 2 x 70 + 2 x 20
 P = 140 + 40
 P = 180

Trapezoid

a = 4

c = 6

b = 10

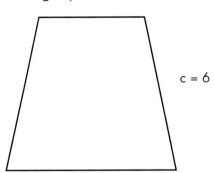

Trapezoid Perimeter = a + b + 2c
 P = 4 + 10 + 2 x 6
 P = 14 + 12
 P = 26

Circle

r = 9

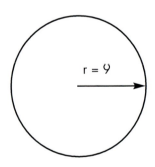

Circle Circumference (Perimeter) = $2\pi r$
 C = 2 x 3.14 x 9
 C = 6.28 x 9
 C = 56.52

Triangle

a = 8

b = 8

c = 4

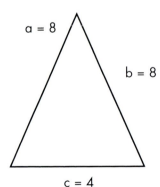

Triangle Perimeter = a + b + c
 P = 8 + 8 + 4
 P = 20

Area calculations

Area is the measure of the surface within a closed boundary. In landscape applications, area calculations can be used for numerous situations, such as determining the number of ground cover plants needed to fill a planting bed, the quantity of sod needed to cover a new lawn area or the amount of product needed to treat an area with fertilizer or weed control compounds.

If measurements are being used to order materials, it may be necessary to add a waste factor, for example for sod installation. (See the chapter "Turf Installation").

Area calculations are usually expressed in square units, such as square inches, square feet, square yards or square metres. Sometimes, square units are shown with the superscript "2," an exponent, such as m^2 (square metres) or ft^2 (square feet).

This section lists formulas used to calculate the area (the value A) for a number of common shapes.

Example calculations — Area

Rectangle

length (l) = 70
width (w) = 20

Rectangle Area = l x w
A = 70 x 20
A = 1400

Trapezoid

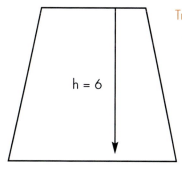

t = 4
h = 6
b = 10

Trapezoid Area = ½ (b + t) h
A = (10 + 4) 6 / 2
A = (14) 6 / 2
A = 84 / 2
A = 42

Circle

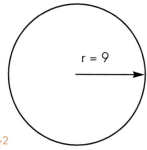

r = 9

Circle Area = πr^2
A = 3.14 x 9^2
A = 3.14 (9 x 9)
A = 3.14 x 81
A = 254.34

Triangle

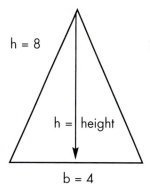

h = 8
h = height
b = 4

Triangle Area = ½ (base x height)
A = 4 x 8 / 2
A = 32 / 2
A = 16

Landscape Irrigation

Area calculations for irregular shapes

Calculating the area for shapes with irregular borders requires a different method than those described above. The results may not be as precise as for regularly shaped areas. To approximate the area of a shape with irregular borders, use the following procedure:

1. Measure a long (L) axis of the area.

2. Measure the width at right angles to the length. Make multiple measurements at equal distances.

3. Add all width measurements and divide by the number of measurements taken to get the average width.

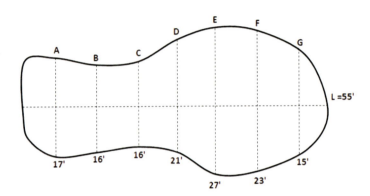

Average width (W) = (A+B+C+D+E+F+G)/7
= (17+16+16+21+27+23+15)/7
= 135 ft/7 = 19.3 ft

Area = L x W
Area = 55 ft x 19.3 ft = 1061.5 sq ft

Computer Aided Drafting (CAD)

Powerful and affordable desktop computers, coupled with sophisticated software designed specifically for landscape applications, have taken over many of the manual tasks associated with creating landscape drawings and performing estimates. While the drafting table has not disappeared, CAD workstations are now commonplace in the offices of many landscape professionals.

Electronic drawings are created with special CAD programs. These programs have drawing tools that automate much of the labor that goes into creating grading plans, planting plans, irrigation designs, and other types of landscape drawings.

When an electronic drawing has been created, it is a simple process to perform estimates by extracting information from the drawing. For example, a click on a line representing the edge of a planting bed can instantly display the perimeter of the bed and the area contained within it. This is especially valuable for estimating the area of beds that have irregular shapes. Manual measuring techniques can be more difficult and inaccurate when shapes are irregular.

Volume calculations

Volume refers to the space contained within a three-dimensional space, such as a pool or mound of soil. There are many landscape applications in which volume calculations are used, such as to determine the amount of topsoil needed in a planting bed, or the quantity of concrete needed to construct a patio. The methods and formulas used to calculate the volume (V) of several common shapes are shown below.

Volume calculations are expressed in cubic units, such as cubic feet, cubic yards or cubic metres. Sometimes you may see cubic units shown with the exponent "3," such as m^3 (cubic metres).

{ Because many suppliers sell product by weight rather than by volume, the volume may need to be converted to weight such as pounds or tons. Refer to the conversion chart found in the Appendices to convert volumes to weights for mulch and rock. Be aware that moisture content may affect the weight of certain products. }

Example calculations — Volume

Cuboids (box shapes)

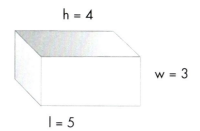

Cuboid Volume = Area of base x height
V = (l x w) x h
V = (5 x 3) x 4
V = 15 x 4
V = 60 cubic units

Cylinder

Cylinder Volume = πr^2 x h
V = 3.14 x $(3)^2$ x 3
V = 3.14 x 9 x 3
V = 84.78 cubic units

Landscape Irrigation

Additional example problems

Linear Calculations

Sample problem:
You need to install metal edging around a circular planting area. The planting area has a radius of 12'. How much edging will you need?

Answer:
Find the circumference of the planting bed.
$C = 2\pi r$
$C = 2 \times 3.14 \times 12$
$C = 75.36'$ of edging

Sample metric problem:
You need to install metal edging around a circular planting area. The planting area has a radius of 3.5 m. How much edging will you need?

Answer:
Find the circumference of the planting bed.
$C = 2\pi r$
$C = 2 \times 3.14 \times 3.5$
$C = 21.98$ m of edging (round to 22 m)

Volume Calculations

Sample problem:
You are preparing a new planting bed 8' by 12'. You will need to fill it with 8" of topsoil. How many cubic yards of topsoil will you need?

Answer:
1. Convert to like units. Convert the depth (8") from inches to feet by dividing by 12.
   8"/12"/ft = 0.67 ft
2. Calculate the volume of topsoil (in cubic ft.) using the volume formula:
   $V = A_b \times h$
   (where A_b is the area of the base found by multiplying the length by the width)
   $V = (8' \times 12') \times 0.67'$
   $V = 96' \times 0.67' = 64.32$ cu ft
3. Convert cu. ft. to cubic yards by dividing by 27 (1 cu yd = 27 cu ft).
   $V = 64.32$ cu ft / 27 = 2.38 cu yds of topsoil

Sample metric problem:
You are preparing a new planting bed 2.5 m by 4.5 m. You will need to fill it with 20 cm of topsoil. How many cubic metres of topsoil will you need?

Answer:
1. Convert to like units. Convert the depth (20 cm) to metres by dividing by 100.
   20 cm/100 cm/m = 0.20 m
2. Calculate the volume of topsoil (in cubic m) using the volume formula:
   $V = A_b \times h$
   (where A_b is the area of the base found by multiplying the length by the width)
   $V = (2.5$ m $\times 4.5$ m$) \times 0.20$ m
   $V = 11.25$ sq m $\times 0.20$ m = 2.25 cu m

Sample problem:
A landscape plan calls for a rock fines walk to be installed. The walk is 6' wide and 20' long. If the rock fines are 4" thick, how many cubic yards will be required to complete the job?

Answer:
To find the solution to this problem, use the formula for volume of a cube: (Volume = Area of the base x height)
V = Ab x h

1. Convert the height (4") from inches to feet so you are working with like units. To convert from inches to feet, divide by 12.
   4"/12" = 0.33'

2. Calculate the volume in cubic feet.
   V = Ab x h
   V = (6' x 20') x 0.33'
   V = 120' x 0.33' = 39.6 cubic feet

3. Convert cubic feet to cubic yards by dividing by 27.
   V = 39.6 cubic feet/27 = 1.47 cubic yards

Sample metric problem:
You are preparing a new planting bed 2.5 m by 4.5 m. You will need to fill it with 20 cm of topsoil. How many cubic metres of topsoil will you need?

Answer:
To find the solution to this problem, use the formula for volume of a cube: (Volume = Area of the base x height)
V = Ab x h

1. Convert the depth (10 cm) from centimetres to metres so you are working with like units.
   To convert from cm to m, divide by 100.
   10 cm/100 cm/m = 0.10 m

2. Calculate the volume in cubic metres.
   V = Ab x h
   V = (1.8 m x 6.0 m) x 0.10 m
   V = 10.8 sq m x 0.10 m = 1.1 cu metres

Solving for an unknown — 3-step method

Working in the landscape industry requires solving many different types of problems. Encountering situations that require solving for an unknown are common. A good problem-solving strategy can help you be more effective. Although there are other methods that work, the 3-Step Method is practical and can be utilized in different scenarios.

The following problem is an example you might encounter on a landscape job. Use the 3-Step Method as shown.

Example: Calculating cubic yards from cubic feet
If 54 cubic feet equals 2 cubic yards, how many cubic yards is 400 cubic feet? Use the 3-Step Method to find the solution.

Step 1: What Information is given?
Read the problem carefully and write down the given or known information. Pay attention to units of measure. A common mistake made when working with word problems is forgetting to use the correct units of measure. Units of measure can be mixed in the same work problem; forgetting to use the correct units of measure throughout the problem often results in the wrong answer. The information given is:

54 cubic feet = 2 cubic yards

Landscape Irrigation

Step 2: What information is being asked?
What do you want to find out?
How many cubic yards = 400 cubic feet

Step 3: Plug in the known values and solve the equation.
This kind of math problem uses a proportions equation. It has three known values and one unknown value, called "X" in this example. The unknown is the value you are asked to find. Set up a proportions equation so that the two known variables are on top, across from each other. Place the other two variables (which include the unknown) below, making sure to line up like units. In the example:

X = 54 cubic feet = 2 cubic yards
    400 cubic feet = X cubic yards

Notice that cubic feet are lined up together and cubic yards are together. Next, cross multiply.

X = 54 cubic feet ⟋⟍ 2 cubic yards
    400 cubic feet   X cubic yards

$$X = \frac{400 \text{ ft}^3 \times 2 \text{ yd}^3}{54 \text{ ft}^3}$$

Cubic feet (ft³) cancel each other out and the equation is left with cubic yards (yd³).

$$X = \frac{800 \text{ yd}^3}{54}$$

X = 14.8 yd³

Answer: 400 cubic feet is 14.8 cubic yards

Example: Weight and volume conversion
A cubic yard of ³/₄" river rock weighs 1.25 tons. How many tons would be required if 1.47 cubic yards are needed?

Step 1: What Information is given?
1 cubic yard = 1.25 tons
Step 2: What information is being asked?
How many tons = 1.47 cubic yards?
Step 3: Plug in the known values and solve the equation.

X = 1 cubic yard = 1.25 tons

1.47 cubic yards = X tons

X = 1 cubic yard = 1.25 tons

1.47 cubic yards = X tons

$$X = \frac{1.47 \text{ cubic yards} \times 1.25 \text{ tons}}{1 \text{ cubic yard}}$$

X = 1.84 tons

Metric Example: Weight and volume conversion
A cubic metre of river rock weighs 2.57 metric tonnes (2,750 kg). How many metric tonnes would be required if 1.18 cubic metres are needed?

Step 1: What information is given?
1 cubic metre = 2.57 metric tonnes
Step 2: What information is being asked?
How many tonnes = 1.18 cubic metres?
Step 3: Plug in the known values and solve the equation.

X = 1 cubic metre = 2.57 metric tonnes

1.18 cubic metres = ? metric tonnes

$$X = \frac{1.18 \text{ cubic metres} \times 2.57 \text{ metric tonnes}}{1 \text{ cubic metre}}$$

X = 3.03 metric tonnes

Calculating plant spacing

The number of plants needed for a bed is basically the area of the bed divided by the space needed by the plant. Follow the planting spacing instructions and calculate the number needed for the bed area.

U.S./Imperial

If planting spacing is given in inches and bed measurements in feet:

Number of plants = area/(spacing in inches/12)^2

Notice that if planting distance is 12", the number of plants is equal to square footage because 12/12 = 1 and 1^2 = 1 (one squared). Refer to the examples shown below.

To calculate the number of flats:
Number of flats= number of plants/plants per flat

Sample problem:
A bed size is 6 ft by 20 ft. Plant spacing is 18" apart on center (O.C.) and plant distance from edges is 9". There are 15 plants per flat.
How many plants are needed?
How many flats are needed?

Answer:
Area = 6 ft x 20 ft = 120 sq ft
Number of plants = area/(spacing in inches/12)^2
= 120/(18/12)^2
= 120/(1.5)^2
= 120/2.25
= 53.3 plants (round to 53)
Number of flats = 53/15 = 3.5 flats.
Round up to 4 flats.

Metric

If planting spacing is given in centimeters and bed measurements in metres:

Number of plants = area in m^2 x 10,000/(spacing between plants in cm)^2

To calculate the number of flats:
Number of flats = number of plants/plants per flat

Sample metric problem:
Bed size is 1.8 m x 6 m. Plant spacing is 45 cm on center (O.C.). Plant distance from edges is 22.5 cm. There are 15 plants per flat.
How many plants are needed?
How many flats are needed?

Answer:
Area = 1.8 m x 6 m = 10.8 m^2
Number of plants = area x 10,000/(spacing in cm)^2
= 10.8 x 10,000/(45)^2
= 108,000/2025
= 53.3 (rounds to 53)
Number of flats = 53/15 = 3.5
Round up to 4 flats.

Test Your Knowledge - Sample Problems

Solve the following problems. The numbers represent a unit of measure (UM). Assume the UM is the same for all numbers on a given figure (for example, cm, in, ft or m).

1) What is the linear perimeter of the rectangle?

2) What is the area of the rectangle?

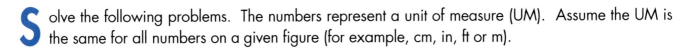

length (l) = 85

width (w) = 15

3) What is the perimeter of the parallelogram?

4) What is the area of the parallelogram?

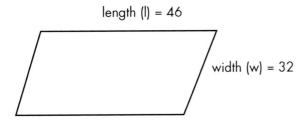

length (l) = 46

width (w) = 32

5) What is the perimeter of the trapezoid?

6) What is the area of the trapezoid?

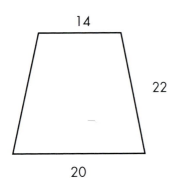

14

22

20

7) What is the perimeter of the circle?

8) What is the area of the circle?

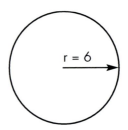

r = 6

9) What is the perimeter of the triangle?

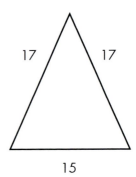

17   17

15

10) What is the area of the triangle?

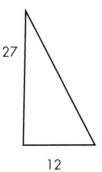

27

12

11) What is the volume of the cuboid?

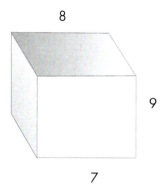

12) If it takes 2.5 hours to install 4 inches of mulch in a 200 square foot planter bed, how long will it take to install 4 inches of mulch in a planter bed that measures 700 square feet?

13) A right triangular area measures 17' 10" x 54' 2". How many square feet are in the triangle, to the nearest whole number?
   A. 463 square feet
   B. 757 square feet
   C. 387 square feet
   D. 483 square feet

Answers to sample problems

1) Rectangle Perimeter = 2l + 2w
   P = (2 x 85)+ (2 x 15)
   P = 170 + 30; P = 200

2) Rectangle Area = l x w
   A = 85 x 15; A = 1275

3) Parallelogram Perimeter = 2b + 2a
   P = (2 x 46) + (2 x 32)
   P = 92+ 64; P = 156

4) Parallelogram Area = b x a
   A = 46 x 32; A = 1472

5) Trapezoid Perimeter = a + b + 2c
   P = 14 + 20 + (2 x 22)
   P = 34 + 44
   P = 78

6) Trapezoid Area = ½ (b + t) h
   A = (14 + 20) 22;   A = 34 x 22
          2   2

   A = 748   A = 374
         2

7) Circle Circumference (Perimeter) C = 2πr
   C = 2 x 6 x 3.14; C = 3.14 x 2; C = 37.68

8) Circle Area = πr²
   A = 3.14 x 6²; A = 3.14 (6 x 6); A = 3.14 x 36
   A = 113.04

9) Triangle Perimeter = a + b + c
   P = 17 + 17 + 15; P = 49

10) Triangle Area = ½ (base x height)
    A = 27 x 12;   A = 324
          2   2
    A = 162

11) Volume = w x l x h
V = 8 x 9 x 7; V = 504

12) Use the 3-Step Method to find the solution.
Step 1: What information is given? 200 square feet = 2.5 hours
Step 2: What information is being asked? How many hours = 700 square feet
Step 3: Plug in the known values and solve the equation.

   X = 200 square feet = 2.5 hours
   700 square feet = ? hours

   X = 200 square feet ⟶ 2.5 hours
   700 square feet ⟶ ? hours

X = 700 sq ft x 2.5 hours
       200 sq ft
X = 8.75 or 8 hours and 45 minutes

13) D. 483 square feet

To find answer, first convert to inches:
17' 10" = (17 x12) + 10 = 214"
54' 2" = (54 x12) + 2 = 650"

Area of triangle = ½ b x h
= ½ x 650" x 214"
= 69,550 sq in

Convert to sq ft:
144 sq in = 1 sq ft
69,550 sq in/144 sq in/sq ft = **483 sq ft**

Summary

Landscape plans contain a lot of valuable information. They may show existing layout or proposed changes, and they can specify materials required, including plant numbers and types, pavers, edging, mulch, etc. Other relevant fixtures and lines are also indicated, such as irrigation pipes, sewer lines, drainage, sprinkler valves, etc. Landscape plans are drawn to scale, meaning a distance on the plan is equivalent to a distance on the work site. The drawing scales vary on plans and can be indicated using different methods. The architect's, engineer's and metric measuring scales are very helpful tools and can be used to determine distances and estimate quantities by making measurements directly on the plan. Be sure that the correct measuring scale is utilized and that the units are read properly.

Basic math skills are required to calculate quantities, such as perimeters (or circumferences), areas, volumes and plant spacing. Use the correct math formula to calculate and estimate quantities of materials to avoid waste and shortages. Math skills are required for converting to different units and also for finding unknown quantities.

Useful tables for converting weight and measure are included in the *Appendices* to this manual.

Chapter 3

Irrigation Plan Reading

What You Will Learn

After reading this chapter, you will be able to:

- Identify symbols on the plan that represent irrigation system components.
- Use the legend to identify specific components and differentiate between like components.
- Determine where flow rates are identified for sprinkler heads.
- Identify which items on an irrigation plan can be counted for take-off and which items must be measured.
- Give examples of items that do not appear on a plan but must be included in a take-off.
- Recognize standard abbreviations for pipe fittings for a take-off.

Chapter 3

Preview

Elements of an Irrigation Plan

Base map

Other Useful Information on Plans

- Symbols
- Sprinkler heads
- Pipes and sleeves
- Valves and other symbols
- Zone flow rate and precipitation rate

Material Take-Offs

- Counted items
- Measured items
- Items that do not appear on a plan

Manual sponsored by **Hunter Industries**

Landscape Irrigation

Overview

An irrigation plan is a "roadmap" that shows the contractor how to install the irrigation system at a site. It contains important information about the layout of the irrigation, and the specific components and materials needed to construct the system. A variety of topics related to reading and interpreting irrigation plans are covered in this chapter.

Elements of an Irrigation Plan

An irrigation plan is a scale drawing that illustrates the layout of an irrigation system. Symbols are used to represent the various components of the system, such as points of connection, valves, sprinkler heads, piping and controllers.

Irrigation plans contain elements also found in most landscape plans. These common elements include:
- Title block
- North arrow
- Legend
- Specifications
- Drawing scale
- Installation details
- Notes
- Company name and/or designer
- Date

To read and interpret an irrigation plan prior to actual installation, you must be able to orient the plan correctly relative to north and to measure distances accurately based on the drawing scale. For more information about these topics, refer to the *"Landscape Plan Reading and Estimating"* chapter.

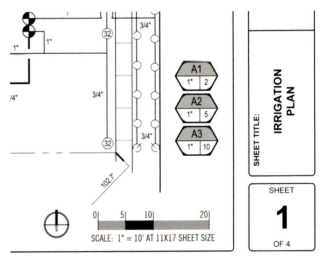

Excerpt from an Irrigation plan showing drawing scale and north arrow.

Base map

On an irrigation plan, the layout for the irrigation system is drawn over a base map. The base map shows important features of the landscape, which can include:

- Property lines
- Structures
- Turf areas
- Planting beds
- Trees
- Decks and patios
- Walkways, roadways and parking areas
- Utilities

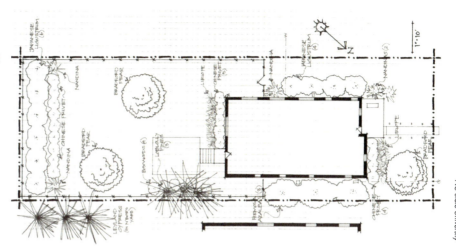

Example of a base map. No irrigation information is displayed yet.

Other Useful Information on Plans

Symbols

The various components of an irrigation system are represented by graphic symbols drawn on the base map. Some of the symbols used are graphic conventions. However, different irrigation designers may use different graphic symbols, and even some of the conventional symbols may be changing. Always check the drawing legend to be certain of a symbol's meaning.

A typical irrigation plan has symbols that represent system components, such as:

- Point of connection
- Backflows
- Controllers
- Valves
- Quick couplers
- Sleeves
- Piping (mainline, laterals, drip)
- Sprinkler heads with a variety of nozzles
- Drip and micro-irrigation systems
- Bubblers

Sprinkler heads

Sprinkler heads are usually drawn as small circles, squares or other geometric shapes. These symbols are often partially shaded or divided to designate the spray pattern of the sprinkler. For example, a full undivided circle would represent a 360-degree or full-circle sprinkler. On the other hand, a circle divided in half (or half shaded) would represent a 180-degree or half-circle sprinkler. See the sample Spray Head Irrigation Legend and the Rotor Legend.

The drawing legend lists the types of heads/nozzles (manufacturer and series) shown in the plan, as well as the radius and flow rate in gallons (litres) per minute (gpm or L/m) of each type of head.

> Note: Although there are some graphic conventions common to most plans, different irrigation designers may use different graphic symbols to represent the same item. Always check the drawing legend to be sure you know which symbols represent which components.

Landscape Irrigation

SPRAY HEAD IRRIGATION LEGEND

SYMBOL	DESCRIPTION	MANUFACTURER PART NO.	NOZZLE	PATTERN	FLOW	RADIUS	PRES
SHRUB POP UP HEADS							
○	SHRUB POP UP	6" SHRUB POP UP	8F	FULL	1.00	8'	30
	SHRUB POP UP	6" SHRUB POP UP	8H	HALF	0.50	8'	30
	SHRUB POP UP	6" SHRUB POP UP	8T	THIRD	0.35	8'	30
	SHRUB POP UP	6" SHRUB POP UP	8Q	QRTR	0.25	8'	30
	SHRUB POP UP	6" SHRUB POP UP	5H	HALF	0.20	5'	30
	SHRUB POP UP	6" SHRUB POP UP	5T	THIRD	0.15	5'	30
	SHRUB POP UP	6" SHRUB POP UP	5Q	QRTR	0.10	5'	30
○	BUBBLER POP UP	4" SHRUB POP UP	STRIP BUBBLER	--	0.20	--	30
●	BUBBLER POP UP	4" SHRUB POP UP	STRIP BUBBLER	--	0.30	--	30
TURF POP UP HEADS							
	TURF POP UP	6" TURF POP UP	10F	FULL	1.60	10'	30
	TURF POP UP	6" TURF POP UP	10H	HALF	0.80	10'	30
	TURF POP UP	6" TURF POP UP	10T	THIRD	0.50	10'	30
	TURF POP UP	6" TURF POP UP	10Q	QRTR	0.40	10'	30
	TURF POP UP	6" TURF POP UP	8F	FULL	1.00	8'	30
	TURF POP UP	6" TURF POP UP	8H	HALF	0.50	8'	30
	TURF POP UP	6" TURF POP UP	8T	THIRD	0.35	8'	30
	TURF POP UP	6" TURF POP UP	8Q	QRTR	0.25	8'	30
	TURF POP UP	6" TURF POP UP	5H	HALF	0.20	5'	30
	TURF POP UP	6" TURF POP UP	5T	THIRD	0.15	5'	30
	TURF POP UP	6" TURF POP UP	5Q	QRTR	0.10	5'	30

NOTE: ALL SPRAY HEADS TO BE INSTALLED WITH CHECK VALVE OPTION

ROTOR LEGEND

SYMBOL	DESCRIPTION	MANUFACTURER PART NO.	NOZZLE	PATTERN	FLOW	RADIUS	PRES
TURF POP UP HEADS							
31	TURF ROTOR	6" TURF POP UP ROTATOR	1600 F	FULL	1.60	16'	30
31	TURF ROTOR	6" TURF POP UP ROTATOR	1600 H	HALF	0.80	16'	30
31	TURF ROTOR	6" TURF POP UP ROTATOR	1600 Q	QRTR	0.40	16'	30
32	TURF ROTOR	6" TURF POP UP ROTATOR	2100 F	FULL	3.00	21'	30
32	TURF ROTOR	6" TURF POP UP ROTATOR	2100 H	HALF	1.50	21'	30
32	TURF ROTOR	6" TURF POP UP ROTATOR	2100 Q	QRTR	0.75	21'	30
33	TURF ROTOR	6" TURF ROTOR	2500 FULL	FULL	4.00	25'	45
33	TURF ROTOR	6" TURF ROTOR	2500 HALF	HALF	2.00	25'	45
33	TURF ROTOR	6" TURF ROTOR	2500 QRTR	QRTR	1.00	25'	45

NOTE: ALL ROTORS TO BE INSTALLED WITH CHECK VALVE OPTION

Sample sprinkler legends

Hunter Industries

Pipes and sleeves

Lateral pipes are drawn as straight lines. Pipe segments connect to other system components such as sprinkler heads, valves and other pipes. The system mainline is drawn with a heavier line than laterals, or as a dashed line. Pipe sizes (diameters) are indicated on the plan next to some or all of the pipe segments drawn. The plan legend will identify the type or class of pipe required, such as Class 160, 200, or Schedule 40 or 80.

In many irrigation systems, pipes cross other pipes without connecting. This is shown on an irrigation plan with a small arc drawn "jumping" over one of the crossing pipes. If two pipes cross on a plan with no arc shown, the two pipes connect.

Pipe sleeves are used when a pipe goes under a walkway, roadway or other hard surface. This allows for mainline and wires or lateral lines to pass through the larger sleeve pipe, and for repairs to be performed without removing the paved surfaces above. On an irrigation plan, pipe sleeves are shown as parallel dashed or dotted lines and are often a heavier class (wall thickness) than mainline or lateral piping to prevent being crushed or damaged. Refer to the Irrigation Equipment Legend and then the sample Residential Irrigation plan to find where the pipe sleeves will be installed.

Valves and other symbols

Remote control valves are typically drawn as circles, divided into quarters, with two opposite sections shaded. Each valve has an information box, usually a hexagon or a box, listing the zone or station number, valve size and flow rate expressed as gallons (litres) per minute. See the sample Irrigation Equipment Legend, as well as the sample Residential Irrigation Plan on pages 28-29 to view the valves and valve information.

A variety of other symbols and abbreviations may be used to represent other valves, backflows, quick couplers, controllers and other components. Using the Irrigation Equipment Legend, locate each of the listed valves on the sample Residential Irrigation Design.

Irrigation Plan Reading   Chapter 3 | Page 39

Irrigation symbols

Different plans may show other symbols. A different legend showing some additional symbols is shown below. Note that some components, which are shown in both sample legends, have different symbols. Be sure to check the legend on each plan!

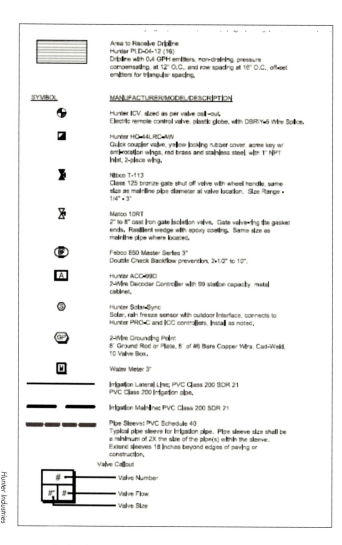

This list shows some additional examples of irrigation symbols.

Irrigation Legend from the sample Residential Irrigation Plan

Zone flow rate and precipitation rate

Information listed on an irrigation plan can be used to determine the flow rate and precipitation rate for any zone in the system.

Flow rate for a zone

To calculate the flow rate in gallons per minute (gpm) or litres per minute (L/m) for any zone, add together the gpm (L/m) shown on the irrigation plan for all the heads in the zone. The gpm for each head is often listed in the drawing legend. Remember that the gpm will be different for heads with different spray nozzles. For example, a full-circle head has approximately twice the output in gpm as a half-circle head of the same series. Refer to the sample Spray Head Irrigation Legend above to view the flow rate for each head.

Flow rates for drip and micro-irrigation zones are measured in volume "per hour" instead of volume "per minute." To calculate the gallons per hour (gph) or

Landscape Irrigation

litres per hour (L/h) for any zone, follow the same procedure for gpm/Lm, counting only the drip irrigation zones shown on the irrigation plan.

Precipitation rate (PR)

There is more than one method of calculating precipitation rates from flow rates. The formula using the "total area method" is:

$$PR = \frac{96.25 \times \text{total gpm}}{\text{total area in square feet}}$$

Additional formulas are given in the *"Irrigation Concepts"* chapter, as well as sample problems showing how to calculate precipitation rates.

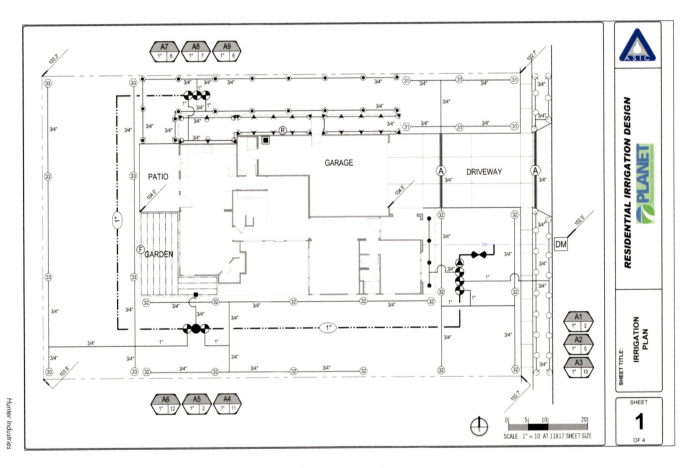

Sample Residential Irrigation Plan showing system layout with irrigation components.

Material Take-Offs

After you become familiar with reading irrigation plans, you can use your plan-reading skills to create a material take-off to estimate the price and/or to order materials. A material take-off is a list of all the materials needed to install the system as it is illustrated in the plan.

An accurate material take-off is essential for producing a cost estimate. The take-off should include all of the system components shown on a plan. Some items can be counted, while others need to be measured. A take-off also needs to include certain items that are not shown on the plan, such as those listed on page 30 under "Items that do not appear on a plan." The need for these items and the quantities can be interpreted from reading the plan or the specifications.

It is common when creating the take-off to increase the quantity of measured items above what is measured from the plan to allow for some inaccuracies in measurement and to account for waste or minor modifications during installation.

Counted items

The quantity of many items — such as valves and sprinkler heads — specified in an irrigation design can be easily determined by counting how many times each symbol appears on the plan. For example, refer to the sample Residential Irrigation Design Plan shown on page 30 and notice the different pop-up and rotor sprinkler heads that can be counted.

Take care when counting symbols, as many symbols are similar in appearance but represent unique items. For example, all sprinkler heads in one zone may look similar (though not identical) on the plan. Notice that some heads may be full-circle, some may be half-circle and some may be quarter-circle. Also, review the details for each item to determine all of the components needed for it, such as the components of a swing joint. When compiling a take-off, similar items with different characteristics (size, angle, etc.), should be listed separately to take into account different nozzles or fittings, such as tees versus elbows.

> Some items for the material take-off may not appear on the plan and need to be estimated.

Measured items

The quantity of pipe by size, specified by internal diameter (ID), and class of pipe (mainline, laterals, drip), sleeves (by size and strength requirements) and wire needed to install an irrigation system can all be measured from a plan. A typical irrigation system includes piping in a variety of sizes. List the total quantity (i.e., the total length) for each size/class of pipe separately on the material take-off. In other words, the take-off should list the total length of all ½" pipe, all ¾" pipe, all 1" pipe, 2" class 200, 2" schedule 40, etc., recorded by size and type.

To avoid errors when estimating quantities of pipe, and to reduce confusion during installation, it is helpful to use highlighters to mark or highlight a plan using different colors to represent different types and sizes of pipe.

To measure the lengths of pipes from an irrigation plan, use a measuring scale (engineer's, architect's or metric scale). For more information about how to properly use a measuring scale (which looks like a three-sided ruler) and the drawing scale on the plan, refer to the *"Landscape Plan Reading and Calculations"* chapter. For now, refer once again to the sample irrigation plan and notice the different piping sizes. Also notice the drawing scale on the plan, which says the scale is 1" = 10'.

Landscape Irrigation

The quantity of wire needed must also be estimated from a plan. Refer to the section, "Wire," below for more information about wire.

Items that do not appear on a plan

Some of the items needed to install an irrigation system are not drawn on the irrigation plan, but should be indicated in detail drawings or referenced in the specifications.

These include, but are not limited to:
- Valve control wire
- Valve boxes
- Pipe fittings
- Bricks, sand or stone screenings used to stabilize and level valves and valve boxes
- Sod or seed to repair trench lines
- Concrete and materials needed to install a thrust block (if a thrust block is needed, it will be noted in the specifications)
- Conduit and junction boxes for electrical wiring
- Water proof wire connectors
- Grounding equipment

The quantities of these materials must be estimated from the plan and included in a take-off. The sample Irrigation Equipment Legend on page 29 specifically indicates items that are not shown on the plan.

Wire

In a traditional installation, a length of wire (hot wire) runs from the controller to each remote control valve along the mainline. In addition, there is a common wire that is shared by all valves and runs from the controller to each valve in series. In a 2-wire system there is no common wire. For more information about wiring, see the *"Irrigation System Components and Maintenance"* chapter.

To estimate the quantity of wire needed for an irrigation system, measure the distance along the mainline from the controller to each remote control valve, then add all these lengths together. Be sure to allow for extra wire for each valve (refer to specifications), which will be coiled in the valve box to facilitate repairs. Then add the length of the common wire, which is the distance from the controller to the furthest valve along the mainline including any spurs or tees. Calculate extra wire to allow for snaking and waste. Snaking the wire allows for expansion and contraction with changing temperatures without stretching or breaking the wire. A waste factor should also be added to estimates; adding 1 percent on a large job to 5 percent on smaller jobs should account for both snaking and waste.

Pipe fittings

Pipe fittings are required wherever a pipe joins another component. This juncture can be a where the pipe joins a sprinkler head, a valve, another section of pipe or some other component, such as a pressure relief valve or a flow regulator.

There is a convention for listing pipe fittings that includes using abbreviations, as well as listing the information in a certain order. Some terms and abbreviations used to designate pipe fittings are listed in the table on page 34.

Examples of insert fittings used for poly pipe.

Irrigation Plan Reading

PVC fittings

Copper fittings

When listing pipe fittings on a take-off, first list the size of each point of connection for the fitting (in inches), then the type of each point of connection (insert, slip, male or female pipe thread), then the type of fitting, such as coupling, 90, or tee.

Note: The sizes of pipes and fittings are the same in Canada, but they are listed in mm instead of inches. For example, 1.5" PVC piping would be labeled on plans as 38 mm.

Some examples of how to designate fittings on a take-off are listed below.

Example 1:
  1" x 1" Ins x Ins poly coupling
  Designates a one inch by one inch, insert by insert, poly coupling. Clamps are required.

Example 2:
  1" x 1" S x S PVC coupling
  Designates a one inch by one inch, slip by slip, PVC coupling. Primer and Glue is required.

Example 3:
  1 1/4" x 1" x 1" Ins x Ins x Fpt poly reducing tee

Designates a one-and-one-quarter inch by one inch by one inch, insert by insert by female pipe thread, poly reducing tee. When listing a tee, begin the listing with the larger end of the straight through portion. Next, list the opposite end of the straight through portion. Finally, list the center (rising) portion. Think of the "T" upside down.

Example 4:
  1 1/4" x 1" x 1" S x S x Fpt PVC reducing tee

Designates a one-and-one-quarter inch by one inch by one inch, slip by slip by female pipe thread, PVC reducing tee.

Sample Materials Take-Off List showing a method of gathering information for pipe and fittings.

Landscape Irrigation

Common Abbreviations and Terms Used with Pipe Fittings

C = Copper

Comp = Compression

Flg = Flanged

Flr = Flared

Fpt = Female pipe thread (threads are not exposed or on the inside the fitting)

Ins = Insert (polyethylene pipe)

Mpt = Male pipe thread (threads are exposed or on the outside of the fitting)

Reducer = Reduces from one size to another

Rt = Ringtite (gasketed joint pipe)

S = Slip (around PVC pipe)

SDR = Sewer and Drain

Spg = Slip (into fitting, as in bushing, used with PVC pipe and fittings)

Summary

An irrigation plan shows the symbols that identify the key irrigation components, in addition to certain items common to landscape plans (such as a title block, a drawing scale and a north arrow). Some components can be counted from the plan, whereas others must be measured from the plan. Since plans are drawn to scale, some quantities, such as pipe, are estimated by measuring using a measuring scale. Some irrigation components, such as fittings and wire, are not shown on the plan, but are listed in the specifications and can be determined from the plan. Whether components are counted, measured or listed, a materials take-off list must be completed to estimate quantities for pricing materials or to place a material order for installation. It is also useful to know that flow rates are indicated on the plans for each type of sprinkler head so that zone flow rates and precipitation rates can be calculated.

Chapter 4

Irrigation Concepts

What You Will Learn

After reading this chapter, you will be able to:

- Define hydraulics.
- Convert weights and volumes of water using known water equivalents.
- Define water pressure.
- Explain how elevation changes affect static (non-flowing) water pressure.
- Convert feet (metres) of head to psi (kPa).
- State the two primary sources of pressure loss in irrigation systems.
- Name at least two factors that contribute to pressure loss through friction in an irrigation pipe.
- State the purpose of using pumps in irrigation systems.
- Define sprinkler precipitation rate, infiltration rate and distribution uniformity.
- Describe why head-to-head spacing is important for sprinkler systems.
- State at least two pros and cons of low volume (drip) irrigation.

Chapter 4

Preview

Water Management and Conservation

Irrigation Systems Overview

Hydraulics
- Water equivalents
- Water pressure

Pressure Loss
- Gravity loss
- Friction loss

Water Distribution
- Sprinkler precipitation rates
- Calculating precipitation rates for an area
- Precipitation rate and infiltration rate
- Head-to-head coverage and distribution uniformity

Low-Volume Irrigation

Alternative Water Resources

Landscape Irrigation

Overview

A basic knowledge of the properties of water and how it moves is important for understanding and managing irrigation systems. This chapter provides an overview of water properties, including pressure and flow. This chapter also covers the importance of proper water distribution and gives examples, showing how to calculate precipitation rates.

Water Management and Conservation

Water conservation is an important part of water management in landscapes. Science and technology have provided improved methods for monitoring water use and using it more wisely. Weather-based control systems automatically respond to changes in the weather, as well as monitoring the needs of the plants. Landscape designers can integrate information about water needs of plants, the climate and microclimate, evapotranspiration rates, irrigation technology, water budgets and more to determine the water needs of the landscape. For more information on water management, see the *"Water Management"* chapter in this manual.

Irrigation Systems Overview

Modern irrigation systems are similar in their basic design. More detailed information about specific irrigation components can be found in the "Irrigation System Components and Maintenance" chapter. A typical irrigation system works as follows:

- A water supply is connected to an irrigation supply pipe called a mainline. The water supply has a backflow preventer at the point of connection so water cannot flow backward and contaminate the supply.
- The mainline distributes water through remote control valves to a network of smaller pipes called laterals.
- Laterals bring water to individual sprinkler heads or other water-emitting devices.
- A controller functions as the "electronic brain." The controller sends signals to the electronic valves, which then send water through the laterals to the sprinkler heads and emitters. The controller regulates when and to which valves the signals are sent.

Ordinarily, there is not enough water available to supply and operate the entire system at the same time. Therefore, the system is divided into different sections, called zones or stations. In most systems, only one zone operates at a time and each zone is usually turned on and off by an automatic valve called a remote control valve (RCV). These valves operate according to a preset schedule that is entered into a programmable timer called a controller. Valves may also be operated manually either by using the controller or by activating at the valve itself.

Hydraulics

Hydraulics is the science of liquids (water) in motion. This section reviews some of the properties and behaviors of water — basic hydraulics — that must be considered in the design of irrigation systems.

Water equivalents

Some important equivalents in measuring water include:
- 1 gal of water weighs 8.3 lbs
- 1 cu ft of water equals 7.48 gals
- 1 cu ft of water weighs 62.4 lbs, which is referred to as the specific weight of water
- 1 ml of water equals 1 cm^3 and weighs 1 g (gram)
- 1 litre of water weighs 1 kg
- 1 m^3 of water weighs 1000 kg

Water pressure

Water pressure is the force that water exerts over a given area. Water pressure is created either by the weight of water (such as in a water tower) or by the use of a pump. Sprinkler heads and other water-emitting devices are designed to operate within a certain pressure range. If water pressure is too low, sprinkler heads discharge large drops of water and may not apply uniform coverage to the area they are designed to irrigate. If water pressure is too high, the spray radius may be exceeded and the sprinkler heads may discharge a fine mist, which can increase water loss from wind drift and evaporation. Once again, the area does not receive uniform coverage of water.

If the supply system pressure is inadequate for proper performance and coverage, pressure regulators may be needed to lower pressure if it is too high or booster pumps may be needed to increase the system pressure.

Water pressure and elevation

Water pressure changes with elevation. This is known as feet of head (metres of head). A water tower provides an example of how water pressure is increased with elevation; the higher the tower, the greater the water pressure at the base. By knowing the conversion factors between pressure and elevation, the static (non-flowing) water pressure can be determined at the base of a tower or the bottom of a pipe at any elevation. For example, 1 ft of water exerts 0.433 psi at the bottom. If the elevation is 2 ft, the pressure is doubled to 0.866 psi (2 x 0.433) at the bottom. Refer to the diagrams below that show two sprinkler pipe configurations. Each has a different length of pipe, but both have the same vertical elevation change. The static pressure is the same for both.

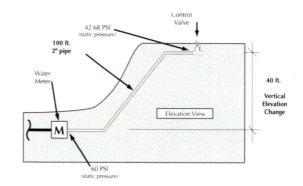

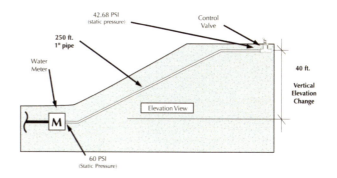

The diagrams show that only vertical changes in elevation affect static pressure.

Landscape Irrigation

Conversions for water pressure

- 1 ft of water (1 foot of head) exerts 0.433 psi (pounds per square inch) at the bottom
- 2.31 ft of water exerts 1 psi at the bottom
- 1 psi equals 2.31 ft in elevation change
- 1 m of water exerts 9.79 kPa (kilopascals) at the bottom
- 1 kPa equals 0.102 m in elevation change

Excessive misting from these heads is a sign the pressure is too high

Troubleshooting Chart for Sprinkler Heads

Sample Calculation — U.S. Standard/Imperial	Sample Calculation — Metric
To convert feet of head to pressure in pounds per square inch (psi), multiply feet by 0.433. Note: Feet of head always refers to change in elevation. Example: What is the pressure (psi) at the base of 200 ft of water? 200 ft x 0.433 psi per foot = 86.6 psi at the base To convert pressure in psi to feet of head, multiply the pressure by 2.31. Example: 100 psi x 2.31 = 231 feet of head *Note:* 2.31 is the inverse of 0.433, so multiplying by 2.31 is the same as dividing by 0.433 because 1/0.433 = 2.31.	To convert meters of head to pressure in kilopascals (kPa), multiply metres by 9.79. Note: Metres of head always refers to change in elevation. Example: What is the pressure (kPa) at the base of 100 m of water? 100 m x 9.79 kPa = 979 kPa at the base To convert pressure, in kPa, to metres of head, divide by 9.79. 800 kPa/9.79 = 81.7 m of head *Note:* In metric, pressure is sometimes stated in units called bars where 100 kPa = 1 bar.

Irrigation Concepts

Pressure is too low.

Pumps and water pressure
As mentioned, water pressure is created by the weight of water, in a tower for example. A second way that pressure is created in irrigation systems is through the use of pumps. In many irrigation systems, the water has to be pumped from a lower elevation point, such as a well or pond, to meet irrigation needs. Pumps provide the pressure needed to operate the sprinklers by converting mechanical energy into pressure and energy needed for water flow. This process is called mechanical pressurization.

Different types of pumps are available and pumps require an energy source to operate. Many irrigation pumps are powered by electricity. To be sure that the pump meets the operational requirements of the irrigation system, the two values that must be known before selecting a pump are:
- Discharge rate: the flow rate that the pump must discharge in gallons per minute or litres per minute (gpm or L/m).
- Discharge pressure: the pressure that the pump must add to the water in psi or kPa.

The term "static head" is used with water pumps and refers to the total vertical distance that the pump must lift the water.

Pressure Loss

Gravity loss
Water moving uphill, against gravity, decreases in pressure as elevation (vertical rise) is gained. If a sprinkler head is located at a higher elevation than the water supply, water pressure at this sprinkler will be lower since the water is moving against gravity to reach the sprinkler head. The greater the increase in elevation, the greater will be the pressure loss. For each foot of uphill elevation, the pressure loss is 0.433 psi. A pump may be required in some situations.

Water naturally tends to move downhill with gravity. If the sprinkler head is located at a lower elevation than the water supply, water pressure will be increased as a result. Remember, whether water is moving uphill or downhill in elevation, the change in pressure per unit of elevation (feet, for example) is the same.

Friction loss
When water is moving through an irrigation system, it is no longer static. It is in a dynamic state. Pressure loss due to friction (friction loss) is the loss of water pressure that occurs as water flows through a restriction, such as a pipe, fitting, valve or other component. A variety of factors determine how much friction loss occurs. For a pipe, the main factors affecting friction loss are:
- Speed of water flow (velocity)
- Inside pipe diameter
- Interior roughness of the pipe
- Length of the pipe

Water velocity, or the speed at which it is moving or flowing, is an important factor in determining friction loss in pipe. In an irrigation system, a velocity of 5 feet per second (fps) (1.5 m/sec) is considered ideal. The velocity should not exceed 7 fps (2.1 m/sec).

Landscape Irrigation

Irrigation Association Friction Loss Chart 2008
Class 160 PVC IPS Plastic Pipe
ANSI/ASAE S376.2   ASTM D2241   SDR 26   C=150
psi loss per 100 feet of pipe

Nominal Size	Shown for convenience Class 315 1/2"	Class 200 3/4"	1"	1-1/4"	1-1/2"	2"	2-1/2"	3"	4"	6"
Avg. ID	0.696	0.910	1.175	1.512	1.734	2.173	2.635	3.21	4.134	6.084
Pipe OD	0.840	1.050	1.315	1.660	1.900	2.375	2.875	3.500	4.500	6.625
Avg. Wall	0.072	0.070	0.070	0.074	0.083	0.101	0.120	0.145	0.183	0.271
Min. Wall	0.062	0.060	0.060	0.064	0.073	0.091	0.110	0.135	0.173	0.255
Flow gpm	Velocity fps psi Loss	Velocity fps psi Loss	Velocity fps psi Loss	Velocity fps psi Loss	Velocity fps psi Loss	Velocity fps psi Loss	Velocity fps psi Loss	Velocity fps psi Loss	Velocity fps psi Loss	Velocity fps psi Loss

When water flows from a larger pipe to a smaller pipe or comes to a 90 degree turn, additional friction losses occur. When the pipe size is reduced and the rate of flow (the amount of water moving through the system) remains the same, the velocity of water flowing through the pipe (in fps or m/s) and friction will increase.

The *length of pipe* affects pressure loss because the longer the pipe is, the greater the cumulative effect of friction loss due to pipe diameter, pipe roughness and velocity will be. This means that when the length of the pipe doubles, the pressure loss also doubles.

Friction loss charts are available from the manufacturers of materials used in irrigation systems. These charts specify pressure loss for each foot (or metre) of pipe, valve or other pieces of equipment for various flow rates and velocities. Refer to the excerpt above from a friction loss chart. Flow rate refers to the quantity of water flowing in gallons per minute (litres/min or cu metres/hr) through the system, and velocity refers to the speed water is flowing in feet per second (metres/second) through pipes of various diameters.

Water Distribution

Water distribution refers to the amount of water delivered to each area. Uniform water distribution is an ideal situation in which each irrigated area receives the same amount of water. Distribution uniformity (DU) depends on proper distribution rates from the sprinkler heads and proper spacing of the sprinkler heads. This section discusses sprinkler precipitation rates, methods to calculate precipitation rates and ways to help achieve uniform coverage.

Sprinkler precipitation rates

In an irrigation system, precipitation rate, or PR, refers to the rate at which sprinkler heads apply water to the landscape area, and PR is measured in inches per hour (mm per hour), the same way that natural precipitation is measured. The precipitation rate should be as consistent as possible throughout a zone to avoid areas of overwatering or underwatering.

Different sprinkler types have different precipitation rates. For example, fixed spray sprinkler heads generally have a high PR, which is 1.0"/hr (25 mm/hr) and above. The PR for rotating stream sprays is medium or moderate (0.5" to 1.0"/hr (12.5 mm to 25 mm/hr). Rotor sprinkler heads have a moderate to low PR. Refer to the chart, which shows the general relationship between precipitation rates and sprinkler types.

Irrigation Concepts

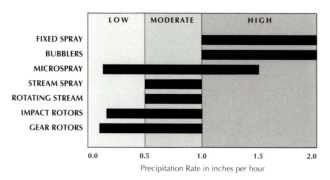

To ensure a uniform precipitation rate throughout a watering zone, follow these guidelines:

- Use sprinkler heads with the same precipitation rates (also known as matched precipitation rates). Matched precipitation rates mean that each sprinkler in a zone is providing about the same amount of water to a given area.
- Use only heads of the same type. In other words, avoid mixing rotor heads and pop-up spray heads on the same zone unless matched precipitation nozzles are used.
- When making repairs on a sprinkler system, if mixing heads from different manufacturers, be sure that precipitation rates are matched by installing comparable flow-rated nozzles.

Note: It is important to understand how the arc of a sprinkler, the sprinkler flow rate and the precipitation rate are related. Sprinklers with matched precipitation rates may have different flow rates. For example, to achieve matched precipitation rates in an irrigation area that has both quarter circle and half circle arcs, the flow rate (in gpm or L/m) of the half-circle head must be double that of the quarter-circle head. Refer to the diagram on this page.

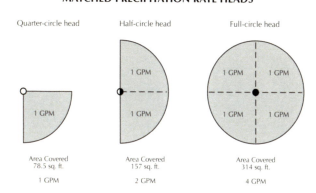

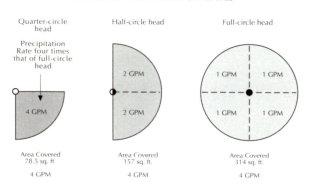

Fixed spray heads have a high precipitation rate.

Rotating stream sprays have a medium PR.

Rotor heads have a low to moderate precipitation rate.

Landscape Irrigation

Calculating precipitation rates for an area

Precipitation rate (PR) is measured in inches (mm) of water applied per hour to the irrigated area. The basic formula used to calculate the PR for irrigation systems is shown below, along with some variations for different sprinkler patterns.

Method 1 — Total Area Method

Sample Calculation — U.S./Imperial Formula	Sample Calculation — Metric Formula
$PR = \dfrac{96.25 \times \text{Total gpm}}{\text{total area in square ft}}$	$PR \text{ in mm/hr} = \dfrac{\text{Total L/min} \times 60}{\text{area in sq m}}$
Where 96.25 is the constant that converts gallons per minute per square foot to inches per hour.	Where 60 is the constant that converts L/min to mm/hr (and 1 L = 0.001 m^3 and 1 mm = 0.001 metres).

Method 1 — Sample Problems

U.S./Imperial	Metric

Calculate the precipitation rate (PR) for an irrigated area measuring 60 ft x 15 ft, containing the following sprinkler heads:
  6 half circle (1.0 gpm nozzles)
  4 quarter circle (0.5 gpm nozzles)
 	
1. Total gpm = (6 x 1.0 gpm) + (4 x 0.5 gpm)
            = 8.0 GPM
 	
2. Total Area = 60 x 15 = 900 sq ft
 	
3. PR = $\dfrac{96.25 \times 8.0 \text{ gpm}}{900 \text{ sq ft}}$
   PR = 0.86 in/hr
 	
Note: The total flow rate (gpm) for the area is calculated by adding the gpm for each head in the area.
	Calculate the precipitation rate (PR) for an irrigated area measuring 20 m x 5 m, containing the following sprinkler heads:
	  6 half circle (3.6 litre/min nozzles)
	  4 quarter circle (1.8 litre/min nozzles)
	
	1. Total L/min = (6 x 3.6 L/min) + (4 x 1.8 L/min)
	             = 28.8 L/min
	
	2. Total Area = 20 x 5 = 100 sq m
	
	3. PR = $\dfrac{60 \text{ min/hr} \times 28.8 \text{ L/min}}{100 \text{ sq m}}$
	   PR = 17.3 mm/hr
	
	Note: The constant used to convert litres per minute per square metre to millimetres per hour is 60.

Method 2 — Individual Head Spacing Method for Full Circle

Sample Calculation — U.S./Imperial Formula	Sample Calculation — Metric Formula
Spacing formula for square sprinkler pattern: PR = $\dfrac{\text{gpm of full circle (360°) sprinkler} \times 96.25}{\text{head spacing} \times \text{row spacings}}$	PR = $\dfrac{60 \times \text{L/min for full circle (360°) head}}{\text{head spacing} \times \text{row spacings}}$ Where 60 is the constant that converts litres per minute (L/min) to milliliters per hour (mm/hr).

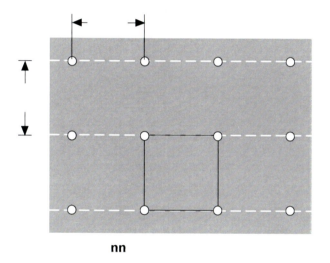

nn

{ "Spacing" in these formulas assumes the row spacing and head spacing is the same. Refer to the diagram. }

Proper head spacing ensures adequate coverage.

Method 3 — Individual Head Method for Any Arc
The following formulas have been modified so they apply to any arc.

U.S./Imperial Formula and Example	Metric Formula and Example
$PR = \dfrac{34{,}650 \times gpm \text{ (for any arc)}}{\text{degrees of arc} \times \text{spacing}^2}$ Note: 34,650 is the constant that converts gpm to in/hr	$PR = \dfrac{21{,}600 \times L/min \text{ (for any arc)}}{\text{degrees of arc} \times \text{spacing}^2}$ Note: 21,600 is the constant that converts L/min to mm/hr
In this example, the head is a half-circle (180° arc) sprinkler with a 20 ft radius delivering 2.5 gpm. The manufacturer recommends 20 ft head spacing and 20 feet between the rows of heads (square spacing). Using the formula: $PR = \dfrac{34650 \times gpm \text{ (for any arc)}}{\text{Arc (degrees)} \times \text{Head Spacing} \times \text{Row Spacing}}$ $PR = \dfrac{34650 \times 2.5 \text{ gpm}}{180 \times 20ft \times 20ft}$ $PR = \dfrac{86625}{72000}$ $PR = 1.20 \text{ in/hr}$ The PR for a full-circle head will be the same since a full-circle head covers twice the area and applies double the flow of the half-circle.	In this example, the head selected is a half-circle (180° arc) with a 6 m radius delivering 10 L/min. The manufacturer recommends a 6 m head spacing and 6 meters between the rows of heads (square spacing). Using the formula: $PR = \dfrac{21{,}600 \times l/min \text{ (for any arc)}}{\text{Arc (degrees)} \times \text{Head Spacing} \times \text{Row Spacing}}$ $PR = \dfrac{21600 \times 10 \text{ L/min}}{180 \times 6m \times 6m}$ $PR = \dfrac{216000 \text{ L/min}}{6480}$ $PR = 33 \text{ mm/hr}$ The PR for a full-circle head will be the same since a full-circle head covers twice the area and applies double the flow of the half-circle.

Precipitation rate and infiltration rate

Infiltration rate is the rate at which water enters the soil. Sandy soils have a higher infiltration rate than clay soils. See the chapter, "Water Management," for more details.

The precipitation rate should not be greater than the infiltration rate. Otherwise, runoff will occur. Some strategies to avoid runoff on clay soils, which have a low infiltration rate, include:

- Using sprinkler heads with a low precipitation rate.
- Using the "cycle and soak" feature on the controller, if available, or set sprinklers to water multiple times in each zone.
  - Break up the total watering time for each zone into several segments or cycles by operating a zone for a short time, allowing the water to soak in, and then repeat the watering and soaking cycle. An example of a cycle and

soak schedule is: water 3 times a day; water 4 minutes each cycle; wait 1 hour between watering cycles (soaking period).

Head-to-head coverage and distribution uniformity

As mentioned previously, uniform coverage of irrigation water, or distribution uniformity (DU), is important to prevent areas from being over-watered or under-watered. Distribution uniformity is a measure of how evenly or uniformly water is applied by sprinklers across the irrigated area. Achieving uniform water coverage is a key principle in designing irrigation systems and head-to-head overlap or coverage is a way to achieve it. Head-to-head coverage means that the spray radius of the sprinkler heads is equal to the distance between heads. For example, if the spray radius of sprinkler heads in a zone is 15 ft (4.5 m), the heads should be spaced 15 ft (4.5 m) apart.

Head-to-head coverage provides uniform water distribution.

Low-Volume Irrigation

Low-volume or drip irrigation provides a watering system that applies water at a slow rate directly to the base of plants. Drip irrigation operates at low pressure and carries water through flexible polyethylene pipe or tubing. It can be discharged through emitters installed only where water is desired, or along the length of inline emitter tubing. This tubing can be placed either on the surface, covered with mulch, or buried underground.

Inline irrigation tubing and low-volume emitter.

Drip irrigation systems require lower water pressure than spray systems to work properly, so pressure regulators are usually required at the valve. Emitters used in drip systems can become easily clogged, so a water filtration (Y-strainer) must be incorporated into drip systems.

One of the advantages of drip irrigation is that it minimizes evaporation and runoff. Drip irrigation is an efficient way to water planting beds, as well as individual trees and shrubs. Drip irrigation is measured in gallons per hour (gph) or litres per hour (L/h) rather than gallons or litres per minute.

Landscape Irrigation

Note that drip irrigation does not necessarily conserve water. Its efficient use of water depends on proper design, installation and management. More information about the components used in a drip irrigation system can be found in the chapter the *"Irrigation System Components and Maintenance."* Below is a list of advantages and disadvantages of drip irrigation compared to common spray systems.

Hunter Industries

This is a pre-assembled, factory water-tested "kit" that has a high-grade valve with a filter and a pressure regulator. It is ideal for drip zones.

Drip Irrigation

Advantages	Disadvantages
• Water is distributed only where needed • Weed growth is reduced, since water is applied only to selected areas • Runoff is reduced or eliminated if runtimes are properly scheduled on the controller • Evaporation is reduced • Low water pressure means leaks are less critical • When properly designed, installed and managed, system benefits and payoffs include savings on water costs and maintenance costs for weed control, reduced "carbon footprint."	• Sub-surface piping cannot be easily inspected for proper function • Pressure regulation is required • Filtration is required • Surface systems are vulnerable to damage and vandalism • May have higher upfront cost (installation) before payoffs are realized

{ Be aware that the performance of the components and products in any irrigation system depends on proper installation, management and installation! }

Alternative Water Resources

In many areas throughout North America, water for irrigation can come from multiple sources. Non-potable water is not considered suitable for consumption by humans, but can be used for landscape irrigation. Non-potable water can come from many sources, including:

- Reclaimed or recycled water (from municipal wastewater treatment facilities)
- Rainwater catchment or harvesting
- Natural water sources, such as ponds or lakes
- Greywater (from dishwasher, shower or laundry use)
- Wells

Irrigation systems using non-potable water must be clearly identified so that human consumption is avoided. The standard system for identifying non-potable irrigation systems is to use purple-colored irrigation components. Use of purple components may include pipes, valve box covers, quick couplers, valves, sprinkler heads, etc. For more information on rain barrels and other irrigations options, see the "Irrigation System Components and Maintenance" chapter.

Non-potable water sources

Recycled water from water treatment plant

Ponds and lakes

Rainwater harvesting

Landscape Irrigation

Summary

Hydraulics is the science that deals with the effects and application of liquids, such as water, in motion. Working with irrigation systems requires a basic knowledge of the properties of water, both at rest and in motion. Water pressure is affected by elevation and the change in pressure can be calculated using standard water equivalents. When water is moving through an irrigation system, water pressure is lost due to friction and gravity.

The rate at which water is applied to an area is called the precipitation rate. To help maintain uniform water distribution, ensure head-to-head coverage and consider the infiltration rate of the soil when maintaining and managing the system.

Low-volume irrigation systems operate at low pressures and apply water at slow rates. Advantages to well-designed and well-managed low-volume irrigation systems are that water loss to evaporation and runoff are minimized and water is applied only where it is needed. Some disadvantages include that pressure regulation and filtration are required.

There are multiple non-potable sources of water for irrigation that include natural sources (such as rainwater harvesting), and reused and recycled sources. Use of alternative resources for irrigation is a good conservation practice where allowed.

Chapter 5

Irrigation System Components & Maintenance

What You Will Learn

After reading this chapter, you will be able to:

- Define point of connection and state why a backflow preventer is placed there.
- List the two causes of backflow and four types of backflow preventers.
- Describe two basic types of controllers.
- Describe the function and capabilities of a central control system.
- Describe the purpose of environmental sensors and how they work.
- Define mainlines and laterals.
- Describe the purpose of remote control valves, shut-off valves and quick couplers.
- Describe two common methods for wiring.
- Describe the difference between spray heads and rotors.
- List at least three irrigation components specifically used with low-volume systems.
- State three different materials from which irrigation pipes are made and the differences in how each is installed.
- Describe how to repair damaged pipes.
- Describe how to solder copper pipe and fittings.
- Describe four common problems that field diagnostics can help identify.
- State why winterizing is important and how to do it.

Chapter 5

Preview

Point of Connection and Backflow

Major Components

Backflow Prevention Devices

Controllers
- Controllers and types
- Central control systems

Piping
- Mainlines and laterals

Valves

Wiring Systems

Sprinkler Heads and Other Irrigation Options
- Spray heads and rotors
- Low-volume systems and components
- Rain barrels and cisterns

Installing Pipes and Fittings
- PVC and poly
- Copper pipe and fittings and how to solder

Irrigation System Repair and Maintenance
- Pipe repair and sprinkler head repair
- Basic field diagnostics
- Winterizing an irrigation system

Manual sponsored by **Hunter Industries**

Landscape Irrigation

Overview

A well-designed and maintained irrigation system is supposed to be a supplement to rainfall, not a substitute. Ideally, the system ensures the optimum amount of water for turf and landscaped bed areas so they will grow and thrive. Irrigation needs are dependent on various factors, including soil type, plant moisture requirements and climate. This chapter provides a description of the major components of an irrigation system, as well as general maintenance and troubleshooting procedures.

Most irrigation systems using city water systems are similar in their basic design. (Note: This chapter does not cover pump and well systems). A typical irrigation system works as follows:

- A water supply is connected to an irrigation supply pipe called a mainline.
- The water supply has a backflow preventer so water cannot flow backward and contaminate the supply.
- The mainline distributes water through remote control valves to a network of smaller pipes called laterals or lateral lines.
- Laterals bring water to individual sprinkler heads or other water-emitting devices.

Ordinarily, there is not enough water available to supply and operate the entire irrigation system at the same time. Therefore, the system is divided into different sections, called zones or stations. The zones operate one at a time according to a preset schedule entered into a programmable timer called a controller. Valves may also be operated manually using the controller or the valve itself.

More detailed information is presented in the sections that follow.

Point of Connection and Backflow

Before describing the major hardware components of an irrigation system, it is helpful to understand the importance of avoiding contamination of water sources by preventing backflow.

Point of connection

The point of connection (POC) is the location where an irrigation system taps into an existing water supply. This can be located in different places, including the house gate valve (may be a ball valve), on an underground water line near a sidewalk, house or building; in a basement, crawl space or any other convenient location. A backflow preventer (see next section) is installed near the point of connection to protect the water supply from contamination.

The point at which a non-potable water source connects to a potable water supply is referred to as a cross-connection. This occurs at the point of connection for an irrigation system.

Backflow prevention

The unwanted reversal of the flow of water through a cross-connection is called backflow. Backflow prevention devices are mandatory on all irrigation systems connected to municipal water supplies, to prevent backflow from occurring. Water in an irrigation system is subject to contamination from pesticides, fertilizers, manures, etc. This means that the potable water supply from which the irrigation system draws its water is in danger of contamination if water from the irrigation system flows back into the source piping (usually the city piping system). The contaminated water can cause illness or even death. For this reason, backflow prevention is an important part of an irrigation system. There are specifications and legal codes that need to be followed when installing or maintaining a backflow prevention device. Always check local codes and regulations prior to designing and installing an irrigation system.

Backflow preventers are usually installed near the point of connection. They should be installed in an accessible location to facilitate servicing, testing and inspection, and they should be protected from freezing. Backflow prevention devices are directional. Therefore, it is important to make sure the arrow points in the direction of flow when they are being installed.

Backflow preventers contain seals, springs and moving parts that are subject to wear and fatigue, so periodic testing is required by code. Backflow can occur in two different ways, as described in the following paragraphs.

Causes of backflow
Backpressure
Backpressure occurs when the pressure in the irrigation system downstream is greater than the pressure in the water supply upstream. This can be caused by a decrease in pressure in the water supply, an increase in the downstream pressure or both. A booster pump in the irrigation system can cause backpressure.

Backsiphonage
Backsiphonage is the reversal of normal flow in the system caused by negative or reduced pressure in the water system. Some possible causes include undersized piping, a line break lower than the service connection or a high water withdrawal rate from firefighting, pipe flushing, etc.

Backflow prevention devices are discussed in more detail in the next section.

Major Components

An efficient irrigation system consists of a carefully matched assembly of pipes, valves, sprinklers, wires and other hardware. In the following sections, the function of each major irrigation component is described and some installation guidelines are given. Separate sections are provided for each of these major components:

- Backflow prevention devices
- Controllers
- Piping
- Valves
- Wiring systems
- Sprinkler heads and other irrigation options

Backflow Prevention Devices

Local codes may vary regarding selection and installation of backflow prevention devices. Check local regulations before installing any backflow prevention device.

Types of backflow prevention devices
There are four basic types of backflow prevention devices in common use today. Each is described below.

Pressure vacuum breaker (PVB)
PVBs have a spring-loaded check valve and a spring-loaded air inlet valve. They are designed to prevent backflow from backsiphonage only and are not effective against backflow due to backpressure.

> Install backflow prevention devices near the point of connection and where they are accessible for inspection and servicing.

Shutoff valves are located at each end of the assembly and the units are equipped with test cocks. PVBs must

Landscape Irrigation

be installed at least 12" (30 cm) above the highest outlet in the system.

Atmospheric vacuum breaker (AVB)
AVBs have a float check, a check seat and an air inlet valve. The air inlet valve opens if there is a loss of pressure in the supply pipe. This allows air (atmosphere) into the outlet piping, preventing backflow. AVBs should not be under constant pressure for more than 12 consecutive hours. Like PVBs, AVBs are designed only to prevent backflow caused by backsiphonage.

Reduced pressure assembly (RPA)
RPAs have two spring-loaded check valves with a pressure differential relief valve between them. They maintain a pressure differential of not less than 2 PSI between the supply (upstream) side and outlet (downstream) side. If pressure builds up on the outlet side, the relief valve discharges water to relieve pressure. Shutoff valves are located at each end of the assembly and the units are equipped with test cocks. RPAs are effective against both backpressure and backsiphonage and are approved to protect water systems from substances hazardous to health.

RPA backflow prevention device. The arrow should point in the direction of flow

They should be installed 12" (30 cm) above the grade, but do not have to be higher than sprinklers or other outlets.

Double-check valve assembly (DCA)
DCAs have two spring-loaded check valves. Shutoff valves are located at each end of the assembly and the units are equipped with test cocks. These backflow preventers are effective against both backpressure and backsiphonage. However, they are not approved to protect water systems from substances considered health hazards. Again, check local regulations.

Anatomy of a Sprinkler System

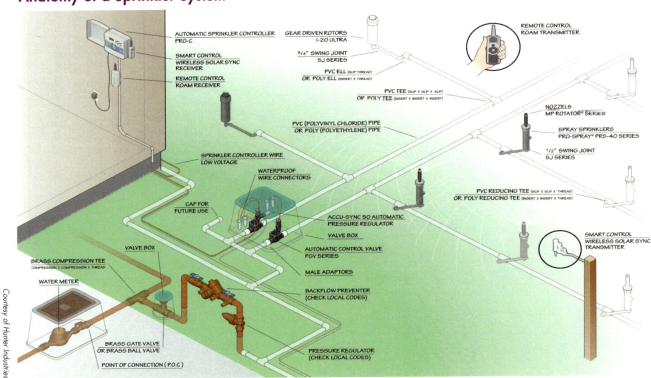

Courtesy of Hunter Industries

Controllers

Irrigation controllers are used to schedule when an irrigation system waters by automatically opening and closing remote control valves according to a programmed schedule. Controllers are connected to valves by wire. The two basic types of controllers in common use are electro-mechanical and electronic.

This controller has three programs with multiple start times and flexible scheduling options. It can also connect to a weather sensor, solar sensor and/or a remote control.

Controllers and types

Electro-mechanical controllers
Electro-mechanical controllers have been in use for many years. They are driven by motors and gears and are considered dependable, but they have limited features and are relatively inflexible in their ability to set different watering rates for different watering zones.

Electronic (solid state) controllers
Electronic controllers are more complex and are controlled by microprocessors. They are also called solid state controllers. They have more sophisticated programming capabilities and allow for more flexible irrigation schedules.

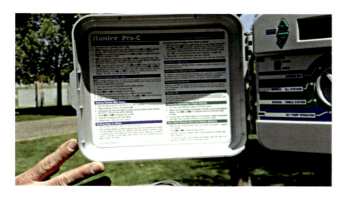

Programming controllers
Electro-mechanical controllers are programmed using a series of dials and switches. Electronic controllers are programmed through a keypad or a dial and keypad interface. Though different controllers have different methods of programming, they all require the following information to be entered:

- Current day and time
- What days to water
- What time of day each cycle should begin
- How long each zone should operate

When a controller is programmed, be sure to modify the program as evapotranspiration (ET) rates change, that is, as weather conditions change. This could be weekly, bi-weekly or monthly. It is usually not necessary to completely reprogram the controller to make adjustments in a program. For example, as weather conditions change — and therefore ET rates change — adjust the amount of time or number of days to irrigate. The easiest way to modify the base program is to adjust run days or run times.

Many controllers have a seasonal adjusting feature that is initially set to 100 percent. For example, to reduce all station run times by half, set the water budgeting percent key to 50 percent. To double the run time of all zones, set the water budgeting percent key to 200 percent.

Most controllers also have a semi-automatic mode that allows a watering cycle to be started manually. In semi-automatic mode, after a program (for example, Program A) is activated manually, the controller will run

‹ Note: Most controllers have basic instructions on the inside panel of the door.

Landscape Irrigation

all zones in that program sequentially, then reset to run existing programs normally. Most controllers have a manual mode, as well, that allows a selected zone to be started manually.

Multiple program controllers allow you to enter different programs for different groups of zones. For example, Program A can irrigate turf zones, Program B can irrigate low water use shrubs and Program C can irrigate trees.

When entering multiple programs, be careful not to overlap run times. If the run time of one program overlaps the start time of another program, the second program will most likely run at the end of the first program.

New weather-based and moisture sensor-based irrigation controllers ("smart" controllers) will automatically adjust run times based on current weather conditions and/or moisture levels. Consult local irrigation suppliers or distributors for more information. Also, refer to the next section, entitled *"Smart controllers."*

Also see the chapter *"Water Management and Auditing"* for more information about irrigation scheduling.

Smart controllers

"Smart" controllers, as defined by the Irrigation Association, are controllers that automatically update the watering schedule to allow for changes in water needs throughout the year.

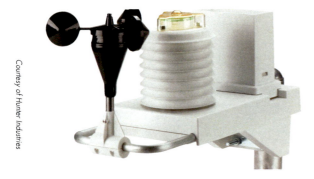

Courtesy of Hunter Industries

This ET system is an optional accessory for some controllers that measures environmental conditions, calculates the local ET and initiates a new watering schedule that replenishes only the water that is actually needed.

Smart controllers estimate or measure depletion of available plant soil moisture in order to operate an irrigation system, replenishing water as needed while minimizing excess water use. Smart controllers use sensors and weather information to manage and adjust watering schedules. There are several methods by which smart controllers receive information needed to modify watering times. For example, information can be weather-based (using an on-site weather station or using nearby weather stations), based on soil moisture monitored in the root zone, or tied to historical weather data.
A properly programmed smart controller requires initial site-specific set-up that includes information such as soil type, plant type and slope. Then it will make irrigation schedule adjustments to run times and required cycles, based on changes in weather, soil moisture or other changing data, throughout the irrigation season without human intervention.

Weather station

Environmental sensors
Environmental sensors are devices that interface with controllers, shutting down an irrigation system when water is not needed. Different sensors are available that can monitor rainfall, soil moisture, humidity, air flow (wind) and temperature. Sensors can be integrated into a complete irrigation management system using smart controllers.

Rain sensors are the most common type of sensors. These sensors have a collection device that gathers rainwater. When enough rainwater is collected, it disables the controller so the system can't operate. Some rain sensors are adjustable so that light showers

Irrigation System Components & Maintenance

will not shut down the system. When rainwater evaporates, the controller again operates as programmed.

Central control systems

Central control systems are sophisticated computer-based systems that operate controllers, sensors and other parts of irrigation systems from a central location. These high-tech systems provide an extremely efficient means of controlling large or complex irrigation installations.

A central control system has a central computer that can be placed in a remote location. This computer communicates (using various methods, such as hard wiring, radio, phone lines or the Internet) with an on-site control device that monitors and controls the various components of the irrigation system.

Central control systems can be programmed off site.

Central control system allows viewing from a computer in a remote location.

Actions that affect an entire system, such as adjusting watering times for different seasons, can be programmed from a central control system. Some systems can interface with sensors that monitor wind, weather, rain and soil moisture. If environmental conditions exceed pre-defined limits, the central control system responds by adjusting watering schedules.

Piping

Mainlines

The mainline is a pipe that carries water from the backflow prevention device to the remote control valves. Typically, piping used for mainlines is made of polyvinyl chloride (PVC) or a semi-rigid plastic, although copper or galvanized steel pipe also has been used in the past. If reclaimed, non-potable water is supplying the system, purple PVC mainline and valve boxes are required. Poly (polyethylene) pipe is acceptable in certain regions with little or no ground freeze, or in residential installations.

The mainline is under constant pressure when the system is charged and is usually the largest pipe in an irrigation system.

Laterals

Lateral lines are the pipes that supply water to sprinklers or emitters. Laterals are under pressure only when an irrigation valve is activated. They are located downstream from remote control valves. PVC or poly pipes are generally used for laterals. Laterals are placed in a trench dug by hand or with a trencher, backhoe/excavator, or installed with a pipe puller. When using a pipe puller, tape or plug the end of the pipe and insert fully into the gripper. When entering or exiting the ground, the pipe should be at a slight angle to avoid excess stress on the pipe. For more information on trencher and pipe puller operation and safety, refer to the chapter, "Landscape Equipment Safety and Maintenance."

Landscape Irrigation

After digging or trenching, clean and level the trench, install the pipe heads and then backfill and compact soil by puddling (applying water to the top of the backfill), jetting (injecting water below the surface of backfill) or tamping (compacting soil with some type of compaction device). This may have to be done in several lifts (layers), depending on the depth of excavation.

This trencher is digging the trenches to install the irrigation pipes. Always ensure utilities are located and marked.

This length of PVC pipe is ready to place in the trench.

This technician is cutting PVC pipe.

PVC pipe is being placed in the trench.

Valves

Valves are devices that regulate the flow of water in an irrigation system. There are many types of valves, including main valves, master valves, flow valves, isolation valves and drain valves. Some valves are operated manually, while others are electrically controlled. Most valves are directional, so when installing a valve, make sure the arrow points in the direction of flow. Valves are usually installed in a buried valve box—a plastic box with a green lid (or purple lid for non-potable water)—providing easy access for maintenance or repair. Several valves often share the same valve box. The most commonly used valves are described below.

Multiple valves in one box.

These valves are equipped with a mechanism that helps prevent microscopic particles from contaminating the diaphragm filter.

Remote control valves (RCVs)

RCVs are electrically controlled valves that regulate the flow of water to different parts of a system. Since there is generally not enough water available to supply an entire system at once, most irrigation systems are divided into different zones. Each zone has a remote control valve. Remote control valves have a solenoid, and when electricity flows to the solenoid, a magnetic field is created causing the valve to open. The two wires coming out of the solenoid are then connected to the field wiring.

This remote control valve shows the solenoid with its two wires.

Water then enters the lateral lines, which are the pipes that supply water to sprinklers or emitters.

Remote control valves are available with or without flow control. Valves with flow control have a stem on the top that allows water flow to be adjusted manually.

Shut-off valves

Shut-off valves are manually operated valves and can be gate valves, ball valves, disk valves or butterfly valves. When installed near the water source, they can shut off an entire system in case work is needed on the mainline or control valves, or in case of emergencies. They are not intended for frequent use. Gate valves should not be left in the fully open position or damage to the seals can occur.

Quick couplers

Quick couplers on the mainline allow water from an irrigation system to be instantly available for a variety of uses. They are valves connected directly to the pressurized mainline, allowing immediate access for the attachment of a hose or a sprinkler, even while the system is operating. Some have a notched key or lug arrangement and some have threaded keys and valve bodies.

Quick couplers

Landscape Irrigation

Wiring Systems

Two basic forms of wiring are used with irrigation systems. The first is a multi-strand or multi-wire system and the second is a two-wire decoder system. Note: Regardless of the type of wiring system used, be sure that the controller is unplugged from the power source before beginning any wiring tasks.

Multi-strand system

The multi-wire system consists of one common wire, usually white, and any number of other zone wires, each dedicated to an individual valve. Each individual zone wire in the multi-wire system is then connected to a singular terminal at the controller. Wire is installed along the mainline for easy access and to minimize damage. Wire for irrigation must be jacketed with an approved direct burial coating. Wire should be snaked under piping. This provides extra wire to prevent stretching or breaking as the ground expands and contracts due to moisture and temperature changes. It is also a common practice to include one or two extra wires for maintenance or expansion of the system.

All wire connections and splices should be made with watertight connectors and housed within a valve box. When splicing wire, always use wire that matches the gauge and color of existing wire.

Two-wire decoder system

The two-wire decoder system is popular in the industry world wide. This system consists of two wires that are run continually from the controller to the end of the system and are connected to a decoder at each valve. Each decoder is assigned an individual address that is recognized by the controller. The same two wires connect the controller, decoders and components from three to more than 50 zones. The system can be compared to a telephone system in that each decoder is assigned a number and the controller can send an electronic signal to individual valves or to multiple valves depending on the information provided by the programmer. The system is more versatile than the multi-wire system because the wires can be stubbed off at the end of the irrigation system for future expansion. In addition to ease of expansion, the two-wire decoder system is easier and less costly both to install and maintain.

Sample Wiring Detail Drawing

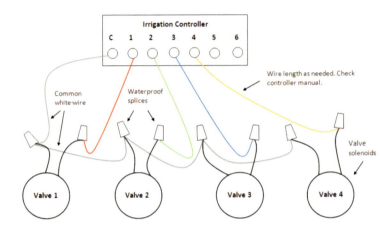

A common wire (white) goes from the controller to each valve. Each valve solenoid has two wires. One wire is used for the common wire connection and the other connects to the individual valve zone wire, as shown. All wire connections and splices are made with watertight connectors.

Sprinkler Heads and Other Irrigation Options

Sprinkler heads emit a spray of water on turf areas and planting beds. They attach to laterals using either a rigid PVC riser or swing pipe as specified by state or provincial code. Sprinkler heads are available in many varieties to match different site conditions, available water pressure, etc. The two main types of sprinkler heads that are described in this section are spray heads and rotors. (Refer to the detailed drawings that show proper sprinkler head installation).

These two different types of sprinkler heads should not be installed on the same lateral unless MPR (matched precipitation rate) nozzles are utilized on the entire zone. It is best to design systems where different types of sprinklers are on separate lateral zones.

Low-volume systems and components and other irrigation options are also discussed in this section.

Spray heads

Spray heads discharge a continuous spray of water at distances typically ranging from 5 – 15' (1.5 – 5 m). The two main types of spray heads are risers and pop-ups.

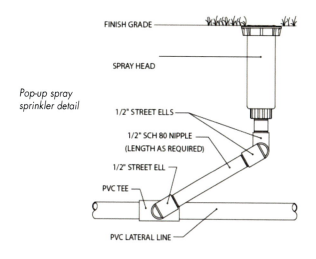
Pop-up spray sprinkler detail

Note: If an irrigation system is supplied with non-potable water, the caps on the heads must be purple. This color is a standard indicator of non-potable water.

Risers are fixed heads mounted on pipes projecting out of the ground. Since they are permanently installed above the height of surrounding plants, they are best suited for planting beds or other areas where they will not appear unsightly, create a hazard or be subject to damage.

Pop-up spray sprinkler

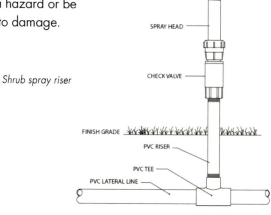
Shrub spray riser

Pop-up spray heads are installed below the turf line or at grade. When the water is turned on, they pop up and spray. When the water is turned off, they retract. They are available in different spray patterns, including full-circle, half-circle, quarter-circle, fully adjustable and in special patterns for long, narrow strips. Pop-ups are commonly used in lawns and planting beds. Refer to the diagrams showing the details.

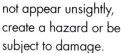

Landscape Irrigation

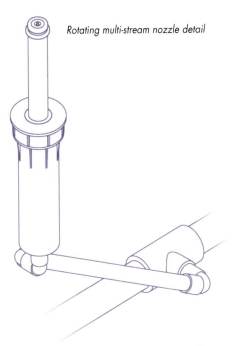
Rotating multi-stream nozzle detail

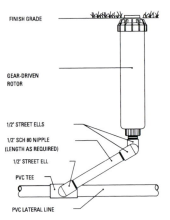
Gear-driver rotor sprinkler detail

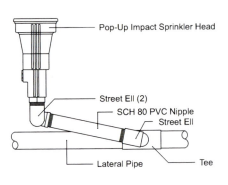
Impact rotor sprinkler detail

Rotating multi-stream sprinkler

Rotating multi-stream nozzles
Multi-stream nozzles can be retrofitted to any existing pop-up spray nozzles providing improved coverage and using much less water. These nozzles can be used to improve or revitalize older irrigation systems without requiring new valves or lateral lines, which is a great economical advantage as well.

Rotating multistream sprinklers may also be called rotator sprays

Rotors
Two basic types of rotors are impact rotors and gear-driven rotors. Rotors rotate in a full or partial circle. They have a larger spraying radius than risers or pop-ups and are best suited for large turf areas. Rotors tend to be more costly than spray heads, but fewer heads are needed to cover a given area. Rotors are available in pop-up models and in fixed versions for mounting on risers.

Impact rotors have a spring-loaded arm that swings sideways when contacted by water sprayed through the nozzle. When the arm swings, it impacts the sprinkler body, causing it to rotate a small amount. Each time it rotates, a new section of lawn receives water. Impact sprinklers can be adjusted to rotate in a full or partial

Rotor sprinklers in a landscape

Irrigation System Components & Maintenance

Rotor sprinklers in a landscape

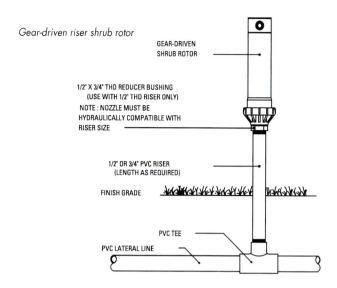

Gear-driven riser shrub rotor

Pop-up rotor retracted in the ground

circle. Impact rotors are easily recognized by the loud, distinct noise they make while operating.

Gear-driven rotors are turned by the water, which causes the gears to turn and then the head to rotate. They do not have the noise of impact sprinklers. Impact and gear-driven rotor heads may be attached to the piping using either a rigid PVC riser or swing pipe, as specified by state or provincial code.

Low-volume systems and components

Low-volume irrigation systems for beds and plantings in native areas require additional equipment compared to sprinkler head irrigation systems and are discussed in more detail in the "Irrigation Concepts" chapter. The additional components for low-volume systems are described below.

Drip valve assembly

Each zone has a drip valve assembly usually, but not always, contained within a valve box. Each assembly is made of the following components:

- Remote control valve
- Filter — Low-volume systems include emitters with small openings that can easily become clogged. To prevent clogging, filters are usually installed.
- Pressure regulator — Most low-volume irrigation systems are designed to operate at pressures below that of the typical water supply. To keep water pressure within the design limits of the system, a pressure regulator is installed.

Drip tubing and piping

Drip tubing and piping is thin-walled poly tubing that supplies water to emitters or microsprays (see below). Diameters range from 1/8 – 1" (3 – 25 mm).

Drip valve assembly with a valve, filter and pressure regulator

Landscape Irrigation

In-line tubing with built-in emitters

Microspray emitter

Multi-stream bubbler component

All images Courtesy of Hunter Industries

Emitters

Emitters are devices that drip water at a slow rate. Output for drip emitters is measured in gallons per hour (gph), with discharge rates generally ranging from ½ – 2 gph (a 1 gph emitter discharges 3.75 litres/hour).

Emitters are typically installed in a location that delivers water to the base of plants. On sloping terrain, they should be placed on the uphill side of the area to be watered.

Emitters are purchased separately and installed along drip tubing wherever water is needed. As plants grow, emitters should be added and extended out with root growth. Pressure-compensating emitters are available for use where water pressure is reduced on long runs or on sloping terrain.

In-line emitter tubing and laser soaker line

In-line emitter tubing has individual drip emitters incorporated into the drip tubing. Emitters are spaced at different intervals (typically 6" or 12" intervals or 15 cm – 30 cm). The tubing comes in ¼", ⅝" or ½" diameter. Rather than supplying water to individual plants, this tubing supplies more uniform water to a larger area for smaller plants, such as annuals and perennials. See also the *"Subsurface low-volume systems"* section below.

Laser soaker line is drip tubing with regularly spaced laser-drilled holes that emit water. In-line and laser line can be laid on the surface or buried in the ground or under mulch, and is designed to operate at pressures up to a range of 20 – 40 psi.

> Many low-volume system components are directional. When installing components make sure the arrow points in the direction of flow.

Microsprays

Microsprays have characteristics of ordinary spray heads but operate at lower pressure, have lower discharge rates and a smaller spray radius. Microsprays are more efficient than surface spray irrigation and less efficient than drip irrigation.

Bubblers

Bubblers are similar to drip emitters, but with a higher discharge rate. Their output can be adjusted from 2 – 6 gallons per minute (gpm) or 7.5 – 22.5 litres per minute. Since this exceeds the soil infiltration rate, they are used to flood small areas. After the bubbler is shut off, water infiltrates the soil. They should only be used in locations where standing water is contained and the surface is flat.

Soaker hoses

Soaker hoses are porous hoses that continuously sweat water. Soaker hoses can be cut to desired length and plugged with an end cap. They operate best on flat sites and work well in raised planters or flower pots.

Irrigation System Components & Maintenance   Chapter 5 | Page 73

Multi-stream bubbler

Subsurface low-volume systems

Subsurface drip irrigation (SDI) systems are low-pressure, low-volume irrigation systems that use buried drip tubes. With subsurface systems, water is provided directly to the root zone. There is no evaporation, no runoff (which means reduced soil erosion) and water use efficiency is very high (up to 97 percent). SDIs may use from 30 percent to 70 percent less water than conventional irrigation systems. The benefits of SDI systems make them a great water conservation and management choice.

Rain barrels and cisterns

In some regions, rain barrels and cisterns are becoming more popular for capturing rainwater for landscape needs. Rainwater "harvesting" is best done in regions that have frequent rain. Rain barrels are usually about 60 gallons (227 litres), whereas cisterns can a have a capacity of 1000 or up to 100,000 gallons or more (3785 – 378,500 litres).

There are several benefits to capturing or harvesting rainwater, including reducing stormwater runoff and its potential for polluting waterways, reducing the demand on municipal water and providing a more natural source of water (no fluoride or chlorine). In addition, they are easy to install. Rain barrel water should be used within a week or two to discourage the growth of algae. Some cisterns may incorporate water filtration and treatment systems.

Note: In some areas, rainwater collection is illegal or otherwise regulated. Check local regulations.

Installing Pipes and Fittings

The section *"Piping"* described the primary piping used in a typical irrigation system — the mainline and laterals. This section describes how to install pipes and fittings. These basic procedures also apply to repairing pipes and fittings covered in a later section.

Polyvinyl chloride (PVC) pipe

The best way to join PVC pipe and fittings is to use PVC primers and cement. A wide variety of products is available for this purpose. Note: Before using any adhesives, read and follow the manufacturer's instructions.

Follow these steps when installing PVC pipe:
- Remove any burrs or rough edges from ends of pipe with sandpaper or with gloved hand.
- Be sure all pipe and couplings are dry.
- Clean the two surfaces to be joined and apply primer or cleaner.

Landscape Irrigation

Using glue to join PVC pipe and fittings.

Crimping tool with a poly fitting.

- Allow primer to sit for the length of time recommended by the manufacturer, then apply the cement. Be sure the surfaces to be joined are completely covered.
- Avoid over- or under-application of cement. Excessive cement can damage pipes and couplings, while too little cement won't produce a strong joint.
- Insert coupling into pipe.
- Join the pieces together, turning the coupling slightly to spread cement evenly. Remove any excess cement from the seam.
- Hold the pieces together to allow cement to set up. Refer to and follow the manufacturer's recommendations.
- Repeat to attach the other pipe.
- Allow sufficient time for curing before burying or charging the line. Again, refer to the manufacturer's recommended time.

Safety guidelines for working with primers and cement

The major hazards from working with adhesives include noxious fumes and irritation from contact with skin.

Avoid using primer and cement in an enclosed area, when possible. Watch for signs of headaches, which can indicate overexposure.

Wear appropriate eye protection.

Avoid contact with skin. Wear rubber gloves and other proper protective equipment.

If you get adhesive on your skin, remove it with a mild cleanser. Avoid using an abrasive cleanser or solvent.

Keep containers closed when not in use.

If applicators are supplied, use them to apply products.

Polyethylene (poly) pipe

Follow these steps when installing poly pipe:
1. Remove any burrs or rough edges from ends of pipe.
2. Position clamp(s) loosely over the ends of the two sections of pipe.
3. Insert couplings into each pipe as far as they will go.
4. Tighten the clamps to secure the couplings. If using worm drive clamps, a screw driver or nut driver can be used. If using pinch clamps, a specialized crimping tool must be used to ensure a secure connection.
5. Double clamping may be necessary when using pinch clamps with high water pressure, when using poly pipe that is greater than 1 ¼" (4 cm) diameter or at valve connections and fittings within 10 ft (3 m) of an automatic valve. When double clamping, offset the tightening points of clamps.

Flux is applied to pipe and fitting before soldering.

Fitting is placed on the pipe.

A mapp torch is being used to apply the solder to the joint and fitting.

Copper pipe and fittings

Installing copper pipe and fittings requires soldering skills, soldering equipment and additional safety precautions.

Soldering equipment

Irrigation installation often requires copper fittings to be permanently joined by soldering or brazing. Soldering uses metals that have a melting point below 800° F (427° C). Brazing uses metals that have a melting point above 800° F (427° C). Equipment commonly used for soldering and brazing includes mapp (methylacetylene-propadiene) gas torches and acetylene B-tanks. Special safety precautions must be followed when using any soldering or brazing equipment.

Mapp gas

Mapp gas is a blend of liquefied petroleum and methylacetylene-propadiene. Mapp gas produces a hotter flame than some other gasses used for soldering and brazing. Mapp gas is available in hand-held 1-pound (0.5 kg) canisters that are easily portable and can accept a variety of torch tips.

Acetylene B-tanks

B-tanks are gas containers filled with acetylene. Like mapp gas canisters, they can be used with different torch tips. At almost two feet tall (60 cm), a B-tank is not as portable as a mapp gas canister.

Landscape Irrigation

How to solder

Before beginning any soldering activities, be sure to wear proper eye and hand protection and other protective clothing, and follow the safety guidelines under *"Safety Guidelines for Soldering."*

Follow these steps when soldering copper pipe and fittings:

1. If this is a repair, excavate an area large enough to comfortably undertake the repair. The excavation depth should be approximately 2" (5 cm) below the bottom of the pipe, the width should be approximately four times the pipe diameter (min. 4" or 10 cm), and the length should be at least 24" or 60 cm (longer if needed).
2. Cut pipe to length using a proper tool, such as a tubing cutter or hacksaw.
3. Using an Emory cloth, sand cloth or wire brush, remove any burrs or rough edges and clean the surfaces to be joined. If soldering to make a repair, remove water from the pipe since water cools the pipe and may not allow a proper seal.
4. Apply soldering flux to the surfaces to be joined.
5. Place the fitting on the end of the pipe.
6. With a torch, apply heat to the fitting so that the flux begins to bubble.
7. Place solder on the joint. As the fitting is heated, the heat will melt the solder and draw it into the joint. Don't heat the solder directly. Move solder around the joint until the whole joint is covered.
8. While still hot, remove excess solder with a damp rag.

> ### Installing threaded fittings for all pipes—PVC, poly or copper
>
> Threaded fittings are joined by applying pipe dope (thread sealant) to threads or wrapping the male threads with Teflon tape then screwing the fittings together. Tape should be applied in a clockwise direction so it does not unravel when fittings are joined. Care should be taken not to over-tighten fittings, which can damage threads or crack fittings or valves.

Common Abbreviations and Terms Used with Pipe Fittings

C = Copper

Comp = Compression

Flg = Flanged

Flr = Flared

Fpt = Female pipe thread (threads are not exposed or on the inside the fitting)

Ins = Insert (polyethylene pipe)

Mpt = Male pipe thread (threads are exposed or on the outside of the fitting)

Reducer = Reduces from one size to another

Rt = Ringtite (gasketed joint pipe)

S = Slip (around PVC pipe)

SDR = Sewer and Drain

Spg = Slip (into fitting, as in bushing, used with PVC pipe and fittings)

Safety guidelines for soldering

The major hazards from soldering and brazing are the harmful fumes produced by gas and metals, and extreme heat from open flames and hot surfaces.

Note: Before using any soldering equipment or combustible gas, read and follow the manufacturer's instructions and Material Safety Data Sheets (MSDS).

Wear proper eye, ear and body protection.

Keep body parts away from open flame and avoid contact with hot materials.

Use only in a well-ventilated area. Metals and gas can produce harmful or deadly fumes.

Keep your head away from fumes.

Properly dispose of used containers. Note: It is illegal to have some types of gas containers refilled. Know the regulations for the type of gas container you are using.

Store all combustible gases in a cool, well-ventilated area out of direct sunlight and away from any source of heat, sparks or flame. Use a restraining device to hold tanks in place and prevent them from falling over.

Irrigation System Repair and Maintenance

Nearly all irrigation systems require periodic maintenance due to wear and tear on equipment, electrical disruptions, damage from landscape equipment or vandalism, changing environmental conditions and other causes. In this section, pipe repair, sprinkler head troubleshooting and repair and winterizing the system is discussed. Controller, valve and all electrical-related maintenance and troubleshooting is covered in the chapter, *"Wiring & Electrical Troubleshooting."*

Pipe repair

This section describes how to repair pipe and fittings. These basic procedures are similar to those used for installation (see earlier section, *"Installing Pipes and Fittings"*).

Excavation
For all pipe repairs, excavate an area large enough to comfortably undertake the repair. The excavation depth should be approximately 2" (5 cm) below the bottom of the pipe, the width should be approximately four times the pipe diameter (min. 4" or 10 cm), and the length should be at least 24" or 60 cm (longer if needed).

PVC pipe repair

Components used to repair PVC are joined with adhesive cement. Always read and follow manufacturer's instructions and safety precautions when using any adhesives. The steps for repairing a broken section of PVC pipe are very similar to those used when first installing PVC pipe and fittings. Follow these steps:

- Excavate as instructed above.
- Cut out the damaged section of pipe. Use a PVC saw or pipe cutters and make sure the cut is straight.
- Remove any burrs or rough edges where the pipe has been cut.

Landscape Irrigation

Poly pipe cutter.

> When repairs are complete, holes or trenches should be backfilled and compacted. Compact soil by puddling (applying water to the top of the backfill), jetting (injecting water below the surface of backfill) or tamping (compacting soil with some type of compaction device). This may have to be done in several lifts (layers), depending on the depth of excavation.

- Be sure all pipes and couplings are dry. You may need to use repair couplings or compression fittings to provide the necessary play needed for this repair. A slip-fix is generally used only on non-gasket fitting laterals, rarely on mainline repairs.
- Clean the two surfaces with a rag (and water if needed), wipe dry and apply primer.
- Allow primer to sit for the time recommended by the manufacturer, then apply cement. Be sure the surfaces to be joined are completely covered. Don't over- or under-apply. Excessive cement can damage pipes and couplings, while too little cement won't produce a strong joint. Avoid contact with skin. Wear rubber gloves and other proper protective clothing.
- Insert the coupling into the pipe.
- Join the pieces together, turning the coupling one quarter around to spread cement evenly. Remove any excess cement from the seam.
- Hold the pieces together for about a minute, or according to the manufacturer's instructions, to allow cement to set up.
- Repeat the above to attach a coupling to the other section of pipe.
- Cut a piece of pipe the same length as the section you removed in Step 1.
- Attach the new section of pipe to couplings using the same procedure you used to attach couplings to old sections of pipe.
- Allow sufficient time for curing before burying or charging the line. Again, refer to the manufacturer's recommended time.

Irrigation System Components & Maintenance

Sprinkler misting means pressure is too high.

Tools and components for poly pipe repair

Poly pipe repair

Follow these steps when repairing a broken section of poly pipe:

- Excavate as instructed previously.
- Cut out the damaged section of pipe. Use a poly cutter and make sure the cut is straight.
- Remove any burrs or rough edges where the pipe has been cut.
- If using pipe clamps, position clamps loosely over the ends of the two sections of pipe or use compression couplings to connect the new section of pipe.
- Insert couplings into each pipe as far as they will go.
- Tighten the clamps to secure the couplings.
- Cut a piece of pipe the same length as the section you removed.
- Position two clamps on each side of the cut, loosely over the new piece of pipe.
- Insert the ends of the new piece of pipe over the two couplings.
- Tighten all four of the clamps to secure the new pipe.

Repairing copper pipe and fittings

Follow the steps listed under *"Copper pipe and fittings,"* with the following additions:

1. Excavate an area large enough to comfortably undertake the repair. The excavation depth should be approximately 2" (5 cm) below the bottom of the pipe, the width should be approximately four times the pipe diameter (4" or 10 cm), and the length should be at least 24" or 60 cm (longer if needed).
2. Remove any water that may be in the pipe as this cools the pipe and may not allow a proper seal.

Troubleshooting and repairing sprinkler heads

Problems with a sprinkler head are often detectable either by a distorted spray pattern or by the presence of brown grass around the head. Some problems can be easily corrected with simple adjustments. Depending on the type of head, it may be possible to adjust the spray angle and radius. The method for adjusting varies with the type of head and the manufacturer. Refer to the table on page 70 for troubleshooting recommendations.

Landscape Irrigation

Troubleshooting Chart for Sprinkler Heads

Problem	Likely Cause	Corrective Action
Distorted spray pattern	Nozzle is clogged with debris	Clear debris. You may need to detach nozzle to remove obstruction. Spray heads have a filter screen under the nozzle. If it becomes clogged, it should be cleaned or replaced.
Heads discharge large drops	Nozzle is clogged with debris	Clear debris. You may need to detach nozzle to remove obstruction. Spray heads have a filter screen under the nozzle. If it becomes clogged, it should be cleaned or replaced.
	Water pressure is too low	Check for leaks in the system. If the system is not leaking, you may need heads that operate at lower pressure.
Heads discharge a fine mist	Water pressure is too high	Install remote control valve with flow control. Install pressure regulator valve on mainline.
Rotary sprinklers do not rotate or rotate too slowly	Water pressure is too low	Check for leaks in the system.
	Bad gear-drive mechanism (gear-drive sprinklers only)	Replace gear drive.
	Break-up pin is improperly adjusted (impact sprinklers only)	Adjust break-up pin.
	Insufficient water is contacting lever (impact sprinklers only)	Adjust lever.
	Lever is impacting back of sprinkler head (impact sprinklers only)	Adjust lever.
Pop-up sprinkler will not pop up	Water pressure is too low	Check for leaks in the system.
	Dirt or other debris in the spindle sleeve area	Remove debris. Internal unit may need to be disassembled for cleaning.
Pop-up sprinkler sticks in up position	Dirt or other debris in the spindle sleeve area	Remove debris. Internal unit may need to be disassembled for cleaning.

Irrigation System Components & Maintenance

Bad seals

Broken sprinkler head

Pressure too high

Basic field diagnostics

Looking at an irrigated area can sometimes reveal problems with an irrigation system. Below are some conditions that may indicate problems.

- If water continues to come out of a head after the zone is shut off, this can indicate a leaking or weeping valve. However, a head located in a low point where water from the entire zone will drain can also cause this. This is called low head drainage and can be eliminated with the use of check valves. A check valve prohibits water from leaving the head when the system is not pressurized.
- If one part of the irrigated area is constantly wet, there may be a leak in the mainline.
- If grass in a particular zone is brown, the zone is not receiving adequate coverage. Some possible causes include:
  - Faulty valve
  - Faulty wiring
  - Broken lateral
  - Broken sprinkler head, which reduces pressure to the entire zone
  - Insufficient watering time on controller
  - If grass is brown around a single sprinkler head, likely causes are a faulty head or a clogged or broken nozzle.

Runoff as illustrated is caused by excessive run time. Correct by decreasing time and/or dividing time into multiple cycles.

Winterizing an irrigation system

In climates where freezing temperatures are common, irrigation systems should be winterized to avoid costly damage. This is done by blowing water out of the system using an air compressor. If water remains in the system, it will expand when frozen and can crack pipes, valves and fittings.

Follow these steps to winterize the irrigation system:
- Turn off the water supply to the system. If the main shutoff valve is outdoors, it should be insulated to protect it from freezing.
- Connect the proper size air compressor to the downstream side of the backflow preventer. Most backflow preventers have a point of connection (POC) with a small valve for connecting an air compressor.

Landscape Irrigation

- Use the controller to open the remote control valve furthest from the point of connection. This will help clear water from the mainline as you proceed.
- Start the air compressor and slowly increase pressure.
- When only air is coming out of the sprinklers, turn off the compressor and shut the remote control valve.
- Repeat for each valve in the system.
- Set the controller to rain mode. This will shut down the signals to the valves without losing the programming. Alternatively, you can turn off the power to the controller. If you do this, you will need to reprogram the controller in the spring.
- Drain the backflow preventer and open any drains at the point of connection.

> After winterizing, all valves—except the main supply valve—should be left in a slightly open position to prevent damage to the seals.

Summary

Irrigation systems continue to evolve, favoring more sustainable options. All conventional irrigation systems have several common components, including backflow prevention, piping, valves, emitting devices, wiring and controllers. Various options are available for each of these components.

Smart controllers are becoming more common and can conserve water and save money and time. After programming, smart controllers can use information from environmental sensors and/or the weather to manage watering schedules for optimal irrigation—not too much, not too little.

Low-volume systems use different piping and tubing solutions and various drip emitters to reduce water loss by evaporation. Subsurface drip irrigation systems are even more efficient by eliminating evaporation and reducing irrigation needs by supplying water directly to the roots.

Irrigation systems typically require periodic troubleshooting, repair and other maintenance due to wear and tear or damage. Field diagnostics, meaning watching the irrigation system in action, can often indicate the likely problem. Leaks in the mainline or laterals require excavation. Often sprinkler head issues can be solved by cleaning and removing obstructions. Valve or valve parts may occasionally have to be replaced.

Protect irrigation systems by properly winterizing them in areas where freezing temperatures are sustained through winter.

Chapter 6

Wiring & Electrical Troubleshooting

What You Will Learn

After reading this chapter, you will be able to:

- Name two common wiring methods for controllers.
- Recognize and understand key terms and concepts used when working with electrical systems.
- Compare the terms used for water concepts and electrical concepts.
- Name and describe the function for at least four common tools or pieces of equipment used for electrical troubleshooting.
- Follow troubleshooting steps given for electrical system field tests for multi-wire systems.
- Follow troubleshooting steps given for two-wire decoder systems.
- Follow instructions for troubleshooting and maintaining valves.

Chapter 6

Preview

Wiring Controllers
- Multi-wire system
- Two-wire decoder system

Electrical Terms, Concepts and Equipment
- Electrical terms and concepts
- Basic troubleshooting equipment

Troubleshooting Multi-Wire Systems

Troubleshooting Two-Wire Decoder Systems
- About troubleshooting two-wire systems
- How to troubleshoot

Troubleshooting Valves

Manual sponsored by **Hunter Industries**

Landscape Irrigation

Overview

Working with irrigation wiring and electrical troubleshooting requires additional skills, knowledge and experience because of the potential hazard and additional safety precautions needed when working with electrical devices. In the chapter *"Irrigation System Components and Maintenance,"* repairing pipes and troubleshooting malfunctioning sprinkler heads is discussed. In this chapter, controller wiring and troubleshooting electrical problems is covered.

Wiring Controllers

There are two methods of wiring that are typically used for irrigation systems; the multi-wire, or "common wire" system and the two-wire decoder system.

Multi-wire system

Guidelines for installing controllers using a multi-wire system (or common wire system)

- Install the controller in an accessible location. Where possible, install the controller near the zones that the controller will operate to minimize the length of wire required.
- Harness wires from the remote control valves and pass them through a conduit in the wall near the controller. Place number labels on each valve wire corresponding to the appropriate valve number.
- Connect the common wire to the common terminal.
- Take the other wire from each valve and connect it to the appropriate zone terminal on the controller. Connect them in the same order as the watering sequence.
- Turn on the power to the controller, and then test each zone.
- Program the controller (see the chapter "Irrigation System Components and Maintenance" for information on programming controllers).

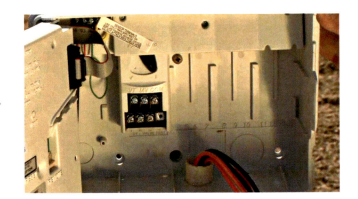

Wires are brought into the controller through a conduit. The white common wire will be wired to the common (COM) terminal.

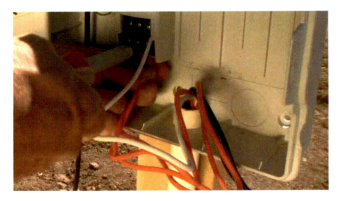

Controller wiring is complete, showing the common wire and the zone wires.

Two-wire decoder system

The two-wire decoder system is ideal for large commercial irrigation installations that have long wire runs from the controller to the decoder and valves. This system can take the place of thousands of feet of wire in large installations. The connections and communication between the controller and the decoders are what run the system. Each decoder has its own unique number or address and some decoders can have up to six unique addresses. Identifying information is passed between the controller and the decoders. Decoders "decode" the signals, respond only to signals unique to their address and tell the valves and other components what to do. The controllers that run these systems can be pre-wired and ready to be plugged in and operated using remote control devices.

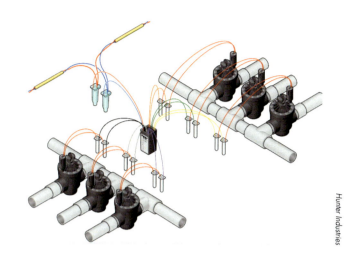

Diagram of two-wire decoder system

Electrical Terms, Concepts and Equipment

Nearly all irrigation systems require periodic maintenance due to wear-and-tear on equipment, electrical disruptions, damage from landscape equipment or vandalism, changing environmental conditions and other causes. This section begins with a brief overview of electricity terms and concepts, and then discusses troubleshooting the maintenance and repair of the electrical components of the irrigation systems.

Electrical terms and concepts

Troubleshooting controllers, solenoids and field wiring includes working with electrical components and measuring electricity. The first step in troubleshooting field problems is to check the circuitry. Before doing so, it is helpful to understand some basic terms and tools that are used when working with electricity, as well as some basic concepts.

Some technicians may find it useful to compare terminology and concepts used with water to those used with electricity. The properties of water and electricity are similar in some ways and can be compared as follows.

Concept	Water Term	Electrical Term
Force, pressure or power that can cause flow	Pressure (psi)	Voltage (volts—V)
Force that reduces or resists	Friction loss (psi)	Resistance (ohms—Ω)
Movement or flow	Flow (gpm)	Current (amps—A)

Landscape Irrigation

Common Electrial Terms

Term	Description
Alternating Current (AC)	Standard household current. Most irrigation controllers use 120 Volt AC (VAC)
Amperage (amps)	Quantitative measurement of the flow of electricity. Similar to the flow of water in gallons per minute.
Circuit	In the common wire (multi-wire) irrigation wiring system, the circuit is the electrical wiring path from the end of the zone wire to a station output terminal, then to the solenoid, and finally back to the end of the common wire connected to the controller's common terminal.
Connection	Combining one wire with one or more wires inside of an approved waterproof wire nut or other connecting device. The best connector is pre-filled with non-oxidizing, water-repelling, non-corrosive grease.
Direct current	Directional flowing electricity, such as current flowing from the positive terminal of a battery through a device and back to the negative terminal. This type of current is found in electronic controllers. The battery is used to maintain the program in older electronic controllers and the time and date in newer controllers.
Field Wiring	All wiring between the controller and electrical devices, solenoids and/or relays that is installed in the ground or away from the controller.
Multimeter	A digital or analog testing device for measuring the characteristics of electricity (voltage, amperage and resistance).
Resistance (ohms)	The resistance encountered by electricity in wiring or devices on a circuit. Analogous to friction loss (loss of water pressure) when water is flowing through pipes.
Terminals	The connection on the panel of the controller to which the field wires are attached. There are station output terminals and common terminals.
Voltage	The quantitative measure of the power of electricity. Analogous to water pressure in irrigation terminology.

Basic troubleshooting equipment

The following equipment is recommended for troubleshooting controllers, solenoids and field wiring.

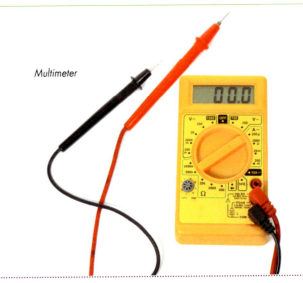

Multimeter

Clamp meter
Essential for troubleshooting two-wire decoder system faults. It measures current (milliamps) in a wire without having to cut the wire. The clamp meter is opened and placed around the wires.

Wiring & Electrical Troubleshooting

Multimeter (Digital volt-ohm meter)
Must be able to read both AC and DC voltage, resistance from 1 to 200 ohms (Ω), and amperage. A relatively inexpensive piece of equipment that provides multiple measures. Models can be digital or analog.

Solenoid with alligator clips
Solder alligator clips to the wire of any good solenoid for a good connection.

Solenoid activator
A good unit has circuit testing capabilities, solenoid activation and a tone generator. A tone generator allows a current/signal through one wire from the field to the controller (or the reverse), which can identify the other end of the same wire. It is useful for determining which clock a valve is wired to, or which field valve a wire runs to.

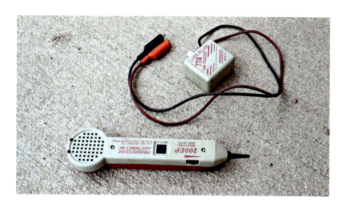

Tone generator and probe

Tone generator with probe
The tone generator reads the opposite end of the wire to which the solenoid activator is connected.

Voltage detector
Reads power level in a wire by placing it near a wire without disconnecting or cutting the wire or the insulation of a wire.

Troubleshooting Multi-Wire Systems

The 12-step process described below provides detailed step-by-step instructions for electrical troubleshooting of controllers. This process is provided courtesy of Control Tech USA (with minor modifications for clarity incorporated).

Irrigation Electrical System Field Test Process

Step	Action
Step 1	Is there a correctly functioning display on the controller when the door is opened? **Yes:** REMOVE ALL POWER FROM THE CONTROLLER, including the 24 volt AC (VAC) backup battery and remove the common wire. Let the controller sit powered down for approximately one minute. While the controller is powered down, test the backup battery with the volt meter, set to DC volts, to make sure the battery is good. Reconnect the 24 VAC power, common wire, and backup battery. Go to Step 5. **No:** Continue to Step 2

Landscape Irrigation

Irrigation Electrical System Field Test Process continued

Step	Action
Step 2	Do a sniff and visual test. Does the controller have a burnt smell or physical signs of damage? **Yes:** Send controller for repair. **No:** Proceed to Step 3.
Step 3	Is there 24 VAC on the secondary side of the transformer? **Yes:** Check terminals and other connections between the transformer and controller. If all tests are good and the controller still does not work, check the fuse or circuit breaker. Reset the controller by powering down for about one minute. First remove the 24 VAC power, the backup battery and the common wire(s), then the battery. Wait at least 1 minute and then reconnect the common wire(s), batteries, and 24 VAC power. If the controller has a display, review it to check that all aspects of the previous program have remained. Proceed to Step 5. If there is no display on the controller, send it in for repair. **No:** Go to Step 4. **CAUTION!** Only a licensed electrician can work with 120 VAC electricity in most areas.

Irrigation Electrical System Field Test Process continued

Step	Action
Step 4	Check for 120 VAC at connections on the primary side of the transformer with a volt meter if allowed in your area. Is the 120 VAC at an acceptable level? **Yes:** Disconnect the primary transformer wires (black and white) from the 120 VAC supply wires. Disconnect the wires on the secondary side of the transformer. Check for continuity through primary side wires by conducting a continuity test with a volt meter or multimeter. Check for continuity through secondary wires. If either side shows "open," replace the transformer and start again at Step 1. **No:** Check to make sure the switch for the power supply is on and check the breaker to make sure it is in the normal position. If the power supply and breaker check out and there is still no 120 VAC at connections to the transformer, call an electrician to repair the primary power.
Step 5  *Multimeter being used to test controller connections*	Test the station outputs with a multimeter (24 VAC) using the field wiring and/or a test solenoid. Do all the outputs read at acceptable levels on the multimeter and activate the test solenoid (if using a test solenoid)? **Yes:** Check the controller switches, keypad keys and functions. If all work normally, check the program and perform and complete the "Field Circuit Resistance (Ω) and Amperage Test Worksheet" to have a reference point for future problems. An example of a filled-in worksheet is shown on page 80. Refer to the Appendix for a blank worksheet. Go to Step 6. **No:** Send the controller for repair. See *Field Circuit Resistance and Amperage Test Worksheet - Sample* on next page.

Landscape Irrigation

Irrigation Electrical System Field Test Process continued

Step	Action
Step 5 continued	

Field Circuit Resistance and Amperage Test Worksheet - Sample

Zone	Ohms (Ω)	Amps (A)	Zone	Ohms (Ω)	Amps (A)	Zone	Ohms (Ω)	Amps (A)
1	25.8	0.42	11	53.2	0.41	21	54.2	0.43
2	27.3	0.23	12	26.0	0.44	22		
3	6.9	1.54	13	54.5	0.41	23		
4	0	0.22	14	29.3	0.44	24		
5	10.6	0.84	15	5.8	1.24	25		
6	25.1	0.23	16	25.2	0.48	26		
7	27.4	0.43	17	26.9	0.44	27		
8	6.6	0.69	18	30.1	0.44	28		
9	25.9	0.43	19	5.4	1.29	29		
10	26.7	0.47	20	26.0	0.44	30		

Step	Action
Step 6	Did all field circuits test okay? **Yes:** Check all controller output connections and splicing and retest the system. Follow the test instructions given for the "Field Circuit Resistance Test." If all tests run okay, run a simple program and make sure the controller and the valves work normally. If the system runs normally, the test is complete. **Field Circuit Resistance Test** This procedure tests the field wiring circuitry attached to a controller. This test helps discover or affirm a field problem. If there is a problem in the field wiring, it must be corrected before operating the bad circuit again. Using a good multimeter: • Set the ohm (Ω) reading between 0 and 200 ohms. • Connect the black lead of the multimeter to the disconnected common wire from the controller. Alligator clip ends or a jumper with alligator clips work best. • Starting with Zone #1 field wire or zone terminal, touch the wire/terminal with the red lead of the multimeter.

Irrigation Electrical System Field Test Process continued

Step	Action

Step 6 continued	• Record the reading in a chart for Zone #1. (The chart should show a number for each zone).
	• Touch each of the remaining field zone wires, as described above.
	• Record each reading for each zone.
	• Determine which circuits are good and which are bad using the following scale:
	
	    0 – 6 ohms Short circuit: bad solenoid or shorted wire path
	    6 – 12 ohms Slow burn solenoid or multiple solenoids on the circuit. Check the circuit.
	    12 – 60 ohms Normal operating range. The zone is good.
	    >60 ohms An "open" or broken or nicked wire exists or there is a "bad" splice, one that is not properly waterproofed.
	
	• Disconnect the wires from the zone terminals with "bad" circuits.
	• Check splicing in valve boxes when readings are high.
	
	No: Disconnect the failed zone wires and common wires(s) from the controller. Find the valve on the failed zone. Disconnect the solenoid wires from the field wires. Test the resistance value (ohms) of the solenoid. Go to Step 7.

Step 7	Do the solenoids have the correct ohms rating? Use the table below. **Yes:** Go to Step 8. ### Solenoid Ohm (Ω) Resistance Values by Manufacturer *Note: This list may not be complete.* | Manufacturer	Resistance Value (older/newer)
Asco (Bermad/ClaVal)	14.4
Buckner	21.7/18.8
Champion	21.7/15.4
Greenlawn	22.7/21.4
Griswold	21.1	

Landscape Irrigation

Irrigation Electrical System Field Test Process continued

Step	Action
Step 7 continued	<table><tr><th>Manufacturer</th><th>Resistance Value (older/newer)</th></tr><tr><td>Hardie/Irritrol</td><td>24.4</td></tr><tr><td>Hunter</td><td>29.7/23.4</td></tr><tr><td>Imperial ATTV</td><td>21.7</td></tr><tr><td>Nelson</td><td>22.2</td></tr><tr><td>Orbit</td><td>20.2</td></tr><tr><td>Rain Bird "A" series coil</td><td>28.5</td></tr><tr><td>Rain Bird "B" series solenoid</td><td>23.8/35.4</td></tr><tr><td>Rain Bird "DV" series solenoid</td><td>51.8/40.4</td></tr><tr><td>Superior</td><td>23.1</td></tr><tr><td>Toro 1"</td><td>28/54.3</td></tr><tr><td>Toro ¾"</td><td>23/54.3</td></tr><tr><td>Weathermatic</td><td>34.3</td></tr></table> **No:** Turn off the water supply. Replace the faulty solenoid and retest according to Step 5.
Step 8	Does the field wiring have the proper ohms reading? It should read "open." **Yes:** Reconnect the zone wire and common wire to the correct terminals at the controller. Turn on the zone from the controller. Test for 24 VAC across the end of the field wire and the common wire in the valve box. Go to Step 9. **No:** There may be a short. Find the problem with the field wiring, repair and retest according to the *"Field Circuit Resistance Test Worksheet."*
Step 9	Is there 24 VAC on the field wire at the zone valve? **Yes:** Reconnect the solenoid wires to the field wire and the common wire. Turn on the zone at the controller. Go to Step 10. **No:** There may be a broken wire. Find the problem using a pulser or 521 wire and valve locator. Repair and retest.

Irrigation Electrical System Field Test Process continued

Step	Action
Step 10	Did the zone valve turn on? **Yes:** Go to the next bad circuit and test according to Step 6. **No:** Turn off the water supply and remove the solenoid from the valve. Activate the zone and check to see if the solenoid pulled in the plunger. Go to Step 11.
Step 11	Did the plunger pull in? **Yes:** Check for mechanical operation of the solenoid and valve according to the manufacturer's recommendations. The valve itself may need to be replaced or rebuilt. **No:** There may be a short to ground situation. Test with a ground fault locator to determine the relative location of the break or exposed wire causing the fault. Repair and retest from Step 11. If zone still does not operate, go to Step 12.
Step 12	Call for help!

Troubleshooting Two-Wire Decoder Systems

The two-wire decoder system consists of two wires that are run continually from the controller to the end of the system and are connected to a decoder at each electric valve. This system was briefly described in the chapter, "Irrigation System Components and Maintenance." Each decoder is assigned an individual address that is recognized by the controller. The same two wires connect the controller, decoders and solenoids from as little as three to more than 50 zones. Each decoder is assigned a number and the controller can send a unique electronic signal to individual valves or to multiple valves depending on the information provided by the programmer. The system is more versatile than the multi-wire system because the wires can be stubbed off at the end of the irrigation system for future expansion. In addition to ease of expansion, the two-wire decoder system is easier and less costly both to install and maintain.

Landscape Irrigation

About troubleshooting two-wire systems

When troubleshooting any wiring system, it is important to have a troubleshooting strategy before going into the field and then to follow the appropriate steps to isolate the problem. The strategy for a two-wire decoder system should be based on the diagnostics or tests run at the controller, which narrow down the area in which the problem lies. Using the diagnostics, coupled with common sense, will save a lot of time when troubleshooting. For example, it is important to know how many single and multiple address decoders are on each individual wire path, as well as the "at rest" current draw for each individual wire path, so that you can quickly determine which path has the problem. A benefit of having multiple wire paths (up to five coming into the line termination box within the controller) is that system problems can be isolated, thus allowing the rest of the property to continue to be properly irrigated.

It is best to have a copy of the irrigation plan as built before beginning any troubleshooting or repairs. The plan shows the layout of the system and whether it is in a loop or star (also called branched or hub and spoke) configuration. The star or branched configuration is easier to troubleshoot. In a loop system layout, problems can be more difficult to isolate because they may occur only under certain conditions, such as when the ground is wet. If a problem is suspected in a looped system, the two ends of the loop must be disconnected at the furthest midpoint. This disconnect should be accessible in a valve box at some point along the two-wire path, and preferably near the midpoint of the loop.

Common problems

Problems in the field could result from a wiring problem or an improperly functioning solenoid or decoder. This discussion focuses primarily on wiring problems, such as wire breaks, skinned wires, faulty splices, etc., which can result in short circuits and ground faults.

The majority of all field problems that occur involve improper splicing. The two-wire decoder system has more than two times the number of splices compared to a conventional multi-wire system. In any situation that requires troubleshooting in the field, always look at the splices of the suspected problem area first. A splice must maintain integrity between the two wires being connected, be completely waterproof and not allow any current leakage to ground.

Some field problems may occur under certain conditions but not others. It is best to troubleshoot under the conditions that are present during irrigation because short circuits or ground faults may not occur when the ground is dry, but may occur when the ground is wet, causing the irrigation system to malfunction.

How to identify the field wiring problem

The three common types of field wiring problems are:
- Current interruption (non-damaged wire)
- Defective decoder or solenoid
- Ground fault interruption (damaged wire).

Each problem has different symptoms and must be diagnosed using specific steps.

Run a test at the controller

The first step is to run a test at the controller to identify the type of problem. When measuring the current using the line test unit, the number of decoders on all of the connected two-wire paths should be indicated. If the number of decoders indicated is lower than the actual number of decoders in the field, then one or more of the two-wire paths has a current interruption. Current is not reaching the decoders beyond the interruption, which prevents them from functioning.

Identify the two-wire path with the problem

To identify the two-wire path having the problem, disconnect all two-wire paths, and then reconnect them one at a time. When a pathway current reading is less than what it should be, for the number of decoders known to be on the two-wire path, then that path has the current interruption. The interruption is either at one of the decoder wire splices or is located between decoders on the two-wire path. Follow the troubleshooting steps to locate the problem.

Wiring & Electrical Troubleshooting

To troubleshoot follow these guidelines

1. **Check splices for current interruption (non-damaged wire)**
   The first points to check are any splices in the two-wire path between the two decoders and the connections at the first non-functioning decoder.
   - If a bad connection is identified, repair the connection and re-test the system.
   - If all the splices and connections appear to be in good order, proceed with the following steps.

2. **Check decoder and/or solenoid**
   If a decoder or a solenoid is defective, a short circuit condition can occur in the two-wire path that may cause the entire system, or only parts of the system, not to function.

   If decoders are working after the non-functioning decoder, then there is a short and the non-functioning decoder needs to be replaced.
   - If the short-circuit condition is actually being caused by a defective decoder, it is possible to measure current flowing into and out of that decoder by placing a clamp meter around the blue wires from the decoder.
   - On the "up-stream" side of the splice, where the suspected defective decoder is located, current will be excessive and on the "downstream" side, current will be low.
   - Confirm by placing a clamp meter around the blue communication wire on the suspect decoder. Replace the decoder if it is found to be defective.
   - If the decoder controlling a valve-in-head sprinkler or a remote control valve seems to be functioning — passing all decoder diagnostic tests and providing proper feedback and logging — but the valve is not operating, check the solenoid coil. If it checks at 10 ohms or less, then the solenoid needs to be replaced because it is acting as a "shorted" solenoid.
   - If both the decoder and the solenoid are replaced and the system does not operate, there are likely additional problems on the line.

Hunter Industries

3. **Check for ground fault interruption (broken/exposed wire)**
   If the current interruption is not due to a bad splice connection, decoder or solenoid, the entire path downstream of the interruption will be affected.
   - At this point, use the clamp meter to isolate the specific location of the problem. The clamp meter measures current in a wire without having to cut the wire. The clamp is opened and placed around both wires of the cable being tested.
   - To locate the interruption on a specific two-wire path, find the area on the path between the last functioning decoder that comes from the controller and the first non-functioning decoder.

   When the interruption has been localized, the exact break must be found manually.
   - This is done by exposing (digging up) the two-wire line as close to the midpoint as possible, between the last functioning and first non-functioning decoders, and checking the voltage.

Landscape Irrigation

- After the current interruption is passed, there will be a significant drop in the voltage reading. The voltage will be weak, but may not necessarily drop to zero beyond the break.
- Once a voltage drop occurs, begin working back toward the last working solenoid using the midpoint method until the break is located. In other words, if there is no significant voltage drop at the first midpoint, continue dividing the line distance in half working toward the first decoder that does not work until a point is identified where the voltage drop occurs.

When the significant voltage drop is located, the problem lies between the low reading location and the last decoder that worked properly, but not beyond the last excavated midpoint.
- Again, move to the middle of the two-wire path and take a voltage measurement.
- Repeat this process until the break is localized. This method of searching reduces to a minimum how much digging is required and the number of places at which measurements must be taken.
- Excavate and repair the two-wire path using the appropriate waterproof connectors and setting a splice box, which then should be noted on the as-built drawings for future repairs.

If the two-wire path is configured in a hub and spoke layout, the various spokes must be isolated by disconnecting each line from the hub at a line termination box and then using the clamp meter method outlined above.

It is at this point that having a good "as-built" plan is crucial.
- As the two-wire path branches out from the controller, the total draw on the entire system is the sum of the draw for each of the individual branches as you work back to the central location.
- For example, if there is a three-way splice serving two parts of the property, where one part has 20 decoders on it, and the other has 10 decoders on it, then the total draw on the incoming or up-stream wire will read 15 mA (30 x 0.5mA).
- On the outgoing or downstream side of the splice, one leg should read 10mA, for the branch with the 20 decoders on it and the other branch should read 5mA, for the branch with the 10 decoders on it.

4. **Check for earth ground voltage fault (short circuit)**
   Having determined which two-wire path has the short circuit condition, go into the field moving along this two-wire path to find where the short circuit condition is occurring.
   - If one or both of the wires in the two-wire path are leaking to ground, there is an earth ground voltage fault. This indicates that somewhere on the two-wire path, current is leaking from the two-wire path to earth ground.
   - Use the line test unit to measure the earth voltage.
   - When using the line test unit, if the needle moves backwards and forwards in step with the alternating of the red/green LED on the line test unit, it means that there are one or more faults in the insulation of the two-wire path cable.
   - If the needle stands below 1 volt, there is probably a ground fault in the insulation of one of the solenoids or their connecting cables.

Using the clamp meter and with the system in the 60 Hz mode, measure each of the two wires on a given two-wire path.
- If one of the wires is drawing more current than the other wire, then it is highly probable that it contains an earth ground fault.
- The ground fault can be found using a midpoint method similar to the procedure described in step 3. Measure the current at the midpoint of the two-wire path.
- If the two wires are both drawing the same amount of current, then you have passed the ground fault, which means you need to proceed with measurements on the upstream (closer to the controller) half of the two-wire path.
- Continue "halving" the distance and measuring again. If one of the two wires is drawing more current than the other, then the ground fault is downstream (further from the controller). This means continue halving the distance further out from the controller.
- Continue working toward or away from the controller with this process until the current draw in each of the wires is equal, at which point you have passed the ground fault location.
- Move to the center of the last segment and measure again. In this way, you can accurately pinpoint the ground fault location and only have to dig a 5' to 10' trench in many cases.

Examples of typical field problems with troubleshooting actions

Problem	Action
Improper two-wire cable jacket stripping (complete erosion of copper conductor)	Improper "stripping" of the outer jacket on the two-wire path cable may result in a lengthwise cut in the inner insulation of the individual conductor. - Over time, this will lead to corrosion of the copper and loss of conduction. - The end result could be loss of control of all decoders beyond this point on the two-wire path. - This would most likely show up during the "test for grounded cables." - It would also create higher-than-normal current (mA) draw on that two-wire path, based on the number of single channel decoders (each drawing 0.5mA) and the number of multiple channel decoders (each drawing 1.0 mA) at rest. - The current change would be visible in the two-wire path current using a clamp meter with the system set to the 60 Hz mode. It would show up as an "imbalance" between the red and black conductors, when each is "clamped" onto individually. - When you pass the point of the damaged insulation, the readings would be equal, indicating the leakage to ground is between the current test point and the point that you took the last previous reading. *Caution:* If the damaged insulation happens to be in a wet valve box, you will definitely know it when you place your hand in the valve box! Occasionally, this may be the way in which the damaged condition is discovered.

Landscape Irrigation

Examples of typical field problems with troubleshooting actions continued

Problem	Action
	NOTE: This is one of the more common problems encountered with the field wiring. Take care when stripping the outer jacket of the cable to reduce system downtime, as well as time and labor to troubleshoot the system and make repairs.
Improper two-wire cable jacket stripping (corrosion of copper conductor causing leakage to ground.)	In a non-system threatening condition, a broken wire, partial short or skinned insulation—as well as mildly shorted decoders—will cause the "field" LED on the controller to be red. This is a quick visual clue that something is not right with the system. • Improper stripping of the outer jacket that causes the inner insulation of the conductor to be "nicked" can cause corrosion of the copper conductor and ultimate leakage to ground. • If the insulation on both conductors has been "nicked," a short circuit could be created during wet conditions, such as during an irrigation cycle, causing the controller to shut down. • This condition may be extremely difficult to find, since under a dry condition (as you would probably have when troubleshooting during the non-irrigation hours) this short circuit would not be evident. • Thus, if the condition continues to exist, it will require troubleshooting when the soil is wet in order to find the trouble spot. Use the same procedure described previously under "Check for earth ground voltage fault."
Simulated Shorted Solenoid/ Shorted Surge Arrestor	If just one of the conductors has its insulation "nicked," then this fault could be found using a clamp meter and having the system in the 60 Hz mode. • Under this condition, there would be an "imbalance" between the two conductors, with the damaged conductor drawing the most current. • After you pass the damaged area on the two-wire path, the two conductors would then have an equal current draw. Thus, you know that the "nicked" conductor is between the point where you now are and the last point where you took a reading. • Remember, nicked insulation can also occur on the blue communication wires from the decoders themselves. • If one of the conductors has completely eroded away, there will be loss of communication and operation of decoders beyond the point of the loss of the conductor copper. Follow the procedure outlined in the previous "Improper two-wire cable jacket "stripping" (complete erosion of copper conductor)."

Troubleshooting Valves

In general, electronic control valves require little maintenance. However, certain conditions can cause valves to open or close partially or not at all. When disassembling a valve for repairs, keep parts orderly and clean so the valve can be reassembled in the same order in which it was taken apart. Always tighten and loosen bolts or screws in a cross pattern. The following troubleshooting chart lists the likely causes of these situations and their remedies.

Troubleshooting Chart for Electronic Remote Control Valves

Problem	Likely Cause	Corrective Action
Valve will not open	Solenoid coil burned out	Replace
	Solenoid bent or solenoid plunger bound	Replace
	Corrosion build-up blocking internal bleed parts	Clean obstructions
	No power to valve	Check controller output and check for continuity
	Insufficient voltage at valve	Replace wiring
	Improper size wiring or voltage drop caused by improperly insulated underground connections	Replace wiring
	Flow control stem fully closed	Open stem (turn flow control down so that when the valve is turned off from the controller, it closes within 2 – 5 seconds)
Valve will not open fully	Flow control stem partially closed	Open stem (turn flow control down so that when the valve is turned off from the controller, it closes within 2 – 5 seconds)
	Restriction in internal bleeding parts	Clean parts (corrosion, foreign materials)
	Plunger in bottom of seat spacer missing, not seated properly or stuck	Install plunger, clean parts
	Improper size plunger	Install correct plunger
	Valve too large—not enough GPM flow and pressure loss to operate properly	Replace with proper size valve
	If pressure-regulated valve, pressure regulator over-adjusted to limit flow	Turn pressure regulator adjusting screw in clockwise direction to increase pressure

Landscape Irrigation

Troubleshooting Chart for Electronic Remote Control Valves

Problem	Likely Cause	Corrective Action
Valve will not close	Obstruction in valve	Check for rock or other debris under valve seat
	Hole through seat spacer plugged—water not entering upper diaphragm chamber	Clear obstruction
	Ruptured diaphragm or diaphragm chamber	Replace
	Valve was disassembled in field and reassembled improperly	Reassemble correctly
	Solenoid plunger spring missing or damaged	Replace
	Solenoid plunger and/or seat disc eroded or otherwise damaged	Replace
	Line has been surged or subjected to extremely high pressures, damaging internal parts	Replace broken or damaged parts, as necessary
Valve will not close fully	Broken or missing seat washers in valve	Replace
	Cut or damaged seat washer or diaphragm	Replace
	Damaged seat in valve body	Replace body
	Seat disc or seat space bent	Replace
	Solenoid plunger seat disc eroded or otherwise damaged	Replace

Summary

Since irrigation systems are typically powered by electricity, electrical issues will inevitably occur for which troubleshooting is required. Be extremely cautious and be sure that only licensed electricians are working with 120 VAC. Two different wiring configurations are used for irrigation wiring: the multi-wire (common wire) system and the two-wire decoder system. Electrical systems, as with hydraulic systems, have their own unique terminology that must be learned. With just a few pieces of basic electrical troubleshooting equipment, many electrical issues can be investigated and resolved.

Occasionally, valves require maintenance, repair or replacement. The issue can be with the valve itself (for example, it could be damaged or dirty) or with the solenoid, so careful troubleshooting is required to identify and correct the problem.

Chapter 7

Landscape Equipment Safety & Maintenance

What You Will Learn

After reading this chapter, you will be able to:

- Explain the importance of prevention for personal safety and for avoiding damage to equipment.
- List the items to check before using equipment each day.
- Name and describe the use of at least four types of large equipment operated in landscape construction.
- Describe the key safety considerations for large equipment.
- Describe the maintenance guidelines for large equipment.
- Name and describe the use of at least three common types of mid-size equipment.
- List and describe the use of at least six different types of hand-operated equipment.
- Describe the key safety considerations for hand-operated equipment and the maintenance guidelines for hand-operated equipment.
- Calculate the proper fuel mix for 2-stroke engines.
- Describe safety and maintenance measures for fuel-powered and electric hand-operated equipment.
- Describe basic troubleshooting for gas-powered equipment.
- Describe general and end-of-season maintenance requirements for gas-powered equipment.
- List the items to check each day before operating a truck.
- List the items to check regularly for safe operation of a trailer.

Preview

Prevention of Injury and Equipment Damage
Large Equipment
- Commonly used large equipment
- Safety guidelines
- Maintenance guidelines

Mid-Size Equipment
- Types of mid-size equipment
- Safety guidelines

Hand-Operated Equipment
- Types of equipment
- Fuels and mixes
- Safety guidelines
- Maintenance guidelines
- Troubleshooting gas-powered equipment

Trucks and Trailers

The Shop Area
- Guidelines for the shop area

Manual sponsored by **Hunter Industries**

Landscape Irrigation

Overview

The use of motorized equipment is an essential part of landscape construction. Since landscape projects are so diverse, you must be familiar with many types of equipment to accomplish a variety of tasks. This chapter covers four major equipment types: large equipment, mid-size (intermediate) equipment, hand-operated equipment and trucks and trailers. The function, maintenance and safe operation of each are discussed.

Prevention of Injury and Equipment Damage

Safety and prevention are key to avoiding injuries and accidents. When working with landscape equipment, adhere to preventive measures that include:

- Always wearing appropriate personal protective equipment when operating and maintaining or repairing equipment.
- Regularly checking and maintaining equipment.

This section discusses common guidelines to follow for all equipment *before* operating. Sample maintenance schedules for different types of equipment are provided in later sections.

Before using equipment each day, follow the manufacturer's recommended checklist. Common pre-start checklist items follow.

Pre-start checklist
- Check engine oil level
- Check hydraulic system oil level
- Check radiator and oil cooler (check for trash build-up)
- Inspect air filter (check for dirt build-up)
- Check engine coolant level
- Inspect belt tension and condition (alternator and others)
- Check seat belt/seat switch interlock operation
- Check tire inflation and tire condition
- Grease fittings (lubricate daily or weekly per manufacturer's recommendation)
- Check fuel level and only use appropriate type of fuel
- Check safety blocks/lockouts
- Ensure that the back-up alarm is functioning

Large Equipment

Large equipment usually refers to equipment with a cab or area which the operator must enter in order to operate the equipment. Several types of large equipment are discussed in this section.

{ Your safety and the safety of others is top priority. Although this chapter provides safety guidelines for operating equipment, always read the operator's manual for all equipment to become familiar with safe operation and maintenance procedures as specified by the manufacturer. }

Commonly used large equipment
Skid steer
A skid steer is a compact, four-wheeled (some can be tracked), multi-purpose vehicle that can perform many functions in landscape construction. With a bucket on the front,

Skid steer

the skid steer is useful for small excavations and grading jobs and for moving bulk materials, such as soil, gravel or mulches. By using other attachments on the skid steer (such as post hole diggers, trenchers or tillers), it can be used to dig footings, foundations, pools and ponds, and to perform numerous other tasks.

Its small size and tight turning radius make it useful for work in small or confined areas. Skid steers also minimize damage to the existing landscape.

Many tasks formerly done with tractors are now done more effectively with skid steers.

Tractor
Tractors are versatile tools for landscape construction. They are available in many sizes, and like skid steers, can accept a variety of attachments for grading, excavating, post hole digging, scraping, tilling, and hauling gravel and other materials. Tractors can be equipped with mowing attachments to cover large turf areas.

Riding trencher
Riding trenchers are used to dig deep trenches up to 5' for a variety of uses, including edging, lighting, irrigation pipe, utilities, etc. Trenchers are available in many sizes and configurations as riding machines, and as attachments for tractors and skid steers.

Riding trencher

Pipe pullers
Pipe pullers install pipe and wire by pulling it through the ground leaving only a small slit in the ground. Unlike trenchers, pipe pullers cause minimal disruption

Pipe pullers are very effective when installing an irrigation system into an existing lawn.

to the area and consequently, are often the preferred equipment for irrigation installations where there is a pre-existing lawn. Check the project specifications, which will state pipe pulling if it is allowed.

Backhoe
A backhoe is a rubber-tired piece of equipment primarily used to dig large or deep excavations, and can be used to dig trenches for irrigation pipe. Attachments are also available for moving bulk materials, compacting, demolition and other tasks.

Excavators, bulldozers and track loaders
This group of landscape equipment tends to run on tracks versus rubber tires and these machines are designed to handle extremely deep excavations and heavy grading and earthwork projects. Training is critical before operating large equipment. A high degree of skill and experience is required to avoid damage to underground utilities. This equipment is used in wide-open spaces.

Excavator

Landscape Irrigation

Mini-excavators

Mini-excavators are utilized when space is limited and when digging no more that 15' (4.5 metres) deep or when digging around underground obstacles and utilities. They typically have rubber tracks and also have a variety of attachment options available, such as breakers, augers, grapples and thumbs.

Safety guidelines for large equipment

Because of their size and power, large pieces of equipment can be dangerous to the operator and to others. Always follow the equipment manufacturer's operating instructions, as well as the safety guidelines listed below.

Safety Guidelines for Large Equipment

Call before digging — trenching, grading or excavating — to check the location of underground utilities. Note: Some states require that operators have the utility notice with them while operating. The contractor can be directly responsible for all repairs to utilities. Check state/provincial requirements.

Use seat belts if supplied. Seat belts are not required on equipment without roll bars (ROPS).

Be seated inside the cab when starting or operating the controls.

Before starting, make sure the transmission and other operating controls are in neutral and the parking brake is applied.

Leave the cab only when equipment is fully stopped, the parking brake is set and the gearshift is in neutral.

Start only after checking to be sure there are no bystanders in the vicinity.

Do not attach chains, ropes or cables to the ROPS (roll over protection system).

Before leaving the cab, lower the backhoe, loader or other attachments to the ground, stop the engine, apply the parking brake and put the gearshift lever and power-reversing lever in neutral.

When transporting material in a loader, keep the load as low as possible. Raise the bucket only when the load is ready to be discharged.

Do not allow passengers to ride on a loader or on other attachments.

Avoid operating equipment on steep hillsides as this could cause overturning.

To prevent tipping when operating on a slope, avoid swinging the bucket to the downhill side. Deposit load/material on the uphill side.

Whenever possible, park on level ground. If you must park on an incline, lower the bucket (if equipped) with the cutting lips in contact with the ground, apply the parking brake and block the wheels.

Check overhead clearances before operating or transporting equipment under power lines or structures.

Do not operate fuel-powered engines indoors without adequate ventilation.

Move slowly over uneven ground. Be alert for holes, ditches or any irregularities that could cause equipment to overturn or loads to be discharged.

Refuel outdoors with the engine shut off. Smoking is NOT allowed while refueling.

Maintenance guidelines for large equipment

Large equipment requires ongoing maintenance to operate efficiently and safely. Basic maintenance items for large equipment are listed below. Additional maintenance requirements will vary depending on specific types and models of equipment. Consult the operator's manual for maintenance information about the specific equipment you are using. In addition, look for fluid leaks on the floor of the shop, which could be engine oil, fuel, hydraulic oil or antifreeze.

Maintenance Checklist:

- Tires: Maintain correct inflation
- Battery: Check terminals, cables and fluid (unless maintenance free)
- Air cleaner: Clean and/or replace elements
- Engine crankcase: Maintain oil level
- Engine oil filter: Replace as recommended by manufacturer
- Radiator: Check coolant level
- Oil cooler and radiator: Clean trash from cooling fins
- Fan belt: Maintain proper belt tension and inspect for excessive wear
- Fuel water trap: Drain periodically
- Fuel filter: Replace as recommended by manufacturer
- Hydraulic filter: Replace as recommended by manufacturer
- Hydraulic reservoir: Maintain oil level
- Hydraulic reservoir breather: Clean periodically
- Foot controls: Clean trash frequently
- Gearboxes: Maintain oil level
- Final drives: Maintain oil level
- Parking brake: Maintain proper adjustment
- Grease fittings: Lubricate as recommended

{ Most large equipment requires a warm-up period before use each day. Check the operator's manual for the warm-up period required for the equipment you are operating. }

{ Properly maintained equipment saves money and down time. }

Checking air filter

Sample maintenance schedule

Following is a sample maintenance schedule for a backhoe to illustrate the frequency of various maintenance procedures for one piece of large equipment.

Follow the information that comes with the equipment.

Landscape Irrigation

Sample Maintenance Schedule — Backhoe

	Maximum Hourly Interval					
	10	50	100	250	500	1000
Check engine oil level	X					
Check hydraulic system oil level	X					
Check radiator and oil cooler for trash build-up	X					
Check tire pressure		X				
Check coolant level	X					
Check belt tension — alternator	X					
Check seat belt/seat switch interlock for operation	X					
Check parking brake adjustment			X			
Check engine oil and filter			X			
Drain water from diesel fuel filter			X			
Replace air cleaner primary element					X	
Replace safety air filter element (inner)						X
Re-torque wheel nuts			X			
Check and readjust hydrostatic control system				X		
Check gearboxes oil level					X	
Check final drive (chain case) oil level					X	
Check final drive chain tension						X
Check and clean oil reservoir breather					X	
Inspect entire unit for hardware loosening						X
Change hydraulic oil filter					X	
Change hydraulic system oil						X
Check cab retaining hardware for proper torque				X		
Inspect fuel lines and replace fuel filter				X		
Adjust valve tappets					X	
Clean and test fuel injectors					X	

Note: This chart is an example only.

Mid-Size Equipment

Mid-size equipment refers to power equipment that is larger than hand-held equipment but does not have a cab area for the operator. Most are walk-behind machines, but some have a seated area (ATVs). Most are powered by fuel, although some are electric.

Types of mid-size equipment

Utility vehicles and ATVs
Utility vehicles are especially effective on large sites, parks and golf courses. They allow access and hauling capacities that cause less damage to turf than trucks and heavy equipment. Many of these vehicles are also battery operated, which makes them a good choice from a sustainability point of view, as well as being quiet. Use caution when operating these vehicles, as they can be dangerous — particularly on slopes.

Compact utility loaders
Utility loaders offer extreme maneuverability in tight spaces and are light enough that they rarely cause damage to existing landscapes. They can be rubber-tired or tracked and typically have a stand plate for the operator. The versatility they offer with attachments makes them one of the most common pieces of equipment in the industry. Available attachments include augers, breakers, dozer blades, forks, stump grinders, rototillers, trencher arms and pipe pullers, in addition to the standard dump bucket. Use extreme care when operating and maintain constant awareness of surroundings to prevent injury to people and damage to property near the work area (lights, windows, etc.).

Power wheelbarrows, buggies and wagons
This class of motorized wheelbarrows has become a standard in the industry and is especially beneficial to reduce fatigue and injury to workers as well as boosting production. Because they do move quickly, operators should be thoroughly trained and observed before being allowed to operate the equipment unsupervised.

Walk-behind trenchers
Walk-behind trenchers are able to dig 2' – 4' (60 – 120 cm) deep. They are more maneuverable in small spaces than larger trenchers, but can be more dangerous for the operator. Training and extreme care should be taken before operating this equipment.

Some examples of mid-size equipment

Compact utility loader in a trailer

Walk-behind trencher

Landscape Irrigation

Safety Guidelines for Mid-Size Equipment

Call before digging to check the location of underground utilities.

Start equipment only after checking to be sure there are no bystanders in the vicinity.

When transporting material in a compact utility loader, keep the load as low as possible. Raise the bucket only when the load is ready to be discharged.

Passengers other than the operator may NOT ride on power wheelbarrows or compact utility loaders or their attachments.

Avoid operating equipment on steep hillsides, as this could cause overturning.

When operating on a moderate slope, deposit load/material on the uphill side and keep the bucket low.

Whenever possible, park on level ground. If you must park on an incline, lower the bucket (if equipped) with the cutting lips in contact with the ground.

Check overhead clearances before operating or transporting equipment under power lines or structures.

Do not operate fuel-powered engines indoors without adequate ventilation.

Move slowly over uneven ground. Be alert for holes, ditches or any irregularities that could cause equipment to overturn or the load to discharge.

Refuel outdoors with the engine shut off. Smoking is NOT allowed while refueling.

Maintenance guidelines for mid-size equipment

Ongoing maintenance is required to ensure equipment operates efficiently and safely. Basic maintenance items for mid-size equipment vary for specific models. Always consult the operator's manual for maintenance information about the specific equipment being used.

Sample maintenance schedule

Refer to the maintenance example that follows for large equipment, and always consult the operator's manual.

Hand-Operated Equipment

There is a great variety of hand-operated equipment for many different uses. Many are powered by motors that require fuel, but some are electric. Safety and maintenance issues are just as important for hand-operated equipment as they are for large equipment.

Be sure to wear all appropriate PPE, which may include hearing protection, face shields, hardhat, safety glasses, chaps, dust mask or full respirator, gloves and steel-toed boots. Always refer to the manufacturer's recommendations for the appropriate safety equipment for any piece of equipment.

Types of hand-operated equipment

Auger
Augers are metal drills used to dig holes in soil. Augers are available in a variety of sizes for different applications. Hand-held augers are useful for digging small holes for fence posts. Larger models, which can be mounted on large equipment such as skid steers and tractors, are used when larger holes are needed for telephone poles, pylons, etc.

Auger

Brick saw
As the name suggests, brick saws are used to cut brick. Brick saws can be hand held or table-mounted, gas operated or electric. Most brick saws have a flat base, which holds a brick, and a rotating circular blade which does the cutting. The brick is pushed into the blade with some brick saws, and for others, the brick is stationary and the blade is guided into the brick.

Some brick saws utilize a wet cutting blade system that uses a continuous stream of water to keep the blade cool. Other brick saws use dry cutting blades that are air cooled and do not require water. Hearing, eye and hand protection, as well as a dust mask, are required. Like chainsaws, brick saws can be dangerous. Safety issues may vary based on the type of brick saw being used, and whether it is mounted. Follow the operating and safety instructions in the operator's manual from the manufacturer.

Chainsaw

Chainsaw
These powerful saws are used for trimming large limbs, removing dead trees and cutting up fallen trees. A large, exposed cutting chain makes the chainsaw one of the most dangerous motorized hand tools to operate and can cause serious or fatal injury. Always read and follow the operating and safety instructions in the operator's manual and refer to the specific safety guidelines listed below for chainsaws. Hearing, eye and hand protection, chaps and dust masks are required. Check local and state/provincial regulations for specific requirements for chainsaw operators.

Circular saw
Circular saws are used to make straight cuts. These handheld units consist of a rotating circular blade that protrudes through a flat base, which keeps the saw blade steady as it slides across wood or other material being cut. Hearing, eye and hand protection and a dust mask are required.

Brick saw

Landscape Irrigation

Circular saw

Demolition (demo) saws (Quickcut)
Demo saws are similar to chainsaws but with a circular rotating cutting blade instead of a chain. Demo saws can cut hard materials such as concrete, brick and brick pavers, wall block, steel and asphalt, and are often used for demolition work and some installation situations. Note that different blades are required for cutting different types of materials, such as concrete versus steel. Hearing, eye and hand protection and a dust mask are required.

Safety precautions may vary between hand-held and table-mounted saws. Follow manufacturer's recommendations in the operator's manual.

Rototiller
Rototillers have rotating blades/tines that turn over soil to loosen it if compacted, and to incorporate amendments into native soil. Walk-behind tillers are available in front tine and rear tine models. Front tine tillers are designed for light duty, while rear tine tillers are commonly used commercially. For large areas, tiller attachments can be used with tractors, backhoes, and skid steers. Before operating a rototiller, always check for bent or loose tines. During operation, always disengage tines before relocating the rototiller.

Sod cutter
Sod cutters are used to remove sod for reuse or disposal. This walk-behind motorized device cuts sod into strips, leaving cut sections intact. A horizontal blade moves through the soil beneath the turf cutting 12" or 18" (30 or 45cm) wide strips of sod as it moves forward. The strips can then be rolled up for easy disposal or reuse. Sod cutters are available in both machine-driven and hand-operated models. Machine-driven sod cutters require less effort to operate and cut sod faster than hand-operated models.

Sod cutters can be used to remove some or all of a problem lawn prior to repair or replacement. They can also be used to remove portions of a lawn for installation of irrigation equipment, walkways, patios, planting beds, etc,. while keeping adjoining turf intact.

Sod cutter

Rototiller

Plate compactor

Cordless reciprocating saw

Tampers and plate compactors

Tampers and plate compactors are hand-operated, motorized devices used to compact soil and base material. The unit is held upright, while a motor raises and lowers the shaft (like a shock absorber) connected to a flat metal plate, compacting the surface beneath it. Tampers are used when compaction is needed in small areas or in narrow trenches.

Plate compactors are similar to tampers, but they are walk-behind units. The engine rests directly on top of a metal plate, which is larger than those on tampers; therefore, plate compactors are used to compact larger areas. The plate compactor applies both compression force and vibration to achieve the highest compaction density of any compaction tool.

General construction tools

Tools including screw guns, drills, circular carpentry saws, reciprocating saws (Sawzall™), and others are electric or battery-powered (cordless) hand tools. These are extremely useful for many construction projects, such as those that require the insertion of numerous screws and those that require precision sawing or cutting.

Cordless drill

Tamper

Landscape Irrigation

Fuels and mixes

Motorized equipment requires some additional knowledge about fuels to be sure equipment is properly maintained. The wrong fuel or fuel mix can damage equipment.

Motorized, gas-powered equipment is usually driven by either a 2-stroke or 4-stroke engine. A 4-stroke engine usually powers larger equipment. Four-stroke engines use gasoline and regular motor oil, which are added in separate places on the engine.

A 2-stroke engine usually powers smaller equipment, such as chainsaws, string trimmers, blowers, etc. Two-stroke engines require gasoline to be mixed with special 2-cycle oil before being added to the fuel tank. It is important that gas and 2-cycle oil be mixed in the correct proportions to prevent damage to 2-stroke engines. The proper mix varies for different engines, so you should always use the fuel mix recommended by the equipment manufacturer.

Gas cans like these can be used to mix gas and oil for 2-stroke engines. Be sure to label cans containing gas/oil mixes, noting that it is a mix and the mix ratio.

Personal protective equipment (PPE) is critical when operating any type of power equipment.

Safety Guidelines for Using Portable Gas Cans

Be sure the can is approved for flammable liquids and is not more than 5 gallons in capacity.

Place the gas can on the ground to fill and/or mix fuel for 2-stroke engines and maintain a safe distance from vehicles.

Smoking is NOT allowed while filling cans.

Fill containers to about 95% full to allow for expansion.

If fuel spills on the container, be sure it is evaporated before placing in a vehicle.

Refuel outdoors with the engine shut off. Smoking is NOT allowed while refueling.

Landscape Equipment Safety & Maintenance

Sample Problems and Calculations

U.S. / Imperial

Sample problem #1
A chainsaw requires a 50:1 gas/oil mix. How many ounces of 2-cycle oil should be added to 1 gallon of gas? Note: The ratio 50:1 means 1 unit (gallon, for example) of oil for every 50 equivalent units (gallons) of gas.

Note: There are 128 fluid ounces in 1 gallon. To get the correct answer, the problem must be worked using the correct units. This example asked for the answer in ounces, so units must be converted to ounces.

Use the 3-Step Method to find the solution.
Step 1: What Information is given?
   50 gal gas to 1 gal oil

Step 2: What information is being requested?
   How many ounces of oil are needed for every one gallon of gas?

Step 3: Plug in the known values and solve the equation.
   X = 50 gal = 128 oz
   1 gal = X oz

Next, cross multiply. Place the value that is multiplied by the two known variables on top, and place the value multiplied by the unknown variable below.

$$X = \frac{50 \text{ gal.}}{1 \text{ gal.}} \times \frac{128 \text{ oz.}}{X \text{ oz.}}$$

$$X = \frac{128 \text{ oz}}{50}$$

$$X = 2.56 \text{ oz}$$

Answer:
It takes 2.56 ounces of oil for every 1 gallon of gas to achieve a 50:1 ratio of oil/gas mix.

Metric

Sample problem #1
A chainsaw requires a 50:1 gas/oil mix. How many millilitres (ml) of 2-cycle oil should be added to 1 litre of gas? There are 1000 ml in a litre.

Note: The ratio 50:1 means that for every 50 units (in this example the units are litres) of gas, one unit (liter) of oil is required. The quantities must be in common units.

Use the 3-Step Method to find the solution.
Step 1: What Information is given?
   50 litres gas to 1 litre oil

Step 2: What information is being requested?
   How many millilitres of oil are needed for every one litre of gas?

Step 3: Plug in the known values and solve the equation.
   X = 50 litres = 1000 ml
   1 litre = X ml

Next, cross multiply. Place the value that is multiplied by the two known variables on top, and place the value multiplied by the unknown variable below.

$$X = \frac{50 \text{ litres}}{1 \text{ litre}} \times \frac{1000 \text{ ml}}{X \text{ ml}}$$

$$X = \frac{1 \text{ litre} \times 1000 \text{ ml}}{50 \text{ litres}}$$

$$X = 1000 \text{ ml}/50 = 20 \text{ ml}$$

Answer:
It takes 20 ml of oil per litre of gas.

Conversions between units in metric are much easier since units are multiples of 10.

Sample Problems and Calculations continued

U.S. / Imperial

Sample problem #2
A string trimmer requires a 32:1 mix. How many ounces of oil should be added to 2.5 gallons of gas?

Answer:
(128 fl oz/32) x 2.5 = 10 ounces of oil should be added to 2.5 gallons of gas.

Explanation: The ratio of 32:1 means that for every 32 units (in this example the units are ounces) of gas, one unit (ounce) of oil is required. The quantities must be in common units. Since one gallon is 128 ounces, divide by 32 to find out how many ounces of oil are needed at a ratio of one unit (ounce) per 32 ounces of gas.

Metric

Sample problem #2
A string trimmer requires a 32:1 mix. How many millilitres of oil should be added to 12.0 litres of gas?

Answer:
(1000ml/32) x 12.0 = 375 ml of oil should be added to 12 litres of gas.

Explanation: The ratio of 32:1 means that for every 32 units (in this example the units are litres) of gas, one unit (litre) of oil is required. The quantities must be in common units. Since one litre is 1000 millilitres, divide by 32 to find out how many millilitres of oil are needed at one unit (litre) per 32 litres of gas.

General Safety Guidelines for all Motorized Hand-Operated Equipment

Before operating any equipment, read the manufacturer's operation and safety instructions.

Dress appropriately for the equipment you are using. Snug-fitting clothes are least likely to get caught while operating equipment.

Wear footwear that meets government-recommended safety standards (CSA standards with green triangle in Canada or ASTM standards in the U.S.).

Many types of equipment require the operator to wear personal protective equipment, including gloves, chaps, eye, hearing and head protection.

Know how to stop the engine quickly.

When changing locations, shut off hand-held equipment.

Be sure children, pets and other bystanders are a safe distance from the work area.

Never leave equipment unattended while the engine is running.

Never put hands or feet near rotating parts or hidden areas, including cutters, belts, pulleys and gears.

Never make adjustments, remove blades or blade guards or perform any maintenance when the engine is running and always disconnect the spark plug wire prior to working on equipment.

Do not operate equipment in the dark or when it is hard to see.

Safety Guidelines for Chainsaws

Keep bystanders and animals out of the area when starting and operating a chainsaw.

Wear eye protection, ear protection, hardhat, gloves and safety chaps.

Be sure the chain tension is properly set. A loose chain can come off the guide bar and cause serious injury. Be sure to wear gloves.

Never drop-start or jerk-start a chainsaw. Hold the chainsaw on the ground when starting.

Hold the saw firmly with both hands. Keep the handles dry and free of oil or fuel mixture.

The bar of the chainsaw should always be longer than the diameter of the object to be cut.

Run the saw at full throttle to maximize productivity and reduce fatigue.

Stand slightly to the side while cutting, in case you lose control of the saw. You will be out of the plane of the cutting chain and guide bar.

When the chainsaw is running, keep your body away from the chain.

Always make straight, clean cuts.

To prevent kickback, make sure the object you are cutting is clear of obstructions and secure. Do not cut near chain link or wire fences.

Do not use the tip of the saw for cutting as kickback can occur.

Never cut a branch from the under side (under cut).

Do not overreach or cut above shoulder height. A chainsaw is difficult to control in these positions.

Be especially careful cutting around small brush. It can catch in the chain and whip around or pull you off balance.

When cutting a limb under tension, springback can occur when the tension is released. Be prepared for this so the limb doesn't strike you.

Before cutting trees, plan an escape path away from the falling tree. Be sure you have secure footing and a clear work area.

Operate a chainsaw in a tree or from a ladder or bucket truck only if you have been trained to do so.

Stop the engine when carrying the saw. Carry the saw with the guide bar and cutting chain pointing backwards and the muffler away from your body.

Disconnect the spark plug before performing any maintenance.

Check the blade at least daily and ensure that it is properly sharpened at all times. Be sure to wear gloves while checking.

Landscape Irrigation

Always hold the chainsaw on the ground when starting.

chainsaws are one of the most hazardous pieces of equipment to operate. Wear PPE and follow operator safety guidelines

Don't be in a hurry when operating a chainsaw — think safety first!

Safety Guidelines for Gas Engines

Disconnect spark plug before performing any maintenance.

Always turn off the engine to refuel. Let the engine cool before refueling.

Be especially careful of gasoline spills on a hot engine, as this can start a fire.

Fuel the equipment in a ventilated area. Avoid spilling gasoline and, if spilled, properly clean up.

Smoking is NOT allowed while operating or fueling.

Refuel only on hard surfaces and not on a grass area.

Whenever possible, move equipment away from fueling area before starting engine.

Operate engines only in well-ventilated areas.

Safety Guidelines for Electric Motors

Check power cord regularly for nicks and cuts. Replace if the insulation is worn or damaged.

Keep power cords away from sharp objects, intense heat, oil and solvents. These can all damage the insulation.

Be sure the power cord is plugged into a grounded outlet.

Always know where the cord is when operating an electric device. If the cord becomes caught and severed, shock or electrocution can result.

Do not use electric equipment in wet areas unless stated for use by manufacturer.

Maintenance guidelines for hand-operated equipment

As stated before, safety and maintenance begin with prevention. Make sure basic daily checks of the equipment are performed before using it, as well as keeping up with required maintenance activities. Maintenance requirements for hand-operated tools vary for each specific tool. For example, a gas-powered rototiller has different maintenance needs than an electric brick saw, but both require some ongoing maintenance to operate efficiently and safely.
Not all of the maintenance items listed below will apply to all hand-operated equipment. That is why it is important to consult the manuals that came with your tools for specific maintenance information about the equipment you are using.

Daily Maintenance Checklist

Before using equipment each day, check that the following items are in proper operating condition.

- Blades and tines
- Fuel (level and mix)
- Oil level
- Grease fittings
- Tires
- Filters
- Guards (including muffler guard)
- Hoses and pipes (blowers and vacuums)
- Fan grill
- Shoulder straps
- Cutting height

General maintenance guidelines

Blades
- Blades for all types of equipment should be checked daily and sharpened if necessary. Using equipment with dull blades is inefficient and can result in poor quality work and plant damage.

Guards and safety devices
- Check daily. Be sure they are aligned correctly, attached securely and not damaged or altered.

Belts and pulleys
- Check daily for proper tension and for signs of wear, including cracking or fraying. Replace worn belts before they break.

Grease fittings (zerks)
- Lubricate regularly. Refer to the user's manual for the location of all grease fittings and for the recommended interval between lubrications.

Nuts and bolts
- Check frequently. Tighten any that have vibrated loose.

Landscape Irrigation

Hand tool maintenance

Hand tools, such as shovels and picks, require periodic maintenance to keep metal parts rust free and edges sharp, and to keep wooden handles from cracking and splintering. Follow these guidelines to keep hand tools in good condition.

- Sharpen shovels and other hand tools periodically with a flat file. Sharp tools will help you work more efficiently.
- Remove dirt and mud from tools using a hose and/or wire brush. Be sure to dry tools before storing to prevent rust.
- Remove rust from metal surfaces with a wire brush and a small amount of machine oil.
- Sand wooden handles with fine sandpaper at least once a year. After sanding, use a rag to rub linseed oil into the handle to help prevent cracking or splintering.
- Apply machine oil to metal surfaces prior to storing tools for the winter.

Maintenance items for all gas engines

Engine oil level
Check daily before starting the engine to make sure it is filled to the correct level. Add oil if necessary. Operating an engine low on oil can shorten the engine life.

Oil and oil filter
Replace on a regular schedule, as they gradually lose their ability to remove impurities. Oil deteriorates over time, decreasing its ability to lubricate engine parts. Operating an engine with old, dirty oil can cause engine damage or decrease engine life. Refer to the user's manual for specific recommendations as to frequency of oil and oil filter changes.

Air filters
Check daily. If the filter is dirty, it needs to be cleaned or replaced.

Spark plugs
Replace at intervals recommended by the manufacturer.

Pull ropes
Inspect daily for signs of fraying. Frayed pull ropes are likely to break and should be replaced.

End-of-season maintenance for gas-powered equipment

Follow these procedures before placing gas-powered equipment in storage for the winter:

- Clean the equipment, removing all dirt and other debris.
- Empty the gas tank by running the engine until it stops.
- Disconnect the spark plug wire.
- Drain the oil and replace it with fresh oil.
- Lubricate parts as recommended in the owner's manual.

Check oil

Check tire pressure

Check spark plugs

Troubleshooting gas-powered equipment

Despite proper maintenance, motorized equipment may malfunction from time to time. Many problems with gas-powered engines have "quick fix" solutions, as illustrated in the table below. If these solutions do not solve the problem, your equipment may require more extensive repair or professional service.

Troubleshooting Guide for Gas-Powered Equipment

Problem	Possible Cause	Solution
Engine will not start	• Empty fuel tank	• Add fuel
	• Spark plug wire loose or disengaged	• Connect wire securely
	• Blocked fuel line	• Remove and clean fuel line
	• Faulty spark plug	• Clean plug and adjust gap, or replace plug
	• Engine flooded	• Wait to restart
	• Control handle not engaged	• Engage handle
	• Dirty air filter	• Clean or replace filter
Engine runs erratically	• Loose spark plug wire	• Connect wire securely
	• Water in fuel	• Drain tank and refill (dispose of unused fuel properly)
	• Fuel line partially blocked	• Remove and clean line
Engine idles roughly	• Carburetor out of adjustment	• Adjust carburetor
	• Clogged gas cap vent	• Clear vent
	• Oil is overfilled	• Drain and fill to proper level (dispose of unused oil properly)
	• Carburetor out of adjustment	• Adjust carburetor
	• Faulty spark plug	• Clean plug and adjust gap, or replace plug
	• Dirty air filter	• Clean or replace filter

Landscape Irrigation

Trucks and Trailers

Since they are used on a daily basis to transport workers, tools and supplies, trucks and trailers are probably the most valuable equipment used by landscape contractors. So, they must be maintained regularly and operated carefully and skillfully.

Trucks

Depending on where you live, you may be required to have a commercial driver's license to drive a truck or truck-and-trailer combination legally. Licensing requirements often depend on the weight of the truck (or combined weight of truck and trailer), the number of people the vehicle is designed to transport and whether you will be transporting hazardous materials. Check the regulations for your area to see if a commercial driver's license is required for truck and trailer operation.

Trucks and trailers are some of the most valuable equipment used by landscape companies. Proper maintenance and operation are necessary to protect this investment.

Daily maintenance

Before operating a truck each day, check the following items for proper operation, adjustment or levels:
- Headlights
- Engine fluids (proper levels)
- Taillights
- Hoses and belts
- Brake lights
- Brakes
- Turn signals
- Horn
- Back-up lights
- Mirrors
- Hazard lights
- Seat belts
- Tires (inflation and wear)

Trailers

Driving with a trailer in tow requires special skills and special precautions. Maximum driving speed should not exceed 55 MPH (90 km/hr), because a trailer makes vehicle handling more difficult. If you are not experienced hauling a trailer, practice driving in an empty parking lot or other area where traffic will not be a concern.

{ Operating a truck with a trailer takes skill that comes with practice. Safe operation also means following the safety checklist on a regular basis. }

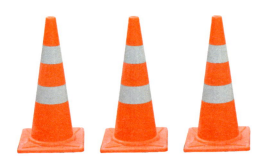

Keep cones as a standard item on your trailer and use them to alert other drivers of equipment loading and unloading.

Landscape Equipment Safety & Maintenance Chapter 7 | Page 121

Backing with a trailer

Backing up with a trailer in tow requires skill and takes practice. Follow these procedures when backing with a trailer.

- Check behind you before backing. Walk around the trailer to make sure the area behind the trailer is clear and use a spotter while backing, if available.
- Turn on flashers. Use horn if vehicle is not equipped with a back-up alarm. Back slowly. Use your sideview mirrors or have another person guide you as you back up, if possible.
- Turn the steering wheel carefully. The trailer will turn in the opposite direction of the truck as you move backwards. Turn the steering wheel right to turn the trailer left, and visa versa. Common errors include oversteering and keeping the steering wheel turned too long. These errors can cause a trailer to jackknife.

Trailer safety

The following safety items should be checked whenever attaching a trailer, and regularly after the trailer is attached.

Check tongue height, making sure trailer is level.

Check the trailer for correct positioning on the hitch. Be sure the hitch is closed and the safety pin is in place.

Make sure the safety chains are crossed and securely attached to the truck and trailer.

Check breakaway cables for proper attachment to the truck and trailer.

Test brakes for proper operation. Make sure that the battery for brakes is fully charged and in good condition.

Make sure all the lights on the trailer are working properly. This includes taillights, brake lights, turn signals, hazard lights and running lights.

Make sure loads and ramps are secure and weight is properly distributed.

Balls and hitches come in different sizes. Make sure the ball and hitch are matching sizes.

Make sure chocks have been removed before moving the trailer.

When the vehicle is parked, make sure the engine is off, brakes are set and wheels are chocked. Place cones at the front and rear corners of the trailer on the side facing traffic.

Manual sponsored by **Hunter Industries**

Landscape Irrigation

Shop Area

Some landscape companies have a large shop staffed with full-time mechanics. For other companies, the shop area is just a small section within the equipment storage area. Whatever your shop consists of, how it is organized and stocked with supplies will affect how equipment operates and ultimately, everyone's ability to get their work done.

Guidelines for the shop area:
- Keep the shop neat and organized, so tools are there when you need them.
- Keep the shop area well ventilated, especially if equipment is operated inside.
- Store potentially hazardous solvents and materials safely.
- Properly dispose of greasy or solvent-soaked rags.
- Keep a fire extinguisher within reach and make sure everyone knows how to use it.
- Have a first-aid kit in plain view.
- Make sure there is adequate PPE for all shop work — for example, ear muffs for sharpening blades, helmets for welding, etc.
- Have a phone within easy reach so that help can be called in an emergency.
- Maintain an organized file of owner's manuals for quick reference when servicing equipment.
- Keep an equipment and vehicle maintenance log to record repairs and schedule regular maintenance.

Equipment that needs servicing

A fire extinguisher must be visible and within easy reach in the shop.

Truck in shop

Summary

The most important assets in the landscaping business are people and equipment. Both are required, which is why safety and maintenance are so important. Think safety first—your personal safety, the safety of others and the safety of the equipment! That means reading the manufacturer's recommendations for safety and personal protective equipment, practicing safe operation recommendations, including proper training before operating equipment, and last but not least, properly maintaining equipment. Properly maintained equipment is safer to operate and extends the life of the equipment.

Gas powered and electric tools and equipment have different safety precautions. Cordless (battery operated) tools are becoming more widely used, and while they eliminate certain safety hazards, proper PPE must be used. Maintenance requirements and schedules vary. Make it a personal discipline to follow maintenance schedules, as well as daily pre-start checklists and safety guidelines.

Chapter 8

Water Management & Auditing

What You Will Learn

After reading this chapter, you will be able to:

- Name four irrigation best management practices (BMPs) recommended by the Irrigation Association.

- Define terms used to describe soil moisture levels, including infiltration rates, saturation, field capacity, permanent wilting point and available water.

- Describe pore space and why it is important to plants.

- Describe how the soil texture affects the infiltration rate of water.

- Discuss the concepts of plant available water and allowable depletion.

- Define distribution uniformity and state its importance.

- State the purpose of a water audit.

- Name at least seven pieces of equipment that are part of an audit kit

- Follow instructions for properly setting up and running an audit.

- Use audit data to calculate low quarter distribution uniformity.

- Use formulas to determine water needs based on evapotranspiration rates and landscape coefficients.

- Use formulas to determine appropriate watering schedules given ET rate, allowable depletion, precipitation rate and irrigation system efficiency.

- Describe some ways water use is managed.

Chapter 8 Preview

Irrigation Best Management Practices

Relationship Between Soil and Water
- Soil properties
- Infiltration rate and field capacity
- PWP, AW, PAW, AD and ET

Irrigation Management
- Precipitation rate
- Irrigation efficiency
- Distribution uniformity

Water Auditing
- Pre-audit inspection
- Auditing items and equipment
- Documentation

Auditing Procedure
- Setting up and running the audit
- Precipitation volume and DU
- Applying results

Irrigation Water Requirements
- How much water is needed?
- Scheduling procedures

Water Management
- Water budgets

Overview

Water management includes the activities of designing (planning), installing, distributing, maintaining and managing the use of water resources to ensure optimal delivery to the plants in a landscape. Understanding water management concepts provides the basis for making good decisions about how much water to apply and how often.

A goal of water management and best management practices for landscape irrigation is to create and maintain efficient irrigation procedures and watering schedules that avoid runoff, overwatering, and underwatering, and are practical and economical over the long term. As water management becomes increasingly more important, science and technology have provided improved tools and methods for monitoring water use to minimize waste.

This chapter discusses the concepts of water management and water auditing and how they can be applied to develop efficient irrigation schedules and practices.

Irrigation Best Management Practices

Best Management Practices (BMPs) for landscape irrigation are typically part of an overall sustainable landscape management program that includes water management and other practices that conserve, reuse, recycle and monitor efficiency of resources, devices and systems. Sustainable landscape management practices also include designing landscapes with plants that can naturally thrive in local climate conditions, grouping plants with similar needs, using planting to minimize energy use (for example shade trees in certain exposures) and using integrated pest management programs that may minimize the use of hazardous chemicals, such as pesticides. See the chapter *"Pest Management"* in the *Landscape Training Manual for Maintenance Technicians*.

This sensor monitors local weather and conserves water by adjusting irrigation runtimes.

Turf and landscape irrigation BMPs compiled and recommended by the Irrigation Association (IA) are described in the following table. An irrigation BMP must meet the criteria of:
- Being applicable to any location
- Protecting water quality
- Conserving water resources
- Being economically feasible after installation and being sustainable through new technology or knowledge.

Irrigation Best Management Practices Recommended by the IA

BMP	Guidelines
Assure quality	• A quality irrigation system means that it is properly managed to distribute supplemental water in a way that adequately maintains plant health while conserving and protecting water resources and the environment. • It depends on implementing the other four BMPs described below.
Design	• Design for efficiency and uniform distribution of water (lower quarter distribution uniformity or DU) and to conserve and protect water resources. • Consider soil type, plant materials, root depth, slope, available water (quality, quantity and pressure), climate and microclimates.
Install	• Install system and components according to irrigation design specifications, manufacturer's specifications and state (provincial) and local requirements using licensed and/or certified contractors.
Maintain	• Service regularly to maintain performance as designed (efficiency and uniform distribution of water) using licensed and/or certified contractors.
Manage	• Manage the system to respond to changing needs by modifying the landscape irrigation schedule to provide the minimum required amount of water.

Relationship Between Soil and Water

When developing an irrigation schedule, soil properties must be considered since different soils take in and drain water at different rates.

Soil properties

Soil is composed of sand, silt and clay particles. Sand particles are the largest and clay particles are the smallest. The percentage of each of these particles in soil determines the soil texture. Sandy clay, silty sand, clay loam and loam are some examples of different soil textures. Loam is not an exact mix of various particle types. Based on the soil texture triangle, loam can vary. For example, it can be approximately 20% clay, 40% silt and 40% sand or about 25% clay, 40% silt and 35% sand. Sand, silt and clay are inorganic components of soil. When these inorganic components are combined with organic matter, this process creates soil structure. Soil structure can be improved by adding more organic matter. (See the chapter *"Plants and Planting"* for more information on soil texture and soil amendments.)

Spaces between soil particles can contain air and water. This is referred to as pore space. The most desirable condition for plant roots is a soil containing 50% pore space. Site construction or other activities that compact the soil diminish pore space.

Infiltration rate and field capacity

When water is applied to the soil surface, it moves downward filling pore spaces. Infiltration rate is the rate at which water moves into soil. Infiltration rate is important to irrigation scheduling because if water is applied to the surface faster than the infiltration rate, runoff occurs and water is wasted.

Furthermore, the rate at which soil absorbs water decreases as more water is applied. The point at which soil pore spaces are filled with water and the soil cannot absorb any more, is the saturation point. In saturated soil, roots of most plants cannot function or remain alive for very long because they do not get enough oxygen. In saturated soil, water displaces the air in the pore spaces. In this condition, with too much water and not enough oxygen, the plants are said to "drown."

Soil remains saturated until it is allowed to drain, which could take a day or more. Field capacity (FC) is the amount of water stored in the soil after it is allowed to drain, or move downward beyond the root zone, due to gravity. Field capacity and saturation point should not be confused.

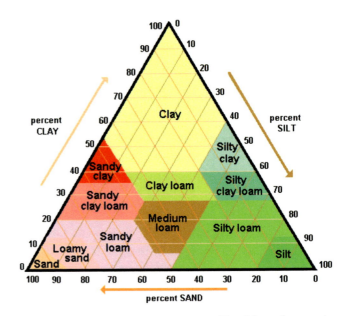

Soil Texture Triangle: Clay percentages are read from left to right across the triangle. Silt is read from the upper right to lower left. Sand from lower right towards the upper left portion of the triangle.

Infiltration rate and field capacity vary with different soil textures. Clay soils have the lowest infiltration rate but retain water the longest. Clay soils should be irrigated at a low rate and require irrigation less frequently. To avoid runoff on clay soils, multiple start times in combination with shorter runtimes must be scheduled. Use the cycle and soak feature, if the controller has this feature. Water is applied until field capacity is approached and then watering is stopped. Once the water soaks in, the next cycle can begin, again for only a short run time. The "Irrigation Concepts" chapter provides a sample watering schedule for clay soils to avoid runoff.

Sandy soils have a higher infiltration rate and drain faster than clay soils. Sandy soils can be irrigated at a lower rate, but should be irrigated more frequently. Nutrients and chemicals can be washed away in fast draining sandy soils, which have poor cation exchange capacity (CEC). A cation is a positively charged element, including K+ and H+. CEC is an indication of a soil's ability to hold nutrients. See the "Plants and Planting" chapter for more information about soil types, including drainage and CEC.

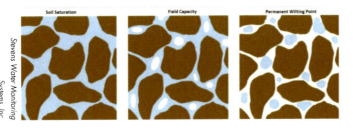

This diagram shows how pore space varies with differing amounts of water. Soil particles are dark, air is white and water is blue. From left to right: soil saturation, field capacity, permanent wilting point.

{ When water is applied after the soil has reached field capacity, the water is wasted. It can damage plants and/or be lost as runoff. }

Sample Infiltration Rate by Soil Texture

Values are approximate

Soil Texture	Infiltration Rate (inches/hour)	Infiltration Rate (mm/hour)
Sand	> 0.8	> 20
Sandy loam	0.4 – 0.8	10 – 20
Loams, fine sandy loams	0.2 – 0.4	5 – 10
Clay loams	0.04 – 0.2	1 – 5
Clay	< 0.04	< 1

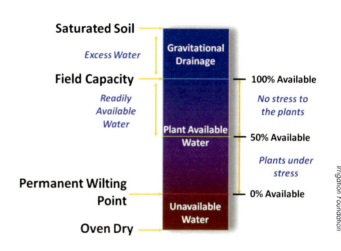

The Soil-Water Relationship

Since infiltration rates vary with different soil types, it is important to avoid providing water at a rate that is higher than the soil can take it in. In other words, the precipitation rate should not exceed the infiltration rate. Maximum precipitation rates for soils with different textures have been suggested by the U.S. Department of Agriculture (USDA) to help avoid runoff. The USDA rates are average values and vary depending on actual soil condition and the condition of ground cover. The recommended maximum precipitation rates should be lower when:

- Irrigating bare ground, compared to ground with cover
- Irrigating soils with smaller particle sizes (silt and clay)
- Slopes steepen

Permanent wilting point (PWP)

The permanent wilting point (PWP) occurs when plant roots can no longer extract water from the soil because the soil has lost too much water. This is expressed in inches of water per foot or millimetres per metre of soil.

Available water (AW)

The difference in the amount of water contained in the soil at field capacity and the amount contained at the permanent wilting point is called available water or AW (see the Soil-Water Relationship illustration). In other words, it is the soil moisture (water held in the soil) that is available to plants. Available water varies with soil type and is measured in inches of water per foot or per inch of soil depth or in millimetres per metre (mm/m). Expressed as a formula:

Available Water (AW) =
Field Capacity (FC) – Permanent Wilting Point (PWP)

Landscape Irrigation

Available water (AW) may also be expressed as a percent of volume.

For example, 1m³ of soil measuring 1m x 1m x 1m, with a water depth of 150 mm has 15% moisture content. This is calculated as follows:

- Convert water depth to metres:
    150 mm/1000 mm/m = 0.150 m
- Calculate volume:
    0.150m x 1m x 1m = 0.150 m³
- Convert to percent:
    0.150 m³/1 m³ = 15.0%

Soil Texture	Average Available Water (inch/inch soil depth)
Coarse (sand, fine sand, loamy sand)	0.06
Moderately Course (sandy loam)	0.11
Medium (loam, silty loam, silt)	0.18
Moderately Fine (silty clay loam, sandy clay loam, clay loam)	0.16
Fine (sandy clay, silty clay, clay)	0.14

Irrigation Foundation

Sample problem: US / Imperial

If field capacity (FC) is 1.5" per foot of soil and permanent wilting point (PWP) is 0.5" per foot, calculate the available water (AW).

AW = FC – PWP
AW = 1.5" – 0.5"
AW = 1.0" per foot of soil

Sample Problem: Metric

If field capacity (FC) is 125 mm/m and permanent wilting points (PWP) is 35 mm/m, calculate the available water (AW).

AW = FC – PWP
AW = 125 – 35
AW = 90 mm/m of soil

Plant available water (PAW)

For irrigation to be effective, water must move downward to the plant's roots. Most of the feeder roots of plants are in the upper soil level (6" – 24" or 15 – 60 cm, depending on the plant). The bottom of this root zone is referred to as the root depth. Plant available water (PAW) is the amount of water stored in the active root zone and is expressed in inches or millimetres. PAW is determined by multiplying the available water by the root depth.

Sample problem: US / Imperial

The root depth (RD) for a specific turf is 9". If the available water (AW) is 1" per foot, calculate the plant available water (PAW). Convert RD to feet (common units):

RD = 9"/12"/ft = 0.75 ft
PAW = RD x AW
PAW = 0.75 ft. x 1"/ft
PAW = 0.75"

Sample Problem: Metric

The root depth (RD) for a specific turf is 20 cm. If the available water (AW) is 90 mm/m, calculate the plant available water (PAW). Convert RD to meters (common units):

RD = 20 cm/100 cm/m = 0.20 m
PAW = RD x AW
PAW = 0.20 m x 90 mm/m
PAW = 18 mm

Allowable depletion (AD)

Allowable depletion (AD) is the amount of loss or depletion from the soil of plant available water (PAW) that is considered acceptable before watering. The Irrigation Association defines allowable depletion as "... the portion of plant available water that is allowed for plant use prior to irrigation." Allowable depletion is measured in inches or millimeters and is sometimes referred to as allowable soil depletion or allowable soil water depletion.

Another irrigation concept, management allowable depletion (MAD), is the percentage used to manage available water for different plants. For example, a medium-value turf may be managed at 50% MAD, whereas a low-value turf may be managed at a 75% MAD. The term "value" used here refers to the importance of keeping the turf in ideal condition. Compare for example, a high-profile golf course versus a rarely used park area. Allowable depletion is determined by multiplying the plant available water (PAW) by the management allowable depletion (MAD):

AD = PAW x MAD

When the allowable depletion is determined, use evapotranspiration information to determine how often to irrigate. AD is also the amount of water needed to replace that lost to evapotranspiration. Again, refer to the "Soil-Water Relationship" illustration above.

Note: Sometimes MAD is referred to as maximum allowed depletion.

Evapotranspiration (ET)

Water is continuously lost to the environment through evapotranspiration (ET). ET is the sum of the water lost through plant leaf surfaces (transpiration) and the water lost from the soil surface (evaporation). ET is measured in inches per day (mm/day). Transpiration and evaporation are a function of temperature, relative humidity, rainfall, elevation, solar radiation and wind. In order to be as accurate as possible, daily monitoring of sites may be needed when these factors are very dynamic. For example, a rainforest is a relatively stable environment, whereas a desert or high plains area tends to be more volatile.

Weather stations can monitor temperature, humidity, wind, solar radiation and more.

Landscape Irrigation

The ET rate determines how much water needs to be replenished, which is then factored into the irrigation schedule. For example, if the daily moisture loss (ET) is 0.25" (6 mm) of water per day, this amount needs to be replenished in addition to other considerations of the irrigation management plan (such as irrigation efficiency). The section, *"Irrigation Water Requirements"* on page 126, shows examples of how ET is factored into determining water requirements and setting irrigation schedules.

Refer to the sample chart and example problem below, which indicate how often to water based on ET rate and allowable depletion.

Sample Daily Evapotranspiration Rate

Day	ET Rate (inches)	Accumulated Loss (inches)	ET Rate (mm)	Accumulated Loss (mm)
1	0.18	0.18	4.0	4.0
2	0.19	0.37	4.5	8.5
3	0.20	0.57	5.0	13.5
4	0.23	0.80	6.0	19.5
5	0.20	1.00	5.5	25.0

Example

U.S. / Imperial	Metric
Assume the plant available water (PAW) is 2" and the management allowable depletion (MAD) is 50%. You should irrigate when water loss equals 1" (50% of the PAW). Using the sample evapotranspiration (ET) chart above, you would irrigate after 5 days when accumulated loss = 1". At this point, it will take 1" of water to return the soil to field capacity (PAW = 2").	Assume the plant available water is 50 mm and your management allowable depletion (MAD) is 50%. You should irrigate when water loss equals 25 mm (50% of the SRC). Using the sample evapotranspiration (ET) chart above, you would irrigate after 5 days (when accumulated loss = 25 mm). At this point, it will take 25 mm of water to return the soil to field capacity (PAW = 50 mm).

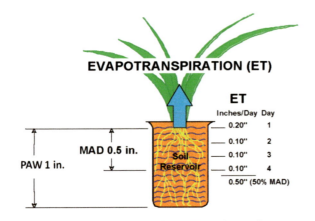

Therefore in 4 days, apply 0.50 inches of water

This picture gives a visual representation of an example where the MAD is 50% of 1", the PAW, or 0.5". Losses due to ET reach 0.5" in four days. If conditions remain similar, irrigation will occur every four days.

Irrigation Management

Precipitation rate

An important concept in irrigation scheduling is precipitation rate (PR). Precipitation rate is the rate that sprinkler heads apply water to the landscape in a given area and is measured in inches per hour (mm per hour). PR was introduced and is discussed in more detail in the *"Irrigation Concepts"* chapter of this manual, where formulas and examples are given. The precipitation rate must be consistent throughout a zone to avoid areas of overwatering or underwatering. This means using sprinkler heads with the same precipitation rates — matched precipitation rates — within a zone to provide the same amount of water to each area.

Irrigation efficiency

Not all water output from an irrigation system is available for plants. Water can be lost from wind drift, evaporation from the air and other causes. Irrigation efficiency is the percent of irrigation water supplied to the landscape that directly contributes to the plant water requirements; in other words, water in the root zone. This relationship can be described by the following equation:

$$\text{Irrigation efficiency} = \frac{\text{Water available to roots} \times 100}{\text{Total water applied}}$$

Efficiency is affected by several factors, including distribution uniformity, irrigation scheduling, irrigation system design, irrigation system maintenance and irrigation management. Irrigation efficiency is also called application efficiency.

Distribution uniformity

Water distribution, introduced in the *"Irrigation Concepts"* chapter, refers to the amount of water delivered to each area. Distribution uniformity (DU) is a measure of how evenly or uniformly water is applied by sprinklers across the irrigated area. DU depends on proper (matched) precipitation rates from the sprinkler heads, proper spacing of the sprinkler heads, system water pressure variations, wind conditions and system maintenance (such as heads being aligned vertically and clean nozzle screens).

Overall irrigation performance or effectiveness depends on both distribution uniformity and irrigation efficiency. Good DU is important for achieving good IE, but does not guarantee good IE. If good DU is achieved, then IE depends on effective management of the irrigation system to avoid overwatering. Distribution uniformity can be estimated from a water audit.

Water Auditing

An effective irrigation system applies the optimum amount of water uniformly over the irrigated area without waste. The purpose of a water audit is to identify problems or inefficiencies in an irrigation system. The information gathered is used to correct system inefficiencies and to develop an efficient watering schedule.

Before conducting an audit, establish goals and procedures of the audit and discuss them with the client. For example, decide whether the system will be tuned up prior to the field audit, based on observed inefficiencies before the audit; or if there will there be a "before" and "after" field audit where adjustments are made after the "before" audit. In other words, the auditor and the client should understand what will be done and, therefore, how to interpret the results.

Landscape Irrigation

Pre-audit Inspection

Prior to an audit, check that the system and controller are in optimal working order:

- Verify that the irrigation system complies with local codes.
- Check the water shutoff, batteries and water connection.
- Identify any problems, defects or deficiencies (conduct visual inspection).
- Correct any major defects or deficiencies (such as mainline or lateral breaks).

Visual inspection

Inspect the irrigation system visually while it is operating. Examine each watering zone as it is put into operation and identify possible problems, including:

- Heads spraying onto sidewalks, driveways or roadways
- Leaks in laterals or other components
- Water pressure above or below manufacturer's specifications
- Broken or misaligned sprinkler heads
- Non-functioning heads
- Heads with reduced water flow
- Heads spraying a fine mist
- Heads that are too high or too low
- Areas that are underwatered or overwatered
- Areas where soil is compacted
- Areas with poor drainage or low spots that hold water

When these problems have been identified, they should be corrected by adjusting or repairing the malfunctioning components. This may include:

- Realigning, raising, straightening sprinkler heads
- Unclogging or cleaning
- Reprogramming
- Repairing

Note: Sometimes these adjustments may be made after a "before" field test to compare to an "after" field test.

Broken sprinkler head

Pressure is too high and causing misting

Pressure is too low and sprinkler in not spraying

Misaligned sprinkler head

All photos: Irrigation Foundation

Auditing items and equipment

Have the following equipment on hand to perform the audit. Audit kits can be assembled or kits can be purchased that include various tools and catch devices.

- Catch devices
- Graduated cylinder
- Pressure gauges with adapters and pitot tubes
- Marking flags
- Tape measures or measuring wheels
- Soil probe
- Anemometer (wind gauge) to measure wind speed
- Clipboard and calculator
- Stopwatch
- Tools for adjusting heads
- Remote control device to activate controller from the field (optional)
- Worksheets

Wind gauge

Catch can devices

Documentation

Record at least the following information about the audit:

- Name and phone number of auditor
- Date and time of testing
- Sprinkler head locations
- Sprinkler head spacing
- Sprinkler make, model and nozzle size
- Current watering schedule
- Soil types and root zone depths, determined by taking core samples
- Wind speed readings
- Test run time
- Approximate catch-can locations
- Volume of water captured in each catch-can
- Pressure readings (with locations) of the heads tested

Use a site map, irrigation plan, property plot map or similar drawing to view the entire system and to record information.

Auditing Procedure

The Irrigation Association (IA) has developed procedural guidelines for conducting landscape irrigation system audits. The IA guidelines are adapted and discussed in this section. Assuming system problems have been identified (see page 122) and corrected, be sure the following conditions are met before beginning water catchment:

- Wind speed is at 5 mph (8 km/hr) or less
- The system is operating under normal conditions
- Test the water pressure at key sprinkler heads, using an appropriate pressure testing device, at the beginning and end of each zone being tested (under normal operating conditions)
- All catch devices (catch-cans) should be the same size and shape; larger collectors provide better repeatable results; if the catch-cans do not have measurements, a measuring device is required to read how much water fell in each cup
- A documentation method for recording set-up procedure and test results

Setting up and running the audit

- Use at least the minimum number of catch devices recommended by the IA, which is 24. More catch-cans with closer spacing may be needed for areas with smaller sprinkler spacing. The number of catch devices should be a multiple of four to simplify calculation of lowest quarter distribution uniformity (discussed in the next section).
- Near the edge of a zone, place collectors 12" – 24" (30 – 60 cm) in from the edge.
- Use the following minimum spacing distances depending on sprinkler head type:
  - Fixed spray: Within two or three feet (0.6 – 0.9 m) of the head and halfway between heads.
  - Rotor heads spaced less than 40 feet (12 m) on center (OC): Within two to three feet (0.6 to 0.9 m) from head and every one-third of the distance between heads.
  - Rotor heads spaced greater than 40 feet (12 m) OC: Within two to three feet (0.6 to 0.9 m) from head and every one-fourth of the distance between heads.
- Unusual or irregularly shaped areas:
  - Rotor sprinklers: Uniform grid of catch devices spaced 10 to 20 feet (3.0 to 6.1 m) using on center spacing (for example, on a golf green or baseball diamond).
  - Spray sprinklers: Uniform grid of catch devices spaced 5 to 8 feet (1.5 to 2.4 m) using on center spacing (for example, curvilinear areas without defined rows of sprinklers).
- Determine a run time to calculate precipitation rate. The IA recommends 3 – 6 minutes for spray sprinklers, 10 – 20 minutes for rotary sprinklers and five revolutions for large rotor sprinklers. Be sure that the sprinklers run for the required time so the calculations are accurate. For rotor sprinklers, record the time required for five revolutions.

- Within each zone, record the water volume collected by each catch-can to the nearest millilitre, since most catchment containers show gradations in millilitres.
- Calculate DU and PR.

Determining average precipitation volume and distribution uniformity

As stated above, distribution uniformity (DU) is a measure of how evenly or uniformly water is applied to the ground across the irrigated area during irrigation. A water audit provides the information needed to determine DU. A commonly accepted calculation is lower quarter distribution uniformity (LQDU or DU_{LQ}). DU_{LQ} is a ratio expressed as a percentage.

{ Note: In large areas with multiple zones that are basically the same (same heads, nozzles, spacing, plants, soil, etc.), information for one zone can be applied to another. Measurements from one-third to one-half of the zones can be applied to the others. }

To determine average precipitation volume from catch-cans

Add the volumes from all catch-cans for a total volume and divide by the number of catch-cans to determine the average for the zone during the run period. The average catch-can volume is used to calculate the DU_{LQ} in the next section.

To determine lower quarter distribution uniformity

From the audit documentation, determine which catch-can readings reflect the lowest quarter, or 25%, of the total number. For example, if 24 catch-cans were used, take the lowest 6 readings (24/4 = 6), add them up and divide by 6.

The formula expressed as percent is:

$$DU_{LQ} = \frac{\text{Average Minimum} \times 100}{\text{Average Total}}$$

Where:

Average Minimum = Average volume of the 25% of catch-cans with the lowest volume in the zone

Average Total = Average volume of the total number of catch-cans in the zone

Example

This example assumes the following volumes in ml were collected and recorded during the audit. Note: An actual audit would use at least 24 catch-cans.

Location	Can 1	Can 2	Can 3	Can 4	Can 5	Can 6	Can 7	Can 8
Reading	35	29	21	17	33	11	23	15

1. Add the values and divide by the number of catch-cans to get the average:
   Average catch = $\frac{(35 + 29 + 21 + 17 + 33 + 11 + 23 + 15)}{8} = \frac{184}{8}$
   Average catch = 23.0ml

Landscape Irrigation

Example continued

2. Identify the lower quarter volumes and find the average:

    Average lower quarter = $\frac{(11 + 15)}{2} = \frac{26}{2} = 13.0$ ml

3. Calculate the percent DU_{LQ} by dividing the lower quarter by the overall average and multiplying by 100:

    $DU_{LQ} = \frac{\text{Average lower quarter}}{\text{Average of all catchments}} \times 100$

    $DU_{LQ} = \frac{13.0}{23.0} \times 100$

    $DU_{LQ} = 56\%$

Measure and document the amount of water collected in each zone during one watering cycle.

Applying results

Correct inefficiencies and defects discovered during the audit. This is an opportunity to educate the client regarding better water conservation and management. The audit results may provide quantifiable numbers that justify renovation to the irrigation system.

If areas were found within a zone that are being overwatered or underwatered, adjust the equipment (either run time on the controller or nozzles in the heads) to achieve more uniform coverage. When the equipment is adjusted for different areas within a zone and the precipitation rate is determined for each zone in the system, schedule the controller to apply the required amount of water. Determining water requirements is the next section.

Irrigation Water Requirements

How much water is needed?

An efficient irrigation schedule should replace water lost from the soil and plants through evapotranspiration (ET). However, because of system losses or inefficiencies, additional water should be added to the ET requirements. Any water added to the soil from rainfall can be subtracted. Irrigation water requirements can be expressed in the following formula:

Irrigation water requirements =
(ET rate + System losses) – Effective rainfall

Water needs based on landscape evapotranspiration rate

Evapotranspiration was introduced earlier in this chapter. It is helpful to understand the concepts of reference ET rates and crop coefficients, the factors that help estimate landscape ET rates.

To determine how much water is needed for the landscape based on landscape evapotranspiration (ET_L), the following relationship is used.

$ET_L = ET_O \times K_L$

Where:
- K_L is the landscape crop coefficient
- ET_O is a reference ET rate for a geographical location and month. The ET_O rate should be obtained from a local agriculture extension service. ET_O rate tables exist and are based on historic weather information. *Note:* The source for the ET_O reference is based on cool season grass.

Three factors are used to generate the landscape coefficient, from which landscape ET can be estimated. They are as follows.

Landscape coefficient =
plant factor x microclimate factor x density factor

$K_L = k_p \times k_{mc} \times k_d$ where:
k_p is the plant factor
k_{mc} is the microclimate factor
k_d is the planting density factor

Each factor needs to be included when estimating water needs.

Therefore the landscape evapotranspiration equation above can be re-written:

$ET_L = ET_O \times k_p \times k_{mc} \times k_d$

The following table gives plant factors for various plant types that are managed at different levels of appearance.

Plant Factors – K_p

Plant Type	Maximum Appearance (low stress)	Acceptable (average)	Low Maintenance (high stress) (managed stress)
Trees	0.90 – 0.95	0.70 – 0.75	0.45 – 0.50
Shrubs	0.60 – 0.65	0.45 – 0.50	0.30 – 0.35
Desert Plants	0.40 – 0.45	0.30 – 0.35	0.20 – 0.25
Ground Cover	0.70 – 0.80	0.50 – 0.60	0.30 – 0.40
Mixed	0.90 – 1.00 (trees, shrubs, ground cover)	0.74 – 0.80	0.50 – 0.55

Crop coefficients for turfgrass (K_T) are different from landscape coefficients. Turfgrass coefficients depend on the type of grass, warm or cool season, the turf height and desired turf quality (for example, golf course versus park). Warm season grasses include Bermuda grasses, and cool season grasses include Kentucky bluegrass and perennial ryegrass. As mentioned, the reference ET rate, ET_O, used to calculate landscape coefficients is based on cool season grass. Another

ET system sensor

Landscape Irrigation

reference ET rate, ET_R, is based on alfalfa. ET_R is typically the reference used for management of agricultural water needs.

Water needs based on irrigation efficiency and distribution uniformity

A well-designed irrigation system uses appropriate emitters and nozzles at proper pressures and with proper spacing. However, given that odd-shaped and smaller areas are more difficult to irrigate efficiently than large open areas, use lower quarter distribution or DU_{LQ} values (determined with an audit as described above) to establish water requirements. The additional water requirements due to system inefficiencies must be added to the ET needs of the plants when determining the irrigation schedule.

Scheduling procedures

The Irrigation Association provides the following irrigation best management practice with regard to scheduling:

> "The irrigation schedule shall be managed to maintain a healthy and functional landscape with the minimum required amount of water."

This means that irrigation scheduling procedures should be designed to account for the water-related factors considered in this chapter, such as ET, allowable depletion, available water, system efficiency, etc.

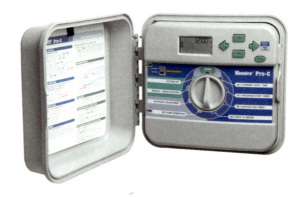

After the water requirements are determined, set the controller to schedule the watering frequency and the run time per zone.

With this information, along with sprinkler precipitation rate and distribution uniformity, the irrigation amount and frequency can be determined. Water budgets and water restrictions must also be taken into account when scheduling.

A number of methods exist to help create an effective schedule that provides the proper amount of water for the plants with the appropriate irrigation runtimes and frequencies. One such method is described below.

Note: The example below assumes no watering restrictions. Watering schedules must be modified when restrictions are in place.

> A well-designed irrigation system uses appropriate emitters and nozzles at proper pressures and with proper spacing.

Sample problem – no watering restrictions

U.S. / Imperial

Assume the following:
- Average ET = 0.19" per day
- Available water (AW) = 2"
- Allowable depletion (AD) = 50% or 1" (1" is 50% of AW)
- System precipitation rate (PR) = 1.8" per hour
- System (irrigation) efficiency = 70%

Calculate the irrigation frequency, water requirements and run time per zone.

1. **Determine irrigation frequency.**
   This step calculates how many days it takes for water loss from ET to reach the allowable depletion (AD). This result is the number of days between watering, which is rounded to an even number to arrive at the adjusted irrigation frequency and adjusted AD.

   AD/ET rate = Irrigation frequency
   1"/0.19" per day = 5.26 days between watering
   Adjusted irrigation frequency = 5 days
   Adjusted AD = 0.95" (5 days at 0.19" per day)

2. **Determine water requirement.**
   The irrigation system must output more than the AD since the system is only 70% efficient. This step calculates the water requirement, which is the actual amount of water the system must output per watering to equal the AD.

   AD/System efficiency = Water requirement
   0.95/0.70 = 1.36"
   Water requirement = 1.36"

Metric

Assume the following:
- Average ET = 4.0 mm per day
- Available water (AW) = 50 mm
- Allowable depletion (AD) = 50% or 25 mm (25 mm is 50% of AW)
- System precipitation rate (PR) = 45 mm per hour
- System efficiency = 70%

Calculate the irrigation frequency, water requirements and run time per zone.

1. **Determine irrigation frequency.**
   This step calculates how many days it takes for water loss from ET to reach the allowable depletion (AD). This result is the number of days between watering, which is rounded to an even number to arrive at the adjusted irrigation frequency and adjusted AD.

   AD/ET rate = Irrigation frequency
   25 mm/4.0 mm per day = 6.25 days between watering
   Adjusted irrigation frequency = 6 days
   Adjusted AD = 24 mm (6 days at 4.0 mm per day)

2. **Determine water requirement.**
   The irrigation system must output more than the AD since the system is only 70% efficient. This step calculates the water requirement, which is the actual amount of water the system must output per watering to equal the AD.

   AD/System efficiency = Water requirement
   24 mm/0.70 = 34.3 mm
   Water requirement = 34.3 mm

Landscape Irrigation

Sample problem – no watering restrictions continued

U.S. / Imperial	Metric
3. **Determine run time per zone.** The precipitation rate is used to determine how long a zone must operate in order to output the required amount of water. Water requirement/PR = zone run time 1.36"/1.8" per hr. = 0.76 hours (approx. 45 minutes) Zone run time = 0.76 hours (approx. 45 minutes)	3. **Determine run time per zone.** The precipitation rate is used to determine how long a zone must operate in order to output the required amount of water. Water requirements/PR = zone run time 34.3 mm/45 mm per hr. = 0.76 hours (approx. 45 minutes) Zone run time = 0.76 hours (approx. 45 minutes)
Results: Assuming there is no rainfall, each zone needs to operate 45 minutes every fifth day to replenish the 1.36" of water lost through ET. If the soil's infiltration rate is lower than the system's precipitation rate, the 45 minutes of operating time should be divided into several cycles to avoid water loss from runoff.	**Results:** Assuming there is no rainfall, each zone needs to operate 45 minutes every sixth day to replenish the 34.3 mm of water lost through ET. If the soil's infiltration rate is lower than the system's precipitation rate, the 45 minutes of operating time should be divided into several cycles to avoid water loss from runoff.

> ET rates for your area can often be obtained from the local water authority or a county extension office. In addition, smart controllers may be tied to a weather satellite that provides ET estimates for your area. The information provided for these systems can be free or provided for a monthly subscription.

Water Management

Water conservation is an important part of water management in landscapes. Science and technology have provided improved methods for monitoring water use and using it more wisely. Weather-based control systems automatically respond to changes in the weather, as well as monitoring the needs of the plants. Landscape designers can integrate information about water needs of plants, the climate and microclimate, evapotranspiration rates, irrigation technology, water budgets and more, to determine the water needs throughout the landscape.

Many states and municipalities have mandated the use of rain sensors for both commercial and residential irrigation systems, meaning the use of some of this technology is no longer optional, but mandatory. Landscape professionals must check mandates before design and installation and monitor compliance during maintenance.

Water budgets

In a growing number of municipalities, the water utility manages water to its customers (residential and commercial) by allocating water and using a tiered pricing structure to encourage conservation. Typically, this means that customers are charged a lower rate for water usage within the range of their allocated water budget and if usage exceeds their water budget, a higher rate is charged for the overage. The water allocation for each customer is determined by reasonable and necessary indoor and outdoor use, and may vary in different cities and areas.

Water budgets also have another meaning to landscape. It can mean the total amount of water needed for the landscape (turf and other plants) to remain healthy, regardless of the source of the water. This information can be used to manage irrigation practices better by comparing water needs of the landscape with water supplied by irrigation and rainfall.

Ideally, landscape water requirements should be considered during landscape design. Design decisions should take into account the water allocation of the customer, as well as other sustainable landscape practices such as selecting plants that are suited to or native to the geographical location, and regional irrigation standards and methods.

Water restrictions and water shortage management

When conditions such as below-average rainfall or below-average snow pack occur, local governments or utilities may enact water restrictions. Check local restrictions to ensure that watering schedules are within the restricted guidelines. As restrictions change, watering schedules need to change accordingly. When a drought occurs, water supplies can be disrupted, causing water shortages. Droughts occur naturally, but the frequency and severity is not predictable. Voluntary water restrictions usually precede mandatory restrictions. Careful monitoring and flexibility are required to modify irrigation schedules during water use restrictions.

Summary

Water management includes the activities of designing, installing, distributing, maintaining and managing the use of water resources to ensure optimal delivery to the plants in the landscape. Irrigation best practices recommended by the Irrigation Association are based on water management and conservation. Soil properties influence the rate in which water enters and soaks into (infiltrates) the soil, and is available to plants. Infiltration rate is important to know for determining optimal irrigation schedules. Field capacity is the amount of water stored in the soil after it is allowed to drain. Additional water applied to the landscape at this point can be damaging to plants or lost as runoff. The soil becomes saturated and excludes air (oxygen) from soil pore spaces. Soil maintained at field capacity is considered overwatering.

Water lost through evapotranspiration (ET) must be replenished. For water to be available to the plants, it must penetrate the upper soil level to be available for the feeder roots. Plants reach the permanent wilting point when the soil has lost so much water that there is none available to the plants. The amount of decrease in the plant available water that is considered acceptable before watering is called allowable depletion and can vary with the aesthetic and functional level that is desired for the landscape.

Replenishing water depends on the precipitation rate of a system, as well as distribution uniformity of the applied water. Conducting audits helps identify system inefficiencies that waste water. The results of an audit can be used to correct system deficiencies and to schedule water application that effectively meets the requirements of the landscape, as determined from ET needs, with an allowance for system inefficiencies and natural precipitation. Some municipalities have initiated water budgeting. Other areas may have water restrictions due to shortages. In these situations, water needs for landscapes must be carefully managed in terms of water use, water waste and plant quality.

Chapter 9

Plants & Planting

What You Will Learn

After reading this chapter, you will be able to:

- List and describe five environmental conditions that should be considered when selecting plants for a site.

- Describe at least six practical functions plants serve, which can be used to enhance the outdoor environment.

- Describe some of the physical characteristics of plants that influence their suitability in specific locations.

- List four physical characteristics you can use to help identify plants.

- Describe the basic structure of plants and how plants grow.

- Identify and describe the information contained in a planting plan.

- Describe the steps required to plant trees and shrubs properly.

- Explain how to stake and guy trees.

- Explain the pros and cons of annuals and perennials and factors to consider when planting them.

- Describe some basic design considerations and maintenance needs for water gardens.

Chapter 9

Preview

Site Conditions

Functional Considerations

Physical Properties and Unique Characteristics

Plant Identification

Plant Growth and Development

Plant Layout

Tree and Shrub Planting

Tree Staking and Guying

Annuals, Perennials and Biennials

Water Gardens and Aquatic Plants

Manual sponsored by **Hunter Industries**

Landscape Irrigation

Overview

Selecting plant materials for a site can be challenging because plants are available in countless varieties, sizes, shapes, colors and textures. This chapter will help you learn to select plants that are well suited to a site based on plant properties and function, or to eliminate plants that are not appropriate, by considering environmental conditions. This chapter also discusses planting techniques that will help plants become established and thrive. Once you have learned the basics, as presented here, you can consult plant lists compiled for your region to find specific plant species that meet your site requirements.

Site Conditions

When selecting plants, begin with a careful analysis of the environmental conditions at the site. Studying the climate, soils and other conditions will help you narrow your plant choices by eliminating those species that are not adapted to the local conditions. Selecting plants suited to local conditions is a "best practice" for creating sustainable landscapes.

Plants that are not well suited to their site may look unhealthy, grow poorly, require excessive maintenance and resources, and fail to provide the functions and benefits that the landscape designer has intended. This section reviews the most important environmental factors to consider.

Climate and microclimate

Climate

The regional climate determines the range of temperatures and amount of rainfall you can expect in an area over a long period of time. Both temperature and rainfall are important considerations for plant selection.

The United States Department of Agriculture (USDA) has created hardiness zone classifications for all of North America. There are 11 hardiness zones based on average low winter temperatures. Zone 1 is the coldest, and Zone 11 is the warmest. The location and range of the hardiness zones is shifting as research on temperature indicates a warming trend. Data recorded between 1990 and 2006 found temperature changes significant enough to shift hardiness zones. The Arbor Day Foundation published an updated hardiness zone map shown here. It can also be viewed online with an animation showing the changes at: www.arborday.org/media/mapchanges.cfm

Zone	Avg. Annual Low
2	-40°F through -50°F
3	-30°F through -40°F
4	-20°F through -30°F
5	-10°F through -20°F
6	0°F through -10°F
7	10°F through 0°F
8	20°F through 10°F
9	30°F through 20°F
10	40°F through 30°F

U.S. hardiness zones map updated in 2006 by the National Arbor Day Foundation.

Plants & Planting

USDA Hardiness Zones and Average Minimum Temperature

Zone	Fahrenheit	Celsius
1	Below -50	Below -45.6
2	-50 to -40	-40.0 to -45.5
3	-40 to -30	-34.5 to -39.9
4	-30 to -20	-28.9 to -34.4
5	-20 to -10	-23.4 to -28.8
6	-10 to 0	-17.8 to -20.5
7	0 to 10	-12.3.0 to 20.4
8	10 to 20	-6.7 to -12.2
9	20 to 30	-1.2 to -6.6
10	30 – 40	4.4 to -1.1
11	Above 40	Above 4.5

Be sure to use the most up to date hardiness zone maps when selecting and planting plants.

Plants are sometimes assigned ratings for the hardiness zones in which they are best suited. Use only plants with a zone rating equal to or less than the hardiness zone you are working in. For example, if you are working in Zone 8, you may consider plants with a zone rating of less than 8, but be cautious.

Hardiness zone ratings alone will not determine if a plant will survive in a given area. Hardiness zones in the U.S. are based on temperature. Precipitation must also be considered. Plants that do well in a wet climate may not thrive in a dry climate (and vice versa) even though they are in the same hardiness zone. Irrigation can allow some plants to live in areas that would normally be too dry for them to survive, but it is best to consider plants that are most suited for a local climatic region when selecting plants.

The Canadian Plant Hardiness Zones are based on average climatic conditions, minimum winter temperatures, length of frost-free period, summer rainfall, maximum temperatures, snow cover, January rainfall, maximum wind speed and effect of elevation.

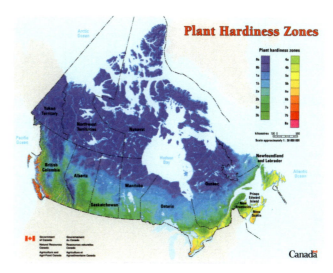

Canada Plant Hardiness Zone Map

The map outlines the nine different zones in Canada; Zone 0 is the harshest and Zone 8 is the mildest. The zones indicate where various types of trees, shrubs and flowers will most likely survive. Significant local factors, such as micro-topography, amount of shelter and subtle local variations in snow cover, are not included on the map.

Refer to the map above and to the Agriculture and Agri-Food Canada web page for an interactive map that pinpoints exact location information:
http://sis.agr.gc.ca/cansis/nsdb/climate/hardiness/intro.html

Microclimate

The term microclimate refers to the climate of an area where sunlight, moisture and wind can vary from surrounding areas. For example, the microclimate in the interior courtyard of an office building will be different than the microclimate of a wooded lot on the shoreline of a nearby lake.

Landscape Irrigation

Plant tags provided by nurseries give important information about plant placement and care.

Every landscape site has its own microclimate or several microclimates. Microclimates can be influenced by walls, fences or overhanging structures, which can block sunlight or rain, creating areas of shade or dry spots. Narrow passageways can create wind tunnels that produce abnormally gusty conditions. An important point is that site conditions can vary substantially, even on a small site and plants suited to one location may not adapt to the conditions elsewhere on the site.

Also keep in mind that microclimates may change over time as the surrounding properties are developed or as landscape plants mature. For example, an area that was once sunny can become heavily shaded and require that changes be made to the type of plants being used.

Therefore, landscapes should always be viewed as dynamic ecosystems and not static ones. As site conditions change, established plants may no longer thrive and changes should be made.

Exposure

Exposure is related to microclimate in that it refers to the conditions to which plants may be exposed in different areas of a site. Sunlight is the most important exposure factor to consider. However, other types of exposure such as wind, water, salt, etc., can also have an impact.

The amount of available sunlight has a strong influence on plants. Many plants, such as potentilla, do not do well in shady locations. Other plants, like hosta, thrive in shade. Shade-loving plants, placed in sunny locations, may wither and die. Sun-loving plants, placed in shady areas, may become weak and spindly.

It is important to analyze the sun and shade patterns of a site. Keep in mind that different locations receive different amounts of sunlight and that sun and shade patterns change throughout the day and throughout the year.

Plants are usually rated by their preference for full sun, partial sun or shade. Locations in open areas or along south-facing walls receive the greatest amount of direct sunlight. These locations require sun-loving plants. Locations along north-facing walls or near large or overhanging structures have limited direct sunlight and require shade-tolerant plants.

Keep in mind that the reflective surfaces of some structures can intensify sunlight. It may be necessary to plant heat-tolerant species in sunny locations where nearby walls, asphalt parking lots, windows, fences or other structures have reflective surfaces.

Soils, substrates and media

Even if you select plants that are well suited to the climate and available sunlight, they may not do well if soil conditions are poor or if the plants are not tolerant of local soils.

Soil conditions

Soil conditions can vary greatly from one site to another or even throughout different parts of the same site. Soil texture, nutrients and pH all affect plant growth.

Soil texture is the way soil "feels," which is determined by the proportion of clay, silt and sand particles. Sand particles are the largest, followed by silt particles, and clay particles are the smallest sized soil particles. Properties, such as water retention and drainage, are associated with soil texture. When practical and possible, amendments are made to soils, which make them more suitable for plants. However, if soil conditions cannot be corrected, such as in excessively wet or dry conditions, use plants that are tolerant of these conditions.

The characteristics of different soil types are described below.

Clay soils tend to drain poorly and dry out slowly, but retain nutrients well. Poor drainage means clay soils are often wet. Many plants do not do well in these conditions because their root systems are deprived of the oxygen they need. Wet soils can also occur in low spots or where the water table is high. Wet soil situations can be improved or overcome by adding certain soil amendments, by constructing special drains, or building planting beds or berms.

Be cautious to avoid using organic matter that will increase the moisture retention of a clay soil.

Sandy soils drain well and dry out quickly. Plants located in sandy soils may need frequent watering, which can wash away nutrients. Sandy soils also have poor cation exchange capacity (CEC). A cation is a positively charged element, including K^+ and H^+. CEC is an indication of a soil's ability to hold nutrients. Soils with a higher CEC have a greater capacity to hold nutrients. The CEC of sandy soils can be improved with soil amendments such as organic matter.

Loam is soil that contains clay, sand and silt in roughly equal proportions and is considered ideal

> Indentify soil texture prior to planting.

Landscape Irrigation

Example of an alternative planting medium

for plants. Loam drains well but doesn't dry out quickly.

Refer to the Soil Texture Triangle, which shows mixtures of sand, silt and clay that are best suited to plants. From the soil texture triangle, it can be inferred that medium loam is approximately 20% clay, 40% silt and 40% sand. Sand, silt and clay are inorganic components of soil. The addition of organic matter to these inorganic components creates soil structure.

For more information on soil types, infiltration rate and field capacity, see the *"Water Management"* chapter in the *Landscape Training Manual for Irrigation Technicians*.

Alternative substrates and media

Given the wide breadth of planting situations that are possible, in addition to planting in soil, there are numerous planting substrates and media available for a variety of uses. Regardless of the composition of the planting medium, the goal is to provide water and nutrients for root absorption to support healthy growth and survival.

Soilless media are usually peat-based and may contain other components, such as bark or composted material. Nurseries, for example, must find the optimum mixtures to grow trees and shrubs in containers. The potting "soilless" mixtures may contain pine bark, sand and peat moss or other composted organic material. Planter boxes may also contain various mixtures of soilless material.

Rooftop gardens — which help insulate and cool buildings, retain moisture, mitigate storm water runoff, buffer noise and extend roof life — utilize "green roof" media. A combination of compost, light weight aggregate and sand is used. Of course, selecting

Soil Texture Triangle: Clay percentages are read from left to right across the triangle. Silt is read from the upper right to lower left. Sand from lower right towards the upper left portion of the triangle.

Plants & Planting

> You can determine the nutrient content and pH of your soil by having it tested. Soil tests are often available through the extension services of colleges, universities and counties, or from independent laboratories.

Use a core sampler to pull a sample of soil for testing.

appropriate plants for roof top gardens is important. Man-made soils are becoming more common. Man-made soil is made by adding organic material to soil that was contaminated and/or depleted by processes such as mining. The process is called "soilification." If using man-made soil, be sure to have it soil tested.

Nutrients
Recall from other chapters that plants require three primary nutrients: nitrogen, phosphorus and potassium—as well as other nutrients in smaller amounts. Soil testing is recommended to get a more accurate view of the soil properties and available nutrients. A soil test provides valuable information about the soil, such as its pH and nutrient content (macronutrients as well as numerous micronutrients including calcium, copper, sodium, magnesium, etc.). Organic matter amendments, such as compost, can provide nutrients, as well as improve soil texture. Fertilizers can correct nutrient deficiencies in the soil.

pH
The pH is a measure of the soil's alkalinity or acidity. The pH scale ranges from 0 to 14 with 7 being neutral. Values above 7 are alkaline (also called "basic"), with higher values being even more alkaline. Values below 7 are acidic, with lower values being even more acidic. Extremes in pH can affect the availability of some nutrients in the soil.

Many plants prefer slightly acidic soils (between pH 6.0 and 7.0), though most plants will tolerate soils that are not strongly acidic or alkaline. While you can temporarily modify pH levels in the soil to some extent, it is best to select plants that are naturally adapted to the pH of the soil where they will be planted.

Urban environments
Selecting plants for urban environments can present special challenges. A variety of conditions that are detrimental to plants may exist, including polluted air, road salts, confined root space and compacted soils from heavy pedestrian or vehicular traffic. Avoid plants known not to thrive in these conditions.

In addition, pay special attention to the mature size of plants used in urban settings and avoid planting large trees or shrubs where they will interfere with overhead wires or signs as they grow. Avoid planting too close to foundations, under eaves or in front of windows where views may be blocked.

Also refrain from using plants that could create hazards or present maintenance problems. For example, shallow-rooted trees can crack or lift pavement along sidewalks or roadways. Trees and shrubs that bear fruits, berries, nuts, pods, etc., can be messy and create maintenance challenges in high-traffic areas.

Wildlife
Large animals, such as deer, may eat or damage plants, making it difficult and expensive to establish new plantings. If deer frequent an area to be planted, you may have to limit your plant selection to species that deer avoid. Other alternatives include enclosing plants in fencing or netting or using some form of repellent.

It is not only large animals that can damage landscape. For example, raccoons and some birds such as crows and geese can destroy lawns by digging for grubs. Moles can create damage by tunneling, but they may

Landscape Irrigation

actually be eating grubs that eat your lawn. Some voles feed on bulbs and roots and cause damage to many plants. Be sure to identify correctly whether the animal is mole or vole, because control methods are very different.

Insect/Disease
Consider plants with natural disease or pest resistance, since prevention is less costly than treatment and replacement. Selecting native species and other species know to thrive in the zone and microclimate of a landscape is a preventive measure for pests and diseases.

Functional Considerations

Plants can serve a variety of practical functions. Below are descriptions of some of the ways plants can be used to enhance the outdoor environment, to produce food, attract wildlife and to put sustainable landscaping practices into effect.

Shade
The shade provided by trees or large shrubs is a welcome relief from oppressive summer sun and heat. In addition, cooling costs for buildings are reduced when their south or west sides are shaded. Deciduous trees are especially valuable for this purpose because they provide shade in summer, but in the cold winter months they lose their leaves, allowing the sun's warm rays to penetrate.

Screens and barriers
A row of trees or shrubs creates a living wall that can serve a number of beneficial purposes, as described below.

Visual screen
Dense vegetation can screen out undesirable views.

Windbreak
A windbreak can block cold winds and reduce heating costs. To create a windbreak, plant a row (more than one row, if space allows) of trees or shrubs upwind

from the structure to be screened and perpendicular to prevailing winter winds.

Sound barrier
Plants can reduce noise from nearby roads or other sources. A combination of tall shrubs and trees planted on a raised bed or berm creates the most effective sound barrier.

Professional Landcare Network | Page 150

Plants & Planting Chapter 9 | Page 151

Colorful accent plants

Hedge as a boundary

Tree as a centerpiece

Accent
Like the centerpiece of a table, an accent plant attracts attention. Accent plants have something interesting or unique about them. It might be a distinct shape, unique foliage, showy flowers or colorful fruit. Use accent plants to create a focal point in the landscape. Additionally, specimen trees and shrubs (which are the highest quality of the species available) should be used in highly visible areas.

Water filtration and/or riparian buffers
Some landscaped areas may be used for capturing stormwater from impervious surfaces. The water is cooled, or both cooled and filtered, prior to its movement into a stream or other surface water. Landscapes that include rain gardens, green roofs, and bio-retention areas are on the rise and all have their place in the protection of water quality.

Riparian buffers are part of the water filtration process and may often be part of a landscape design. They typically reduce erosion or control the amount of sediment and pollutants that may enter a stream.

Hedges
Planting shrubs in a row creates a mass of vegetation where individual plants are often indistinguishable. These rows, or hedges, can be used to define outdoor living areas, create a sense of privacy, delineate boundaries or pathways and create wind blocks, sound blocks, or screens. If a formal or sculpted appearance is desired, select shrubs that tolerate pruning or shearing.

Erosion control
Soil erosion can be a problem where soil is exposed and subject to being washed away by water or blown away by wind. Slopes with sparse vegetation or bare soil are especially susceptible to soil erosion.

Plants can reduce or eliminate soil erosion because their root systems act like a net, holding soils in place. Plants that have a dense root system are especially effective in preventing soil erosion.

Habitat and wildlife
Plants provide food and shelter to many animals, such as squirrels, birds, butterflies and others. Wildlife can be either an asset or a nuisance, depending on the location and the type of animals that plants attract. Birds and butterflies are welcome visitors in most locations, but bees and other stinging insects can be undesirable in places such as schoolyards, swimming pool areas or busy pedestrian areas. Deer and other large animals can enhance the character of rural landscapes. However, in residential or urban settings, they can be destructive to the landscape or considered invasive, and present a hazard to people and the environment.

For example, if you are intentionally trying to attract birds or butterflies, incorporate plants they are known to like, such as cotoneaster or butterfly bush. If bees would create a nuisance, avoid species that attract them, such as privet or linden.

Landscape Irrigation

Xeriscape and water-efficient landscaping

Xeriscape™ is an approach to quality landscaping that conserves water and protects the environment. It is a way to create attractive, water-efficient landscapes in dry areas where water conservation is an increasing priority. Xeriscapes include plant materials, which can survive with little or no supplemental irrigation once they are established.

The Seven Principles of Xeriscape

1. **Use water-wise planning and design**
   Group plants by similar shade, exposure, slope and water needs. Classify microclimates into "hydrozones" based on available water. In some regions, water use is not permitted to exceed certain amounts. The goal is to select plants that will thrive in a particular hydrozone.

2. **Improve the soil**
   Add organic matter, such as compost, when planting trees, shrubs and turf. This will improve the soil structure and provide nutrients for the plants.

3. **Select appropriate plants**
   Native plants are naturally adapted to local soils and rainfall. Use xeric plants in the hydrozones with the least moisture, which are often sunny, south and west-facing areas. Plants needing more moisture should be located along north or east-facing walls or slopes. Avoid mixing plants with differing water requirements within a hydrozone.

4. **Limit high water use turf areas**
   Keep lawn areas to an appropriate size and use. In arid regions, consider using more drought-tolerant grasses, such as Buffalo Grass and wheat grasses, instead of higher water-demanding varieties.

5. **Irrigate efficiently and effectively**
   Do not overwater. Install different irrigation zones for turf and shrub areas. Water in the early morning (best time) or evening to reduce loss from evaporation. Water less frequently to promote deep root growth and to reduce moisture stress.

6. **Use mulches**
   Cover the soil surface to retain moisture, reduce runoff and moderate soil temperatures.

7. **Maintain the landscape**
   Fertilize in accordance with soil test results. Avoid mowing turf too low. Also avoid using insecticides and herbicides unnecessarily. Prune for optimum plant health and at the right time of year for the plant.

Plants & Planting   Chapter 9 | Page 153

Flowers can attract butterflies, birds and bees.

Edible plants are planted with annuals.

Edible landscapes

Increasingly, homeowners want landscapes that do more than provide a pretty setting around their homes. They want landscapes that are useful and a recent, practical trend is to add edibles along with traditional landscape plants.

Fruits, vegetables and herbs are now incorporated into landscapes whether in a separate kitchen garden or planted alongside traditional landscape plants. Edibles bring added diversity in color, texture and fragrance to the landscape setting and they provide the locally-grown, plant-ripened produce many people prefer.

Incorporating edibles into the landscape is a relatively easy process since many vegetables and herbs require the same care and attention as other annuals. There are other beneficial aspects of planting edibles next to other landscape plants. Certain non-edible companion plants attract beneficial insects or repel undesirable ones and provide other benefits that promote plant health among edibles.

Physical Properties and Unique Characteristics

Physical properties are the features that describe a plant's appearance, including size, shape, color, etc. Unique characteristics refer to any special features—thorns, fruit, flowers, etc.—that can make a plant especially desirable or undesirable in a particular location.

Size at maturity

Ideally, plants should be in scale with their surroundings. Large trees may be appropriate in a park, but are out of scale in a small yard. Small areas require small plants, while more spacious landscapes can accommodate plants in a wider variety of sizes. A common mistake is to select plants that eventually outgrow their planting sites. Decide the mature size that is appropriate for a given location and then select plants that will not exceed these dimensions. Consider both height and width.

Other common problems include placing plants too close together or too close to structures. Place trees and shrubs the suggested planting distance apart so they do not crowd each other as they grow to maturity. This distance should also apply to spacing next to buildings and other permanent structures or features.

Manual sponsored by **Hunter Industries**

Landscape Irrigation

These large trees are suitable for the spacious area on this college campus.

Plants are often classified by their size at maturity. A typical system of classifying woody plants (plants that do not die back each year) by height is given below.

Tall woody plants: plants larger than 25' (7.5 m) tall at maturity

Medium woody plants: plants between 8' and 25' (2.5 m – 7.5 m) tall at maturity

Small woody plants: plants less than 8' (2.5 m) tall at maturity

Growth rate should also be considered when selecting plants. Fast-growing plants are sometimes preferred because they have a greater impact in a shorter time. However, many fast growing plants have undesirable characteristics, such as weak wood or susceptibility to pests. Weak-wooded trees can be a hazard because limbs can break and destroy property.

Shape
Different plant species develop distinct shapes or forms. Plants are often described as being round, oval, spreading, pyramidal, columnar, multi-trunked or weeping. In general, plants with a regular or symmetrical shape have a formal appearance. By contrast, plants with an asymmetrical shape have a more informal or naturalistic appearance.

Foliage
In addition to color, a plant's foliage has other properties that can be used to create various effects in the landscape.

A mass of small leaves produces a fine-textured appearance. The use of fine-textured plants in a small landscape can make the area seem larger than it really is.

Plants with large leaves stand out in the landscape, especially against a background of fine-textured plants. Large-leafed plants have a coarse texture, appear to be close, and can make a landscape seem smaller than it really is.

Some plants have unique foliage that attracts attention. Plants with shiny leaves tend to stand out, as do plants with variegated leaves that have streaks or splotches of white or yellow.

Color
Variations in color can make a landscape more interesting. Since most plants have green foliage, green is obviously the predominant color in the landscape. Still, even with green, there can be much variation from one type of plant to another. Some plants have a blue-green appearance while others are bright green or yellowish. When plants with color variations are planted near each other, their differences become more apparent.

Plants that produce leaves that are not green — purple-leaf plum, for example — can create an interesting contrast in a landscape if not overused.

Furthermore, plants go through seasonal color changes, which can create interest throughout the year. As we all know, the fall colors of some deciduous trees and shrubs can be quite dramatic. Incorporating evergreens in a planting scheme

Plants & Planting Chapter 9 | Page 155

provides year-round color. Leaves are not the only part of plants that contribute color. Flowers, fruits, berries and bark can all add color in ways that are sometimes subtle and sometimes spectacular, depending on the plants and how they are used.

Color should be used with some restraint. While splashes of color can add drama, too many colors can look busy and chaotic.

Flowers

Flowering plants, including trees and shrubs, add a special quality to the environment. In addition to the beauty flowers add to a landscape, the fragrance many flowers produce allows us to enjoy the outdoors with senses other than sight.

Some plants produce a profusion of colorful, showy flowers. Others have flowers that are barely noticeable. Different plants flower at different times of the year. Some plants produce flowers throughout an entire season while the flowering period of other plants is short lived. Landscape designers often plan landscapes in which one or more plants are flowering throughout the growing season.

Flowers attract birds and butterflies, which add to our enjoyment of the outdoors. Flowers can also attract bees, however, which are beneficial for pollination but can be a nuisance in some locations.

Fruit

In the right location, fruiting trees and shrubs may be desirable, both for their fruits and ornamental qualities. Fruiting plants can be messy, however, and should be avoided in high traffic areas or locations where there may be maintenance concerns. Fruiting plants can also attract wildlife.

Thorns

Plants with thorns or sharp, pointy leaves can be a nuisance or an asset depending on the location. Thorny plants are not appropriate near schools or swimming pools or along walkways. However, they create effective barriers, keeping people out of certain areas or discouraging them from taking shortcuts through planting beds.

Manual sponsored by Hunter Industries

Plant Identification

Plant identification requires recognizing the different physical traits that vary from one plant species to another. There is no quick or easy way to learn to identify plants. Only through study, exposure and practice will you be able to distinguish between different plant species.

A good regional plant guide or plant key is an invaluable resource when studying plant identification. These materials provide detailed descriptions of individual plant species and their identifying characteristics. Identifying characteristics can vary with season. For example, when deciduous trees have lost their leaves, other characteristics—such as bark or buds—may be used for identification.

Below is a short list of some of the physical characteristics used to identify plants.

Leaves can vary in size, shape and color and their arrangement on the stem can be opposite, alternate or whorled. They can grow individually or in groups or clusters. Some leaves have smooth edges, while others are rough, indented or serrated.

Buds have different sizes and shapes. Some are smooth while others are hairy. Some plants have sticky buds.

Branches of most plants are round, but some are square. Some plant species have thorny branches. Some have hollow branches.

Bark of some plants has a distinct color. Some plants have smooth bark, while others have rough, blotchy or peeling bark.

{ Spending time in a nursery or botanic garden can help you learn plant names and characteristics. }

Plant Growth and Development

Some basic knowledge of horticulture can benefit anyone who works with plant materials. Horticulture is the science and art of cultivating ornamental plants. This section provides some basic horticultural principles, such as plant classification, plant structure, plant growth and plant growth control.

Plant classification

Several terms are commonly used to classify plants, some of which are defined below.

Herbaceous or woody

Plants are categorized as either herbaceous or woody. Herbaceous plants have soft stems, while woody plants have hard, rigid stems.

Vines

Climbing or trailing herbaceous plants with stems that require support are called vines. Woody plants with stems that require support are classified as liana, but are commonly referred to as vines.

Tree or shrub

Woody plants that are self-supporting are either trees or shrubs. Trees are tall and generally single-stemmed. Shrubs are typically multi-stemmed, are smaller than trees and commonly have upright branches.

Life cycle

Plants that complete their life cycle in one growing season are referred to as annuals. Plants that complete their life cycle in two growing seasons are biennials. Plants that live more than two years are perennials. Most woody plants are perennials, while herbaceous plants are found in all three categories. For more information, refer to the section *"Annuals, Perennials and Biennials."*

Deciduous or evergreen

Woody perennials that lose their leaves for a portion of the year are deciduous. Plants that retain their leaves throughout the year are evergreen, even though evergreens may lose some of their leaves in the fall.

Be sure to read current material, as plants can be reclassified or genus and/or species names can change over time. Some nurseries and retail centers use different names, for example, *Actea simplex* versus *Cimicifuga simplex* for the same plant. All plants in the genus *Cimicifuga* were recently transferred to the genus *Actea*.

Plant structure

While plants come in a wide variety of sizes and shapes, most have the same basic structure. Nearly all plants produce flowers, though there are exceptions. Terms that define plant structure are introduced in this section.

Evergreen branches

Close-up of leaf showing veins

Climbing vine

Roots and shoots

Flowering plants have two basic parts: the root and the shoot. The root is the part of the plant that is normally underground. The shoot is normally above ground. The shoot consists of stems and leaves. Leaves grow from enlarged portions of the stem called nodes. Flowers are specialized stems with leaves adapted for reproduction. Buds are small leafy or flowering stems.

The function of the root system is for structural support, for absorption of water and nutrients and for storing carbohydrates the plant's food. In most plants, the absorption process takes place mainly in the small root hairs.

When the original root becomes the primary root, it is called the taproot. In many plant species, the primary root stops growing when the plant is still young and a fibrous root system develops.

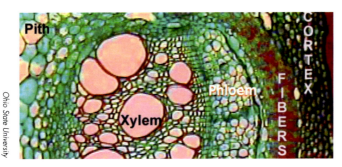

Plant cells and tissues

Cells and tissues

Plants are composed of many different kinds of cells. Masses of similar cells are called tissues. Complex tissues are made of multiple types of cells. A complex tissue that conducts water is the xylem. A complex tissue that conducts food is the phloem.

In perennial woody plants, the phloem and other tissues constitute bark and the xylem forms growth rings. Between the phloem (bark) and xylem (wood) is a group of growth cells called the cambium layer.

The vascular system of plants, which transports water and food (carbohydrates and nutrients), is composed primarily of xylem and phloem tissues. This system feeds and helps support the plant. Typically, the vascular system forms a continuous ring in the stem, where the inner portion of xylem surrounds cells in the center, called pith.

Plant growth

Plants absorb water and nutrients through their roots. These materials move through the vascular system by translocation, the movement of solutions from one part of the plant to another.

The leaves of plants transform light, carbon dioxide and water into energy-rich compounds. This process is called photosynthesis. By-products of photosynthesis are oxygen and water, which are released into the atmosphere through leaves. The release of water vapor through plant leaves is called transpiration. When air, water and nutrients are present in a suitable environment, the result is plant growth.

Pruning

Some amount of control over plant growth can be achieved by pruning. In addition to regulating growth, pruning is done to remove dead, diseased and undesirable portions of a plant.

There are two basic types of pruning: reduction and thinning. Reduction involves cutting back the terminal portion of a branch to a larger branch. Thinning removes a branch to a lateral or main trunk. Reduction can produce a bushy or compact plant. Thinning out encourages longer growth of the remaining branches.

It is best to prune deciduous, woody plants in late winter after severe weather has passed but before buds break. Summer flowering trees and shrubs should be pruned as soon as possible after they bloom. This helps ensure blooming the following year.

Some species, such as maples, benefit from summer pruning. This controls growth and prevents excessive sap flow from the wounds that occur with spring dormant pruning. For some species, such as birch, remove only dead wood. Most evergreens are best pruned before mid-summer in order to prepare them for winter. For more information about pruning, see the chapter *"Tree and Shrub Maintenance"* in the *Landscape Training Manual for Maintenance Technicians*.

Plant Layout

Proper plant layout involves correctly reading planting plans, as well as making appropriate adjustments while planting at the site.

Planting plans

Planting plans are scale drawings that show the types and locations of plant materials to be installed on a site. You must be able to read and understand planting plans, correctly orient the plan relative to North and measure distances accurately based on the drawing scale.

On some planting plans, plants are shown as simple circles. On other plans, plants are represented by more complex symbols. In general, larger symbols represent trees, while smaller symbols represent shrubs. A small cross is drawn in the center of each symbol marking its exact location for planting. Ground covers are often shown, not as individual plants, but as textures filling an area. Plants are drawn to scale at their maximum size (width) at maturity.

Most planting plans include a plant list, which is a table listing some or all of the following information:
- The quantities of plants to be used
- The scientific names of plants
- The common names of plants
- Planting size
- Plant spacing
- Containment of plants at delivery (i.e., balled and burlapped, flats, etc.)
- The symbols or abbreviations used to represent plants in the drawing
- Additional remarks

Planting plans sometimes include planting details. These are illustrations that guide the landscape contractor in soil preparation, planting techniques, mulching needs and staking or guying requirements.

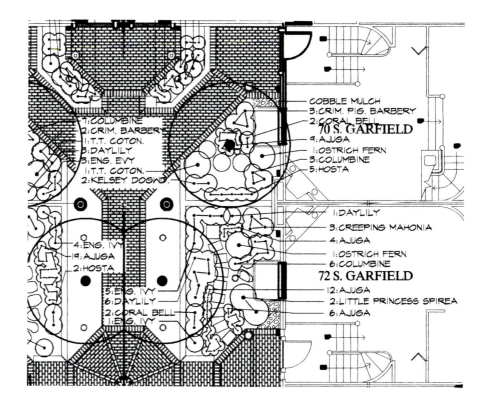

Sample portion of a planting plan.

PLANT LIST

Key	Qty.	Botanical Name	Common Name	Size/Planting Method	Remarks
Shade Trees					
FAA	2	*Fraxinus americana*	Autumn Applause Ash	2 ½" cal., B&B	5 trk., full crown
QRF	8	*Quercus robur fastigiata*	Columnar English Oak	½" cal., B&B	matched
TCG	2	*Talia cordata* 'Greenspire'	Greenspire Linden	2 ½" cal., B&B	5 trk., full crown specimen
Ornamental Trees					
ARH	2	*Amelanchier* 'Robin Hill'	Robin Hill Serviceberry	2" cal., B&B	4 trk., ht matched specimen
Evergreen Trees					
AC	2	*Abies concolor*	White Fir	8' ht., B&B	nursery grown, full, narrow form
PP	2	*Picea glauca* 'Conica'	Dwarf Alberta Spruce	4" ht., #7 cont.	matched specimen
Deciduous Shrubs					
CSK	36	*Cornus stalonifera* 'Kelsey'	Kelsey Dogwood	15" – 18" spd., #5 cont.	7 canes min.
SPMK	24	*Syringa patula* 'Miss Kim'	Miss Kim Dwarf Lilac	24" – 36" spd., #5 cont.	6 canes min.
Evergreen Shrubs					
TM	50	*Taxes media densiformis*	Dense Yew	18" – 24" spd., #5 cont.	full form acclimated
Ground Covers					
HH	74	*Hedera helix*	English Ivy	12" – 18" spd., #1 cont.	5 runners min.

Field adjustments

A planting plan covers many, but not all, aspects of plant placement. Therefore, for best results, technicians must learn to exercise their own good judgment when planting. For example, the person actually planting should determine which side of the plant is the front and then plant accordingly.

Also, while the contractor should always try to locate plants accurately according to the planting plan, sometimes adjustments need to be made in the field. Obstacles such as underground utilities, building overhangs or sprinkler heads may be encountered, requiring plant locations to be slightly altered. If adjustments are necessary, it is important to ensure that other aspects of the landscape plan are not impacted.

Calculating plant spacing

The number of plants needed for a bed is basically the area of the bed divided by the space needed by the plant. Follow the planting spacing instructions and calculate the number needed for the bed area. Examples showing how to calculate plant spacing are found in the "Landscape Plan Reading and Calculations" chapter.

Tree and Shrub Planting

Before planting, be sure to check the project specifications — plant names, quantities, sizes, fertilization, etc. — for all trees or shrubs. Also, refer to the label supplied by the nursery for additional planting recommendations. Plant materials that meet the national standards and specifications should be healthy and not damaged.

Follow these basic procedures for planting deciduous and evergreen trees and shrubs. See photos on next page.

1. Call for locates on public utilities and also locate private utilities.

2. Prune the tree, if necessary. Only corrective pruning should be done at this time. Remove all dead or damaged wood.

3. Excavate the planting pit.
   - The pit should be at least twice the diameter of the root ball and no deeper than the height of the root ball.
   - Locate the root flare and adjust the depth to ensure that excess soil is not on the surface of the root system. Ensure that the pit is not excavated beyond the depth required or settling may occur. For trees in a container, the bottom of the hole should be level. For balled and burlapped (B&B) trees, the hole should be "crowned" in the center with compacted soil to prevent settling. Refer to the planting diagram under "Guying" in the next section to view details for planting a B&B tree.
   - Increase the width of the pit for hard or compacted soils.
   - Scarify (roughen) the sides of the pit.
   - Before placing the tree in the pit, double check the depth of the pit and adjust as needed.

4. Place the tree or shrub in the center of the pit.
   - Lift the tree by the root ball or bucket, not by the trunk.
   - Set the plant plumb and place a small amount of backfill in the pit and compact to stabilize the plant before removing the burlap.
   - Remove all container material.
   - If the plant is root bound, score the sides of the root ball with a sharp knife. With shrubs, cut from the bottom of the root ball part way up.
   - Remove all nylon string, straps or other material that is non-biodegradable and dispose of it properly.
   - Ensure that root/trunk flare is exposed above the grade, as it is often buried too deeply in the nursery container and when balled and burlapped.

Note: If specifications call for fertilizer tablets, place them in the pit, next to the root ball, before backfilling. If other fertilizer types are specified, continue to the next step. A soil test can best determine the need for fertilizer and lime.

5. Fill the pit with backfill mix.
   - Backfill mix consists of 2/3 excavated soil and 1/3 organic material.
   - Remove any large stones, sticks and other foreign debris from the backfill.
   - If a soil test determined the need for phosphorus and lime, these are best added to the backfill because they do not readily move through the soil.
   - Add some backfill, and then water deeply so the backfill will settle. Repeat this procedure a few times until pit is full. It is usually done in thirds.

Landscape Irrigation

Locate and expose the root flare.

If the tree is in a bucket, remove the bucket after the tree is placed in the hole.

Use ²/3 excavated soil and ¹/3 organic material as backfill.

Fill the hole being sure to compact the backfill a few times using foot pressure. Water is often applied when filling the hole to help settle soil and avoid air pockets.

Notice that the hose is pushed down into refilled pit, as far as possible, so that the water reaches the root ball.

- Tamp the soil around the root ball using a shovel handle and foot pressure to remove air pockets.
- Thoroughly water to settle and eliminate air pockets. Different methods include creating a watering basin by building a 4" (10 cm) wall of soil around the perimeter of the planting pit. A watering basin is not necessary in irrigated turf areas. Another method is to insert a hose deeply into the pit.

6. Sometimes deciduous trees are wrapped with paper tree wrap up to the first branch to prevent sun scald injury. Remove the wrap the following spring.

7. Stake or guy trees if required for windy locations or unstable soil. See diagram in the next section.

8. Avoid using trees with weak trunks or poor quality root balls.

9. Fertilize, mulch and water.
   - Fertilize if required by the planting specifications. Fertilizer should be high in phosphorous and low in nitrogen. Follow label instructions.
   Note: The International Society of Arboriculture (ISA) does not recommend fertilizing at the time of planting.
   - Water thoroughly after planting.
   - Add a 2 – 3" (5 – 7.5 cm) layer of mulch to the watering basin, keeping mulch away from the trunk of the tree so as not to cover the root/trunk flare.

Tree Staking and Guying

Healthy trees do not usually require staking. When choosing trees, avoid those with weak trunks or poor quality root balls. Trees planted in locations exposed to high winds or located on steep slopes should be staked. Trees planted in very sandy soil or very wet clay soil should also be staked. Stakes, wires and straps or tree ties should be removed after one to two growing seasons depending on wind conditions and development of the root structure. Upright staking is adequate for smaller trees, whereas larger trees require guying. Refer to and follow the project specifications and details if staking or guying.

It is important to use the proper personal protective equipment (PPE), including eye and ear protection, gloves and a hardhat.

> When staking and guying, refer to and follow project specifications for tree planting and staking.

Staking

1. Drive stakes into the soil just beyond the perimeter of the planting pit.
   - For trees under 8' (2.5 m) use two stakes placed perpendicular to the prevailing winds.

   Note: ISA recommends staking as stated here. However, always read and follow the project specifications and review the planting plan detail before staking.

   - For trees over 8' (2.5 m) use three stakes spaced evenly around the tree at 120-degree angles. One stake should be located in the direction of prevailing winds and, therefore, the other two stakes are at an angle to prevailing winds.
   - Use 6' – 8' (1.8 – 2.5 m) wooden posts or steel T-posts.
   - Stakes should be driven 18" (50 cm) deep into undisturbed soil.

Always wear a hardhat, gloves, and ear protection when driving stakes and wear eye protection when installing tree straps and guy wires.

Tree strap was left on too long and is girdling the tree.

Landscape Irrigation

Pounding metal T-post into ground

Placing tree straps

Tightening guy wire

Tree planting and staking detail — no scale

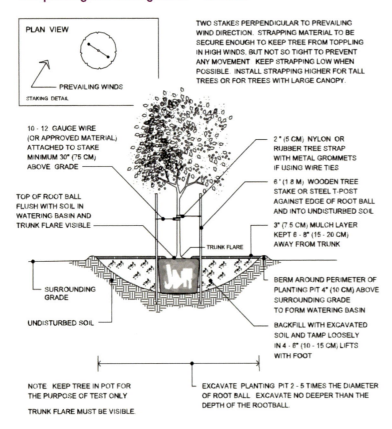

2. Install the ties or tree straps and wires.
   - Different types of tree ties and straps are available. Ties made of flexible material minimize damage to the trunk and provide flexibility. Use the tree ties or straps specified and follow manufacturer's recommendations for installing.

   Note: Avoid using hose and wire as tree straps. The wire can wear through the hose causing damage to the tree. Tree straps should be placed at least 3' (90 cm) above grade.

Guying

1. Drive three anchors (or duck bills) into soil just beyond the perimeter of the planting pit.
   - Anchors are placed at 120-degree angles. One anchor should be located in the direction of prevailing winds.
   - Use a round steel drive rod for the duck bills and a heavy hammer to drive anchors 18" (50 cm) deep into undisturbed soil.

2. Install the tree straps and guy wires.
   - Slide cable through a length of PVC pipe (used as a safety cover) and attach to cable clamps.

- Use 1 ¼" (3 cm) nylon or rubber tree straps with metal grommets.
- Tree straps should be placed at least 3' (90 cm) above grade.
- Use 10 – 12 gauge guy wire.
- Adjust turnbuckle as needed without over tightening.
- Hang flagging from wire to increase visibility.
- Remove stakes, wire and straps after one year if the tree is well established or as specifications define.

INSTALLING CABLE GUY

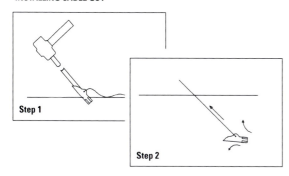

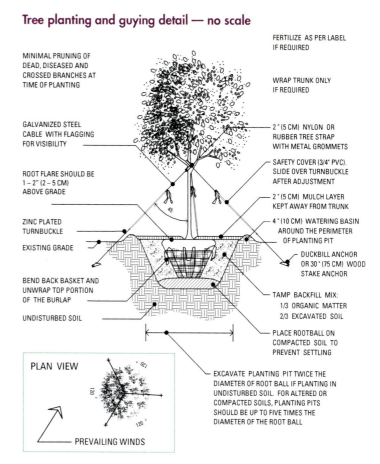

Annuals, Perennials and Biennials

When a splash of color is desired in a landscape, annuals, biennials and herbaceous perennials provide an excellent solution. Whether using annuals or perennials, follow these guidelines to create the best effect in your landscape.

- Most plants perform best in fertile, well-drained soils. To improve texture, amend clay or sandy soils with organic matter—compost, peat, manure, etc.—at a rate of 3 cubic yards per 1000 sq ft (2.5 cu m/100 sq m).
- When creating an island-shaped bed, place the tallest plants in the middle of the island and the shortest plants around the perimeter.
- When planting a bed along a fence or foundation, place the tallest plants at the back of the bed and the shortest plants along the front edge.
- Create visual interest by selecting plants with a variety of forms, colors and textures.
- Place like plants in clusters to accentuate their form, color and texture.
- Use a triangular or random configuration when planting, rather than straight rows.
- Group plants with similar cultural requirements, e.g., don't mix sun-loving plants with shade-loving species.

Landscape Irrigation

Annuals

Annuals complete their life cycle within one growing season, or year. There are summer annuals and winter annuals. Annuals bloom only once in their life cycle before dying out. Examples include pansies, sunflowers and marigolds. The same flowers must be replanted to bloom the next year. Before planting, it is important to amend and prepare the bed properly. The relative advantages and drawbacks of annuals are:

 PRO

- Available in a large variety of colors
- Many species will bloom throughout an entire season
- Easy to replace
- Best source of color
- Can often be used to attract beneficial organisms to the garden

 CON

- More labor intensive
- Require more water
- Expensive to plant on a yearly basis
- May require supplemental slow-release Nitrogen fertilizer
- May require additional pest management practices
- Require different annual rotations from year to year to help maintain soil health
- Many varieties require regular deadheading (removal of spent blooms) to maintain flowering.

Biennials

Biennial weeds and flowers grow in two seasons. During the first season, they remain in a vegetative state and rarely flower or set seeds. In the second season, biennial plants flower, set seeds, and then typically die. Hollyhock is an example of a biennial plant. Black-Eyed Susan is also biennial.

Biennial plants typically reseed themselves and will therefore continually renew themselves. The relative pros and cons of biennials are:

 PRO

- Require less labor once established
- Reseed and continually renew themselves
- Require less water
- Cost effective over time
- Many native varieties are available

 CON

- Require vigilance to remove plants before going to seed so new groups of plants can be established

Perennials

Perennials bloom, die back and come up again the next year. Examples include peonies, salvia and columbine, to name only a few. Since they come up each year, there is no need to replant them. The relative advantages and drawbacks of perennials are:

 PRO

- Require less labor once established
- Often require less water than annuals
- Greater variety of sizes available
- Cost effective over time
- Many varieties can be split and divided
- Many native varieties are available

 CON

- Colors are generally more subdued and the time frame for color is more limited during the season.
- May be difficult to replace with plants of similar species, color and size, if needed

Water Gardens and Aquatic Plants

This section offers a brief discussion of some key points about water gardens and their maintenance. Water gardens require regular monitoring and maintenance to stay in balance. Like soil, the water environment contains many organisms, including algae, microorganisms, insects, plants and animals such as amphibians or fish. Leaves, soil, fertilizers, animal waste and other material also enter the pond or water garden, providing nutrients or presenting challenges to maintain balance. Smaller ponds are easily imbalanced by excessive nutrients, whereas larger ponds can more effectively buffer nutrient materials that enter.

Water plants

Proper balance can be maintained in water gardens with water (aquatic) plants. The water plants remove nutrients from the water, which helps avoid overgrowth of algae. Plants are vital and necessary. Water plants grow at different depths and the design should accommodate plants adapted to growing at different depths. It is best to choose native plants that are suited to the climate. Avoid non-native plants, many of which have become invasive and cause environmental problems when they find their way to natural rivers or streams.

Design considerations

Options for ponds or water gardens include containers, pond liners, pre-formed ponds, or ponds made from concrete, tile or brick. Design considerations for water gardens include pumps and filters that help circulate and clean water, spray jets or waterfalls to increase oxygen, and small fish to eat algae or mosquito larvae.

Maintenance

Maintenance tasks include:
- Occasionally pruning and removing plants or dead leaves.
- Removing excess organic material that has accumulated on the bottom.
- Cleaning filter(s) according to manufacturer's instructions.
- Adding water, as needed, to maintain proper level.
- Providing cold-season maintenance, as needed.
- During the winter, most hardy plants can be left. In colder climates, sink plants in the deepest part of a pond to prevent freezing or keep them in water indoors in a cool but not freezing location.

Water garden with landscape lighting

Summary

Plants are living organisms and require specific conditions to thrive and remain healthy. There is a vast array of plant varieties, ranging from flowers, to shrubs and trees, to aquatic plants, and more. They vary in size, color, shape and function. Growth conditions are diverse, and the care and maintenance needs can be greatly different. Selecting plants suited to the climate and micro-climate is always a good strategy. Soil tests can determine appropriate amendments to help correct the soil.

Keep in mind that not all plants are grown in native soil. Plants raised at nurseries, in planter boxes or on rooftop gardens, are grown in soilless media consisting of various mixes of peat moss, sand and other organic material.

Other factors to consider when selecting plants include erosion control; wildlife habitat; proximity to urban dwellings, streets, etc.; pest resistance; and shade, color, privacy and edibility.

Being able to recognize and identify plants is very beneficial. Learning to identify plants is an ongoing process that requires exposure to different varieties. Taking classes and strolling through botanic gardens can help.

Understanding the basics of plant structure and growth — a reminder that plants are living organisms — helps to underscore the importance of proper tree planting, staking and guying techniques. Correct planting depth, fertilization, backfilling, watering and ensuring that the root flare is not covered are essential. Staking and guying for newly planted trees can be helpful during the first growing season while the roots are becoming established. It is important to use proper techniques to monitor the effects on the growing tree, and to remove stakes and guy wire at the appropriate time.

Flowering plants are a great source of color and add visual interest to landscapes. They can be selected to accent areas having different micro-climates, for example, sunny versus shady areas. Flowering plants can also be selected on the basis their life cycle — annual, biennial or perennial — depending on maintenance needs, cost and flower preferences.

Plants also play an important role in water features, such as ponds. Aquatic plants help keep the water balanced and prevent algae overgrowth. Proper maintenance is required to preserve a healthy environment for water plants.

As always, proper personal protective equipment, appropriate for each task, must be worn!

Chapter 10

Turf Installation

What You Will Learn

After reading this chapter, you will be able to:

- Describe advantages and disadvantages of establishing turf from seed or sod.

- List and describe several factors concerning maintenance, intended use, site conditions and appearance, to be considered when selecting a grass species.

- Describe why a soil test is important.

- List the five main steps for preparing an area for seed or sod.

- Describe three methods for applying seed.

- Calculate the amount of seed needed to seed an area properly.

- Describe the steps for installing sod.

- Describe how to care for and maintain newly installed sod or newly seeded areas.

Chapter 10

Preview

Seed or Sod?

Selecting Grass Species

Site/Soil Preparation
- Soil testing
- Tilling and amendments

Seeding
- Preparation
- Applying seed
- Quantity of seed
- Care and maintenance

Sodding
- Preparation
- Installation
- Care and maintenance

Video training at www.LandscapeTechnician.net

Landscape Irrigation

Overview

Turfgrass is an asset in many landscapes. Turf can be purely ornamental or it can be used as a surface for outdoor activities. Regardless of the purpose and use, establishing healthy turf requires careful planning and implementation. This chapter discusses the considerations for selecting turfgrass, and procedures for installing turf and keeping turfgrass healthy.

Seed or Sod?

Turf areas can be established from either seed or sod, which is turf that is grown off-site, then cut and replanted at a new location. The relative advantages and drawbacks of each method are listed below.

Turf from Seed

PRO
- Less expensive
- Less labor intensive
- Easy to blend different species
- Cost-effective erosion control

CON
- May not produce complete uniform coverage during the first growing season
- Can take several weeks to fill out
- Difficult to establish on slopes
- More susceptible to weeds
- Has temperature requirements for germination and should be planted during specific windows of time depending on location and turf species

Turf from Sod

PRO
- Produces immediate results
- Less susceptible to weeds
- Can be established anytime ground is not frozen

CON
- Limited mix of species available
- Greater initial expense
- Requires more time and labor to install
- Sod can introduce a different soil layer that may cause water saturation to change
- Incorporation of plastic netting in sod in certain locations
- Can introduce new diseases and pests to site
- Increased water requirements

Selecting Grass Species

Turf grass comes in many species and each species has its own characteristics and qualities. When selecting turfgrass seed or sod, it is important to match the type of turf to local conditions and intended use. Consider the following important factors when selecting the variety of turf.

Grass Species Selection Criteria

Site Conditions and Intended Use	Turf Factors	Turf Considerations
	• Shade tolerance • Heat tolerance • Drought tolerance • Soil tolerance • pH tolerance • Traffic tolerance	• Will turf be shaded by trees, buildings, other structures? • Will turf be grown in an area of intense heat and sunlight? • Will turf be required to withstand dry conditions or will regular irrigation be available? • Will turf be grown on clay or sandy soil? • Will turf be grown on acid or alkaline soil? • Will turf be primarily ornamental or will it have foot traffic? • Will the turf area be used for sports or other activities?
Maintenance Needs	**Turf Factors** • Water, fertilizer and mowing requirements • Disease and/or insect resistance	**Turf Considerations** • Will regular maintenance be available? • Will turf be subject to conditions where there is a potential for insect and/or disease problems?
Importance of Appearance	**Turf Factors** • Color • Texture	**Turf Considerations** • Is it important for turf to maintain a uniform green color throughout most of the year? • Should turf be fine textured? Is medium- or coarse-textured turf acceptable or desirable?

Healthy lawn

Needy lawn

Turf ready for harvest

Landscape Irrigation

Site/Soil Preparation

Whether choosing seed or sod, proper site/soil preparation is extremely important for establishing healthy turf. Good soil preparation reduces water consumption, promotes faster and healthier root development and helps reduce future problems such as weeds, disease and yellowing. Prior to installing sod or seed, it is worthwhile to evaluate existing drainage conditions.

Soil testing

Evaluating the soil conditions is an important first step in a successful turf installation. A professional soil test can provide valuable information about the pH, nutrient deficiencies and compaction rate of the soil at a site. This information helps landscape contractors make decisions on tilling methods, amendments and/or fertilizers necessary to prepare the soil for grass.

A soil test can often be arranged through a local county or university extension service. Be sure to explain the purpose of the test to those performing it. Use a core sampler to get samples from several locations around the turf area before installation. Samples should be at least 6" (15 cm) deep. Most test sites want the sample dry and without excess debris (such as grass) for the best test reliability. Be sure samples are a good representation of the actual soil.

Tilling and amendments

To prepare the turf area for either seed or sod:

1. Remove weeds and existing grasses.

2. Add amendments and fertilizers as determined by the soil analysis. Amendments can include peat, compost, composted manure, straw, sawdust or other materials. Amendments are typically applied at a rate of 3 – 5 cubic yards per 1000 square feet (2.5 – 4.2 cu m/100 sq m) of soil.

   Note: Some manures, especially horse manure, may contain seeds from weeds of undesirable grasses. Others may also be high in salts. All manures should be aged and composted before using.

3. Rip and/or till the soil to a specified depth.

4. Remove surface stones and debris greater than 1" (2.5 cm) in diameter.

5. Rake the soil to a smooth, even surface. If turf is to be seeded, smooth soil at finished grade. For sod installations, grade below paved areas and sprinkler heads to allow for thickness of sod.

Wear appropriate PPE, in this case safety glasses, ear protection, gloves and steel-toed boots.

A rototiller is used to till the soil and work in soil amendments in preparation for seeding or sodding. For hard compacted soil, tilling is also done to loosen the soil prior to adding the amendments.

Turf Installation   Chapter 10 | Page 173

Add soil amendments as recommended by the soil analysis to help balance the soil. Till amendments into the soil.

Remove surface stones and debris larger than 1" (2.5 cm) and rake to a smooth grade.

Seeding

Although growing turf from seed takes longer for a uniform cover to be established, it is less expensive than sodding, and grass species can be easily mixed or blended if desired.

Seeding can offer other important roles in landscape management. For example, ryegrass is a quick-to-cover crop for erosion control. Also see the section below on hydroseeding.

Preparation

Follow the soil preparation procedures described above. Select good-quality seed that has been tested for at least 90 percent germination and 85 percent purity.

Applying seed

There are several methods used to apply grass seed, including:

Broadcast spreader

Broadcast seeding

Broadcast seeding is a simple procedure whereby seed is spread evenly over the surface of the soil using some type of seeder or spreader. After the seed has been applied, the area should be raked to cover as much seed as possible with soil. Ideally, seed will be covered by ¼" (6 mm) of topsoil and rolled to ensure proper seed to soil contact.

When spreading seed with a broadcast spreader, go over the area with half of the seed required and then spread the other half in a perpendicular direction to the original pathway. On sloping or small areas, this may not be practical.

The seeded area then is typically covered with straw or other organic mulch to retain moisture and minimize seed movement. On slopes or in other special situations, erosion control measures such as blankets, netting, starter fertilizer, etc., may be required.

Seed drilling

This system uses a seed drill, a specialized mechanical device, to bury seed in the ground at a uniform, pre-set depth. It can be used on untilled soil and in areas where seed applied by broadcast methods may be displaced by wind or water. Seed drilling is relatively slow and expensive, but may be practical in areas such as large fields.

Manual sponsored by **Hunter Industries**

Hydroseeding

Hydroseeding is increasingly used in areas in need of erosion control. Hydroseeding is typically a two-step procedure for seeding and mulching. In the first step, seed, fertilizer and water are mixed together and sprayed onto the prepared ground using specialized equipment called a HydroSeeder™/ hydromulcher. In the second step, specially prepared very fine wood mulch and water are applied as a mixture over the seeded area.

New materials are being developed to be added to the seed mixture before spraying. These materials provide an improved growing medium and better bonding of the seeds so that they are not washed away or blown away.

This method has advantages for large areas, rocky mountainous areas or dense soils where tilling is not possible and on slopes where using other seeding techniques may be difficult.

Quantity of seed

The amount of grass seed required depends upon the type of grass being planted. Species that spread by underground rhizomes, such as bluegrass, require about 2 lbs of seed per 1000 sq ft (1.0 kg/100 sq m) of lawn. Species that grow in clumps, such as tall fescue, require up to 6 lbs of seed per 1000 sq ft (3.0 kg/100 sq m) of area.

Calculating Required Seed — Sample Calculations*

Example:
Sample problem — US/Imperial
  A rectangular lawn area measures 80' by 120'. To seed the lawn at a rate of 3 lbs per 1000 sq ft, how many lbs of seed are needed?

Steps to find answer:
1. Find the area of the lawn.
   $A = l \times w$
   $A = 80' \times 120'$
   $A = 9600$ sq ft
2. The seeding rate is 3 lbs/1000 sq ft. Calculate how many 1000 sq ft sections are in the lawn area.

   9600 sq ft/1000 sq ft = 9.6 sections
3. Multiply the number of 1000 sq. ft. sections by the seed rate.

   9.6 x 3 lbs = 28.8 lbs of seed

For more information on making landscape calculations, refer to the chapter "Landscape Plan Reading and Calculations" in this manual.

Metric example:
Sample problem — Metric
  A rectangular lawn area measures 25 m by 35 m. To seed the lawn at a rate of 1.5 kg per 1000 sq m, how many kg of seed are needed?

Steps to find answer:
1. Find the area of the lawn.
   $A = l \times w$
   $A = 25$ m $\times 35$ m
   $A = 875$ sq m
2. The seeding rate is 1.5 kg/1000 sq m. Calculate the weight (W) of seed required. Multiply area by seeding rate.

Notice that the area of the lawn is smaller than 1000 sq m, the size given for the seeding rate. This means that the amount of seed needed will be less than 1.5 kg. It is a good "common sense" check.

$W = A \times$ rate
$W = 875$ sq m $\times 1.5$ kg/1000 sq m
$W = 1.31$ kg of seed

Care and maintenance

After seed has been applied, it must be kept moist. It should be watered lightly several times a day. During the germination period (1 – 3 weeks), it is important to suppress weeds either manually or chemically. Take special care to review the labeling on products to ensure that they are specifically appropriate for newly seeded areas.

After one month, reseed areas where grass did not become established. Begin mowing when grass reaches a height that is 33 percent higher than the optimal growing height (approximately 4" or 10 cm for most cool-season grasses and shorter for warm-season grasses). Cut 1/3 of grass height. Be sure the subgrade is dry enough before mowing to avoid damaging the grade by causing ruts. Refer also to the chapter *"Turf Maintenance."*

Leaving clippings benefits the turf by adding nitrogen and other nutrients. Excessive clippings (clumps) may be removed.

Sodding

Sodding an area obviously produces immediate results, but the process is usually more expensive and labor intensive than for seeding. Small areas may be the exception.

Preparation

Prepare the soil as described earlier. Use only good-quality sod that does not tear or break during handling, is free from weeds and disease and has a uniform thickness and color. Keep sod moist and install within a day or two of delivery. If sod cannot be planted the same day it is delivered, be sure to place pallets in the shade and keep moist and cool.

Installation

Follow these guidelines for sod installation:

- Roll the properly prepared and graded area with a water-filled roller before laying sod if this step is called for in the specifications or if the soil is not stable (too soft).
- Begin by laying sod around the perimeter.
- Next, lay sod along the straightest or longest edge, and at a perpendicular angle to the slope of an area.
- Be sure each piece is fit tightly against adjoining pieces and knit seams tightly.
- Stagger pieces in next row as in a brick pattern so that the shorter joints of each roll do not align.
- Butt the short ends together tightly.
- Do not overlap any edges.
- Use a sharp knife to cut sod to fit along curves or in irregularly shaped areas.
- For sod with netting, ensure that netting is not showing.
- Roll sod with a water-filled roller to remove air pockets.
- Water soak the sod immediately and thoroughly. Sod along curbs or other paved surfaces will dry out more quickly and may require additional water.
- Fill any gaps between edges of sod with sand or soil to keep the sod from drying out.

See photos on the next page.

Landscape Irrigation

Rolls of sod are ready to install

Butt ends of sod securely together to avoid gaps in the sod.

Stagger pieces of sod in a brick-like pattern

Use a sod knife to cut around sprinkler heads and other obstacles.

Roll sod with a water-filled roller to remove air pockets.

After installation, water sod thoroughly.

Care and maintenance

For the first two weeks, keep sod and top soil evenly moist by watering once a day (more in hot and/or dry conditions). Avoid heavy or concentrated use during this time.

After two weeks, sod should have developed a root system and watering can be cut back. This can be confirmed by pulling back the sod to see if small fibrous white roots are starting to grow. This is a sign that the root system is starting to develop. Deep rooting is promoted by less frequent watering, resulting in increased drought tolerance. Begin mowing when grass is securely rooted.

Be sure grass and soil are dry before mowing. Allowing the soil to dry sufficiently avoids damaging the subgrade with equipment. Cut 1/3 of grass height. Mow diagonally to the seams. Water promptly after the first mowing. If clippings are excessive, remove the excess.

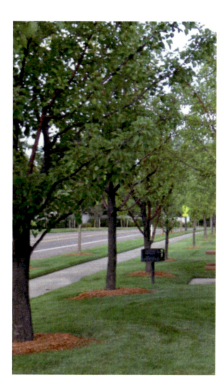

Summary

Turf is installed for different reasons for various functions. There are advantages and disadvantages to establishing turf from seed or sod. Whether sodding or seeding, the site conditions, maintenance needs and appearance should be considered when selecting the grass species. Soil testing is an important first step that provides information on soil properties and soil nutrients. The soil test helps determine how to prepare the soil before planting.

If seeding, there are several ways to apply the seeds. Maintenance needs may be high for up to three weeks until seeds germinate and start to become established. Be sure to calculate correctly the amount of seed required for the area.

For sod installations, watering requirements are higher for the first two weeks while the root system becomes established. Whether sodding or seeding, follow proper guidelines for first mowing.

Appendices

Extras & Resources

What You Will Find Here:

- Work Orders & Communication
- Field Circuit Test Worksheet
- Irrigation Drawings
- Material Safety Data Sheet (MSDS)
- Snow & Ice Management
- Resources
- Glossary

Work Orders & Communication

Work orders are forms — either paper or electronic — used to record activities and accomplishments at a job site. The work order is a communication tool providing information about the status of the project. This information is used for billing and for company records. Filling out work orders is a daily task that is typically done by a crew leader.

How to fill out a work order

Important information to include in work orders:
- Name of the job
- Date
- Location of the job site
- Time spent at the job site
- Materials used, including product names, styles, sizes and quantities
- Equipment used
- Time spent by each employee on specific tasks
- Description of the work completed or in progress

Hints for producing useful work orders

- Write clearly and legibly.
- Keep work orders in a notebook or folder so they stay clean and safe from spills or other damage.
- When filling out work orders that use carbon or multiple copy paper, use a pen and write firmly. Make sure all copies are legible.
- Fill out work orders every workday.
- Be sure descriptions of work to be done and work completed are detailed enough to be meaningful to anyone reading it.

Company Name & Logo

Company address,
phone, e-mail, Web site info

Sample Work Order

Job Name: _____ Date: _____
Address: _____ Job No.: _____
_____ Authorized by: _____

Location & description of work to be performed:
_____
_____
_____
_____
_____
_____

Location & description of work completed:
_____
_____
_____
_____
_____
_____

Job Completed: ❐ YES ❐ NO   Return Required: ❐ YES ❐ NO

Materials Used

QTY	Item	EACH	Total

Equipment Used

QTY	Item	EACH

Additional Job Information:
_____
_____
_____
_____
_____
_____
_____
_____

Work Completed By:			
Employee Name/No.	Start	Stop	Total

Landscape Irrigation

Field Circuit Resistance & Amperage Test Worksheet

A worksheet like this is used to record readings when testing the station outputs with a multimeter. Readings can indicate possible problems. Numbers recorded on the worksheet can also serve as a reference point for future problems.

Zone	Ohms ( )	Amps (A)	Zone	Ohms ( )	Amps (A)	Zone	Ohms ( )	Amps (A)
1			17			33		
2			18			34		
3			19			35		
4			20			36		
5			21			37		
6			22			38		
7			23			39		
8			24			40		
9			25			41		
10			26			42		
11			27			43		
12			28			44		
13			29			45		
14			30			46		
15			31			47		
16			32			48		

Adapted from Control Tech USA, Parker CO

Irrigation Drawings

The following illustrations were provided by Hunter Industries and have been adapted by John van Roessel, P.Ag., Landscape Industry Certified, JVR Landscape Inc., for use in this manual.

Irrigation Heads

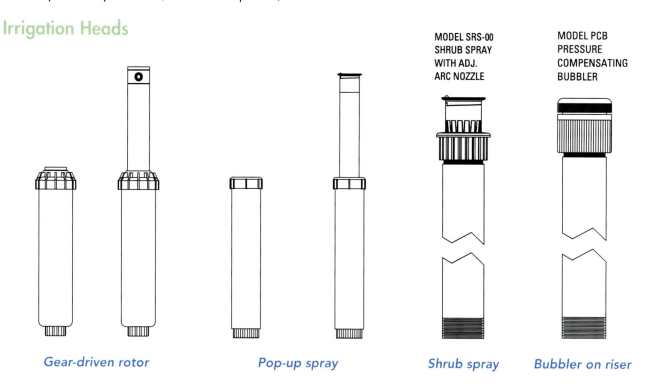

Gear-driven rotor   *Pop-up spray*   *Shrub spray*   *Bubbler on riser*

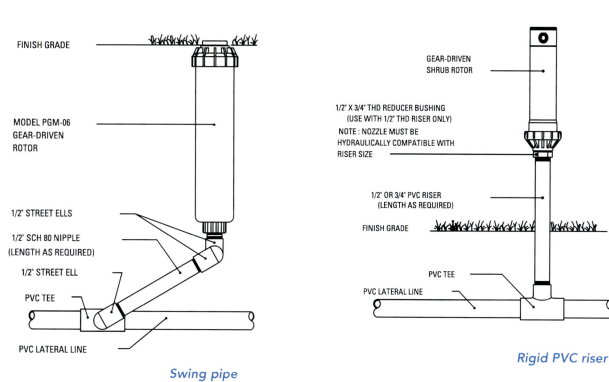

Swing pipe   *Rigid PVC riser*

Manual sponsored by **Hunter Industries**

Landscape Irrigation

Saddle

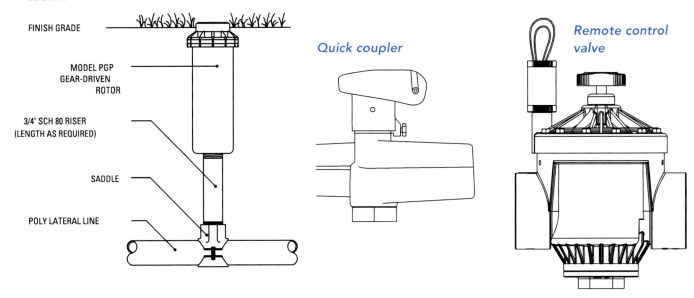

Quick coupler

Remote control valve

Mini-click rain sensor

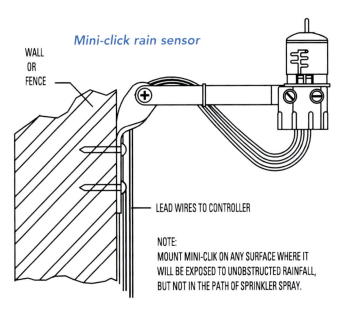

NOTE:
MOUNT MINI-CLIK ON ANY SURFACE WHERE IT WILL BE EXPOSED TO UNOBSTRUCTED RAINFALL, BUT NOT IN THE PATH OF SPRINKLER SPRAY.

Valve box installation detail

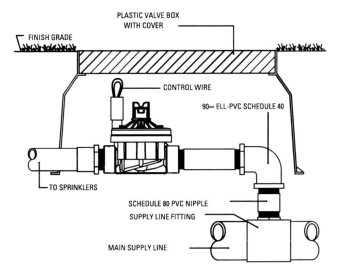

Electronic Controller

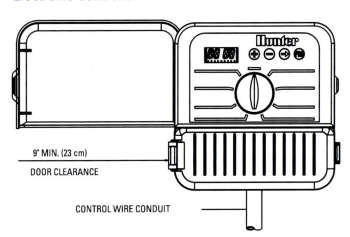

Professional Landcare Network | Page 184

Irrigation Installation Drawings

The irrigation details on this page have been provided by Keesen Water Management, Inc., Denver, CO.

Point of connection

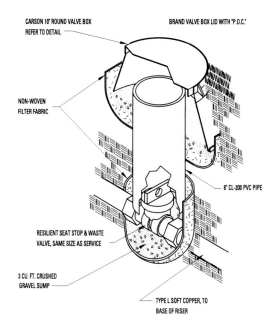

Backflow preventer detail

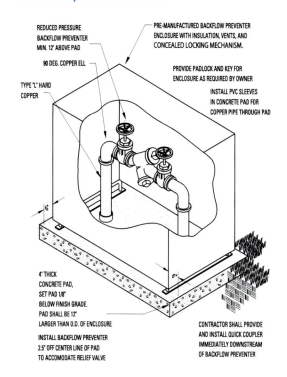

Valve box detail

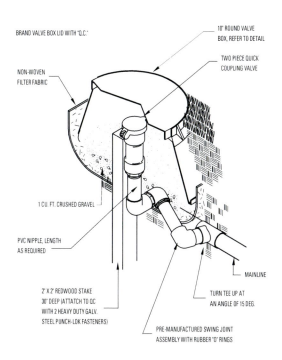

Manual drain valve

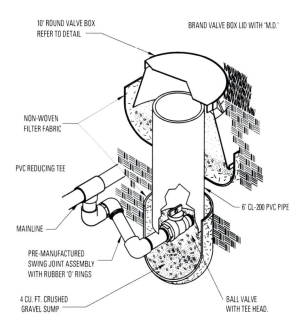

Material Safety Data Sheet

Material Safety Data Sheet

MAPP GAS (Petroleum Gas, MAPD)

Section 1. Chemical product and company identification

Product name	: MAPP GAS (Petroleum Gas, MAPD)
Supplier	: AIRGAS INC., on behalf of its subsidiaries 259 North Radnor-Chester Road Suite 100 Radnor, PA 19087-5283 1-610-687-5253
Product use	: Synthetic/Analytical chemistry.
Synonym	: MAP,MAPP,Methyacetylene-Propadiene, Mixture of Methylacetylene and Propadiene
MSDS #	: 002015
Date of Preparation/Revision	: 4/29/2010.
In case of emergency	: 1-866-734-3438

Section 2. Hazards identification

Physical state	: Gas.
Emergency overview	: DANGER! FLAMMABLE GAS. MAY CAUSE FLASH FIRE. CONTAINS MATERIAL THAT CAN CAUSE TARGET ORGAN DAMAGE. CONTENTS UNDER PRESSURE.
	Keep away from heat, sparks and flame. Do not puncture or incinerate container. Contains material that can cause target organ damage. Use only with adequate ventilation. Keep container closed.
	Contact with rapidly expanding gases can cause frostbite.
Target organs	: Contains material which causes damage to the following organs: upper respiratory tract, skin, eyes. Contains material which may cause damage to the following organs: the nervous system, central nervous system (CNS).
Routes of entry	: Inhalation

Potential acute health effects

Eyes	: Liquid or cold gas may cause frostbites.
Skin	: Liquid or cold gas may cause frostbites.
Inhalation	: Acts as a simple asphyxiant.
Ingestion	: Ingestion is not a normal route of exposure for gases
Potential chronic health effects	: Not applicable
Medical conditions aggravated by over-exposure	: Pre-existing disorders involving any target organs mentioned in this MSDS as being at risk may be aggravated by over-exposure to this product.

See toxicological information (section 11)

Section 3. Composition, Information on Ingredients

Name	CAS number	% Volume	Exposure limits

MAPP GAS *(Petroleum Gas, MAPD)*

Propylene	115-07-1	40 - 50	ACGIH TLV (United States, 1/2009).
			  TWA: 500 ppm 8 hcur(s).
			ACGIH TLV (United States, 1/2005).
			  TWA: 500 ppm 8 hcur(s). Form: All forms

Methyl Acetylene	74-99-7	27 - 33	ACGIH TLV (United States, 1/2009).
			  TWA: 1640 mg/m³ 8 hour(s).
			  TWA: 1000 ppm 8 hour(s).
			NIOSH REL (United States, 6/2009).
			  TWA: 1650 mg/m³ 10 hour(s).
			  TWA: 1000 ppm 10 hour(s).
			OSHA PEL (United States, 11/2006).
			  TWA: 1650 mg/m³ 8 hour(s).
			  TWA: 1000 ppm 8 hour(s).
			OSHA PEL 1989 (United States, 3/1989).
			  TWA: 1650 mg/m³ 8 hour(s).
			  TWA: 1000 ppm 8 hour(s).

1,2-Propadiene (Allene)	463-49-0	13 - 15	TLV (Philippines, 1/1978).
			  TLV: 1800 mg/m³ 8 hour(s).
			  TLV: 1000 ppm 8 hour(s).
			Ministry of Labor (Republic of Korea, 6/2008).
			  STEL: 1250 ppm 15 minute(s).
			  STEL: 2250 mg/m³ 15 minute(s).
			  TWA: 1000 ppm 8 hour(s).
			  TWA: 1800 mg/m³ 8 hour(s).

Isobutane	75-28-5	2 - 5	ACGIH TLV (United States, 1/2009).
			  TWA: 1000 ppm 8 hour(s).
			NIOSH REL (United States, 6/2009).
			  TWA: 1900 mg/m³ 10 hour(s).
			  TWA: 800 ppm 10 hour(s).

N-Butane	106-97-8	2 - 5	ACGIH TLV (United States, 1/2009).
			  TWA: 1000 ppm 8 hour(s).
			NIOSH REL (United States, 6/2009).
			  TWA: 1900 mg/m³ 10 hour(s).
			  TWA: 800 ppm 10 hour(s).
			OSHA PEL 1989 (United States, 3/1989).
			  TWA: 1900 mg/m³ 8 hour(s).
			  TWA: 800 ppm 8 hour(s).

Propane	74-98-6	1 - 5	ACGIH TLV (United States, 1/2009).
			  TWA: 1000 ppm 8 hour(s).
			NIOSH REL (United States, 6/2009).
			  TWA: 1800 mg/m³ 10 hour(s).
			  TWA: 1000 ppm 10 hour(s).
			OSHA PEL (United States, 11/2006).
			  TWA: 1800 mg/m³ 8 hour(s).
			  TWA: 1000 ppm 8 hour(s).
			OSHA PEL 1989 (United States, 3/1989).
			  TWA: 1800 mg/m³ 8 hour(s).
			  TWA: 1000 ppm 8 hour(s).

Section 4. First aid measures

No action shall be taken involving any personal risk or without suitable training. If it is suspected that fumes are still present, the rescuer should wear an appropriate mask or self-contained breathing apparatus. It may be dangerous to the person providing aid to give mouth-to-mouth resuscitation.

Eye contact : In case of contact, immediately flush eyes with plenty of water for at least 15 minutes. DO NOT remove contact lenses, if worn. Obtain medical attention without delay preferably from an ophthalmologist.

Skin contact : Immediately warm frostbite area with warm water (not to exceed 40.5 C, 105F). Remove contaminated clothing and shoes. Wash clothing before reuse. Clean shoes thoroughly before reuse. Get medical attention.

Frostbite : Try to warm up the frozen tissues and seek medical attention.

MAPP GAS *(Petroleum Gas, MAPD)*

Inhalation : Move exposed person to fresh air. If not breathing, if breathing is irregular or if respiratory arrest occurs, provide artificial respiration or oxygen by trained personnel. Loosen tight clothing such as a collar, tie, belt or waistband. Get medical attention immediately.

Ingestion : As this product is a gas, refer to the inhalation section.

Section 5. Fire-fighting measures

Flammability of the product : Flammable.
Auto-ignition temperature : Lowest known value: 286.85°C (548.3°F) (Butane).
Flash point : Lowest known value: Closed cup: -108.15°C (-162.7°F). (propene)
Flammable limits : Lower: 2% Upper: 13%
Products of combustion : Decomposition products may include the following materials:
  carbon dioxide
  carbon monoxide

Fire-fighting media and instructions : In case of fire, use water spray (fog), foam or dry chemical.

In case of fire, allow gas to burn if flow cannot be shut off immediately. Apply water from a safe distance to cool container and protect surrounding area. If involved in fire, shut off flow immediately if it can be done without risk.

Contains gas under pressure. Extremely flammable. In a fire or if heated, a pressure increase will occur and the container may burst or explode. Gas may accumulate in low or confined areas or travel a considerable distance to a source of ignition and flash back, causing fire or explosion.

Special protective equipment for fire-fighters : Fire-fighters should wear appropriate protective equipment and self-contained breathing apparatus (SCBA) with a full face-piece operated in positive pressure mode.

Section 6. Accidental release measures

Personal precautions : Immediately contact emergency personnel. Keep unnecessary personnel away. Use suitable protective equipment (section 8). Shut of gas supply if this can be done safely. Isolate area until gas has dispersed.

Environmental precautions : Avoid dispersal of spilled material and runoff and contact with soil, waterways, drains and sewers.

Methods for cleaning up : Immediately contact emergency personnel. Stop leak if without risk. Note: see section 1 for emergency contact information and section 13 for waste disposal.

Section 7. Handling and storage

Handling : Use only with adequate ventilation. Use explosion-proof electrical (ventilating, lighting and material handling) equipment. High pressure gas. Do not puncture or incinerate container. Use equipment rated for cylinder pressure. Close valve after each use and when empty. Keep container closed. Keep away from heat, sparks and flame. To avoid fire, eliminate ignition sources. Protect cylinders from physical damage; do not drag, roll, slide, or drop. Use a suitable hand truck for cylinder movement.

Storage : Keep container in a cool, well-ventilated area. Keep container tightly closed and sealed until ready for use. Avoid all possible sources of ignition (spark or flame). Segregate from oxidizing materials. Cylinders should be stored upright, with valve protection cap in place, and firmly secured to prevent falling or being knocked over. Cylinder temperatures should not exceed 52 °C (125 °F).

Section 8. Exposure controls/personal protection

Engineering controls : Use only with adequate ventilation. Use process enclosures, local exhaust ventilation or other engineering controls to keep worker exposure to airborne contaminants below any recommended or statutory limits. The engineering controls also need to keep gas, vapor or dust concentrations below any lower explosive limits. Use explosion-proof ventilation equipment.

Personal protection

This example of an MSDS contains only part of the information for this product. Prior to using MAPP gas or any hazardous product, obtain the complete MSDS from the manufacturer and be familiar with the content. Always have any MSDS immediately available.

Landscape Irrigation

Snow & Ice Management

In snowy regions of North America, many landscape contractors provide snow removal services in the winter months. Most vehicles used for landscape services can be easily adapted for snow removal.

Snow removal contracts can vary widely. Be sure you are familiar with the specifications of any snow removal contracts you work on, such as when plowing, sanding or other services should begin. To clarify expectations, have the customer provide a map showing where to plow and where to do hand work. The map becomes an addendum to and part of the contract. A copy of the map is taken to the field with the crew.

Pre-season preparation

Preparation for snow removal should begin before the first snow falls. Familiarize yourself with areas to be plowed before the ground is covered with snow. Note the location of obstacles that could be hidden by snow, including storm drains, fire hydrants, fences, shrubs, curbs, speed bumps, manhole covers, etc. Mapping obstacles ahead of time can help prevent accidental damage to property during snow removal operations. It is also wise to designate locations where plowed snow is to be piled that will not harm landscape, such as rock or mulch beds without plantings or in specific parking spaces.

Trucks and plows

While large equipment is sometimes used for snow removal, most companies offering contract snow removal services use a truck-mounted blade to clear snow-covered areas such as driveways, parking lots and roadways. The angle and height of the blade is adjustable for different plowing situations. Since plowing snow is often done in freezing and potentially dangerous conditions, be sure to dress appropriately and be prepared for emergencies. Appropriate clothing includes insulated boots, a hat, gloves and sunglasses.

Snow removal is standard winter work for many landscape contracting firms.

Safety

Safety is a major concern during snow removal. Always dress warmly, be aware of the symptoms of hypothermia (see the "First Aid and Safety" chapter) and carry emergency supplies in your vehicle, as listed below.

- Cell phone
- First-aid kit
- Flares
- Tool kit
- Plow repair kit specific to your blade. It should include:
   - hydraulic fluid
   - hydraulic hose
   - miscellaneous pins
   - quick coupler
   - miscellaneous repair parts
- Tow strap
- Jumper cables
- Shovel
- Flashlight
- Ice scraper
- Windshield washer fluid
- Sand or salt
- Maps
- Food
- Drinking water

Plowing techniques
Different situations require different plowing techniques. Basic snow removal techniques are discussed below.

Windrowing
Windrowing is a plowing technique used to clear large areas such as parking lots. The operator makes consecutive back-and-forth passes across the area with the blade positioned at an angle to throw snow forward and to the left or right of the vehicle.

Back dragging
Back dragging is the technique used to move snow away from buildings, garages, etc. The blade is put in a straight and raised position while the operator drives forward to the building. The blade is then lowered and the truck backs up, pulling snow away from the building. Since dragging snow is less effective than pushing snow, back dragging should only be done to clear an area large enough for the truck to back into (two or three truck lengths).

Cleanup
Cleanup is the last stage of snow removal and is done to remove snow left over from plowing operations. The blade is put in the straight position and snow is pushed forward to be deposited at the edge of the area.

Guidelines for plowing snow
Some basic guidelines for snow plowing are listed below.
- To begin a pass, accelerate slowly without spinning tires, then lower the blade.
- In parking lots, begin making passes in the center, pushing snow toward the edges. Avoid piling snow in the middle of the lot.
- To avoid drifting, pile snow on the downwind side of the area being cleared.
- Avoid piling snow on streets, sidewalks or neighboring properties.
- When possible, pile snow in low areas so snowmelt does not travel long distances across paved areas before entering a drain inlet. Melting snow can

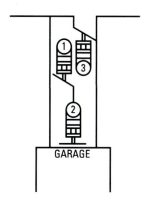

Proper configuration for plowing drives

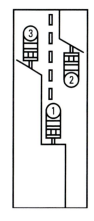

Proper configuration for plowing wide drives

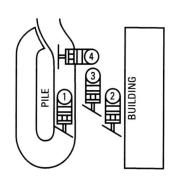

Proper configuration for plowing lots

create an ice hazard when it moves across paved areas and refreezes.
- Avoid covering storm drains, fire hydrants, mailboxes or any structures with snow.
- In some locations, it is illegal to plow snow across a road. Know the regulations for your location.

This chart indicates the size of snow plow that different types of equipment and vehicles can accommodate.

Plow Size

Type of Vehicle	Plow Size in feet (metres)
Tractors	7.0 (2.1)
4WD Utility Vehicles	6.5 (1.98)
Trucks:	
½ ton – 1 ton 2WD	7.0 – 7.5 (2.1 – 2.29)
½ ton – 1 ton 4WD	7.0 – 8.0 (2.1 – 2.44)
1 ½ ton – 2 ton	8.5 – 9.0 (2.59 – 2.74)
2 ½ ton – 3 ton	10.0 (3.05)

Truck maintenance

Plowing snow causes a lot of wear-and-tear on a vehicle. Therefore, vehicles used for plowing require frequent inspections and maintenance. Regularly check the following items on all vehicles used for plowing.
- Tires: for proper pressure and tread wear
- Engine belts: for cracks and proper tightness
- Hoses: for leaks
- Fluids: for proper levels, including oil, windshield washer fluid, radiator coolant, brake fluid, transmission fluid and battery fluid
- Battery terminals: for corrosion
- Windshield wipers: for wear
- Lights: for proper operation, including headlights, taillights, turn signals, brake lights and any auxiliary lights
- Plow blade and assembly: for loose nuts and bolts, cracks, leaking hydraulic fluid and proper hydraulic reservoir level
- Truck undercarriage: for damage at plow assembly attachment points

{ Trucks used in snow removal may require extra attention beyond standard vehicle maintenance. }

Shovels

Snow shoveling is a simple and inexpensive way to remove snow, but it is slow and labor intensive when compared to snow removal with plows or snow blowers. Snow shovels are suitable for small areas, after light accumulations and in locations inaccessible by snow blowers or plows.

Snow blowers

The operation and maintenance of snow blowers is similar in many ways to lawnmowers and other motorized lawn maintenance equipment. Before using a snow blower, read the owner's manual for operating, maintenance and safety instructions, in addition to the guidelines listed below.

Safety guidelines for snow blower operation
- Wear appropriate clothing and protective equipment. Dress in layers. Use goggles or safety glasses and earplugs.
- Wear sturdy footwear that provides traction on slippery surfaces.
- Know how to stop the engine quickly.
- Thoroughly inspect the area to be blown and remove any visible debris.
- Avoid putting hands or feet in the discharge chute or near rotating parts. Serious injury could result.
- In wet or heavy snow, slow down to avoid overworking or clogging the snow blower.

What's wrong with this picture? Operator failed to wear safety glasses and ear protection!

What's right with this picture? Operator directs snow from the blower in the downwind direction.

- If the chute becomes clogged, turn off the engine and disconnect the spark plug. Avoid putting your hand into the chute to dislodge snow because the unit may spin when snow is dislodged. Use a wooden or plastic rod to loosen snow.
- Direct snow away from people, pets, vehicles or other objects or property that could be damaged by flying debris.
- In windy conditions, start upwind and direct snow in the downwind direction.
- Use a snow blower only over smooth paved surfaces. On other surfaces, snow blowers can pick up and throw gravel or other debris.

Ongoing maintenance for snow blowers
- Disconnect the spark plug before performing any maintenance on a snow blower.
- Check the oil level before each use and add oil, as needed.
- Oil and filters should be changed regularly, generally after 20 to 30 hours of use. Refer to your owner's manual for specific recommendations as to frequency of oil changes.
- Inspect the air filter regularly and clean or replace it if dirty.
- Regularly check all nuts and bolts and tighten any that have vibrated loose.
- Replace the spark plug at the interval recommended in the owner's manual.
- Keep all moving parts well lubricated.

End-of-season maintenance for snow blowers
Follow these procedures before placing a snow blower in storage at the end of the season.
- Clean the equipment, removing all dirt and other debris.
- Empty the gas tank by running the engine until it stops.
- Disconnect the spark plug wire.
- Drain the oil and replace it with fresh oil.
- Lubricate parts, as recommended in the owner's manual.
- Store in a dry location.

Snow blowers can be very effective in removing snow from smooth, paved surfaces, such as sidewalks and other areas that are too small for a plow truck to maneuver.

Landscape Irrigation

Sand and deicing products

Sand
Sand can be spread on slippery surfaces to improve traction for vehicles and pedestrians. Sand is effective at temperatures too cold for deicing products. However, stockpiled sand can freeze, making it unusable. Using a sand-salt mix, available from most suppliers, will avoid this problem.

Sand requires cleanup after snow melts and can clog sewers, storm water inlets and can end up in streams and rivers. Residual sand on drive lanes can also contribute to air pollution.

Deicing products
Deicing products can be used to melt or soften ice on surfaces such as roads and walkways. Deicers work by lowering the freezing point of water. Most deicers, such as sodium chloride, magnesium chloride and calcium chloride, are salts. Some deicers, such as acetates, work by softening the ice and snow, making removal easier. The effectiveness of deicers is influenced by a number of factors, including air temperature and the temperature of the surface where it is applied.

As temperatures decrease, deicing products become less effective. For example, salts can melt five times more ice at 30° F (-1° C) than at 20° F (-7° C). Deicing products should not be used if temperatures are below their effective range. For salts, this range is approximately 15° F to 20° F (-7° C to -9° C). This range may vary for other products. Deicers may be blends of chloride salts and acetates. It may be necessary to talk to your supplier about product information, such as the amount of the different components in a blend and the lowest practical melting point. Be attentive both to outdoor temperature and the temperature rating in which the deicer works. Also, use only the quantity needed. Typically, less product is needed at warmer temperatures, which reduces the impact on the environment and also reduces costs.

> Because product deicers can corrode vehicles, always wash and clean vehicles soon after they have been exposed to product deicers.

Deicers can corrode vehicles and other metal objects and have harmful effects on concrete surfaces and structures. They can also increase soil and water salinity, deplete oxygen in water sources and injure plants.

Vehicles should be cleaned soon after exposure to product deicers. Tracking some deicing products onto carpet, tile and other surfaces may cause damage, as well.

Reducing the environmental impact of snow and ice management

There is a continuing shift in the landscape industry and many other industries toward conservation of resources and reducing the environmental impact of human activities. In the area of snow and ice management, use the following guidelines to help reduce the environmental impact of snow and ice management:

- Perform ongoing vehicle maintenance to be sure equipment runs efficiently.
- Plan driving routes to minimize fuel use and emissions.
- Use the vehicle that is the best size and most efficient for the work being done.
- Use the deicing product that is appropriate for the job, which means knowing what is in the product and how and when to use it.
- Use the minimum amount of product needed to get the job done, which is both cost effective and minimizes the impact on the environment.

Resources

Professional industry organizations serve as valuable resources for current technical information. To help readers find additional information on landscape-related topics discussed in this manual, recommended resources that are available from industry associations are listed below.

Professional Landcare Network (PLANET)

The following materials may be ordered from the Professional Landcare Network. Call 800-395-2522 or visit www.landcarenetwork.org.

Basic Sidewalk Clearing with Snowblowers DVD, Snow and Ice Management Association, 2001.

Basic Snowplowing Techniques DVD, Snow and Ice Management Association, 2000.

The Complete Estimating Book 3rd Edition, Charles Vander Kooi, 2004.

How to Price Landscape and Irrigation Projects, James Huston, 2003.

An Illustrated Guide to Pruning 2nd Edition, Edward Gilman, 2002.

Intermediate Snowplowing DVD (Eng./Span.), Snow and Ice Management Association, 2002.

Landscape Specifications Guidelines 5th Edition, Landscape Contractors Association of MD-DC-VA, 2000.

Patios, Driveways, and Plazas – David R. Smith, Interlocking Concrete Pavement Institute, 2002.

Pricing for the Green Industry 2nd Edition, Frank Ross, 1997.

Principles of Pruning Ornamental Trees & Shrubs DVD (Eng./Span.), Professional Landcare Network, 2007.

Taylor's Guide to Ornamental Grasses, Holmes, Roger (Editor), 1997.

Taylor's Guide to Perennials, Ellis, Barbara W., 2000.

Taylor's Guide to Shrubs, Fisher, Kathleen, 2000.

Taylor's Guide to Trees, Roth, Susan A., 2001.

Troubleshooting Diseases of Flowering Plants, University of Florida, 1998.

Troubleshooting Foliage Plant Diseases, University of Florida, 1998.

Troubleshooting Lawn Pests, University of Florida, 2002.

American Nurseryman Publishing Company

The following materials may be ordered from the American Nurseryman Publishing Company. Call 800-621-5727 or visit www.amerinursery.com.

Landscape Plants for Dry Regions, Jones, W. and C. Sacamano, 2000.

Perfect Plant, Perfect Garden, Scott-James, Anne, 1988.

Right Plant, Right Place, Ferguson, Nicola, 1984.

Perfect Plant, Perfect Place, Lancaster, Roy, 2002.

Associated Landscape Contractors of Colorado

The following book may be ordered from ALCC. Call 1-303-757-5611 or visit www.alcc.com.

Specifications Handbook for Landscape, Irrigation and Maintenance Contracting. Associated Landscape Contractors of Colorado, Revised Edition 2003.

Landscape Irrigation

International Society of Arboriculture
The following book may be ordered from ISA. Call 1-217-355-9411 or visit www.isa-arbor.com.

Best Management Practices, International Society of Arboriculture, 2004, Champagne, IL.

Irrigation Association
The following materials may be ordered from the Irrigation Association. Call 703-536-7080 or visit www.irrigation.org.

Handbook of Water Use and Conservation, Vickers, Amy, WaterPlow Press, 2001.

Handbook of Technical Irrigation Information, Hunter Industries, 2009.

Irrigation 5th Edition, Irrigation Association, 2000.

Turf and Landscape Irrigation Best Management Practices, Irrigation Association, 2010.

Turfgrass Water Conservation, Gibeault, Victor A. and Stephen T. Cockerham, ANR Publications, 1985.

Xeriscape Update: Planning and Practice, Zoldoske, David and Verne P.J. Farley, 1990.

Additional resources

The Complete Business Manual for Landscape, Irrigation & Maintenance Contractors with Labor and Production Times, Vander Kooi, Charles, 2005.

Drip Irrigation for Every Landscape and All Climates: Helping Your Garden Flourish, While Conserving Water!, Kourik, Robert, 1993.

Grade Easy: An Introductory Course in the Principles and Practices of Grading and Drainage, Untermann, Richard K., American Society of Landscape Architects, 1997.

Handbook of Architectural Civil Drafting, Nelson, John A., Chapman & Hall, 1983.

Horticultural Science, Fourth Edition, Janick, Jules, W.H. Freeman, 1986.

Landscape Management: Planting and Maintenance of Trees, Shrubs, and Turfgrasses. Feucht, J.R. & J.D. Butler, Van Nostrand Reinhold Co., 1988.

Native Trees, Shrubs and Vines for Urban and Rural America: A Planting Design Manual for Environmental Designers, Hightshoe, Gary L., John Wiley & Sons, Inc., 1987.

Principles and Practices of Grading, Drainage, and Road Alignment: An Ecologic Approach, Untermann, Richard K., Prentice Hall, 1996.

Simplified Site Engineering, 2nd Edition, Parker, Harry & John W. MacGuire, John Wiley and Sons, Inc., 1997.

Southwestern Landscaping with Native Plants, Phillips, Judith, Museum of New Mexico Press, 1987.

Sunset Western Garden Book, Sunset Books Inc., 1995.

Vocational Skills Training for Segmental Paver Installation, Jones, Stephen, Pave Tech, Inc., 2003.

The Xeriscape Flower Gardener: A Waterwise Guide for the Rocky Mountain Region, Knopf, Jim, Johnson Books, 1991.

Xeriscape Gardening, Water Conservation for the American Landscape, Stephens, Tom, Doug Welsh and Connie Ellefson, Macmillan Publishing, 1992.

Xeriscape Handbook: A How-To Guide to Natural Resource – Wise Gardening, Weinstein, Gayle, 1999.

Xeriscaping Guide for Dry-Summer, Cold-Winter Climates, Bennett, Jennifer, 1998.

Plant Hardiness Zones

For more information about Plant Hardiness Zones and close-ups of regional zones, go to the Web site for the United States National Arboretum: http://www.usna.usda.gov and click on Gardens and Horticulture.

For detailed information about the Canadian plant zones go to the Canadian Soil Information System Web site: http://sis.agr.gc.ca/cansis/nsdb/climate/hardiness/intro.html

Glossary

Allowable depletion
The amount of depletion of plant available water (PAW) from the soil that is considered acceptable before watering. Determined by multiplying the plant available water by the management allowable depletion (MAD). Allowable depletion is expressed in inches or millimetres.

Amendment
Any substance, such as manure, peat or mulch, used to alter the properties of soil.

Annual
A plant that germinates, grows, produces flowers and seeds, and completes its life cycle within one growing season.

Available water
The difference in the amount of water contained in soil at field capacity and the amount at the permanent wilting point.

Backfill
Soil used to fill a planting hole after the plant has been positioned. Amended soil is often used as backfill.

Backflow
The flow of water back from the water distribution system, the irrigation pipes, to the potable water source.

Balled and burlapped (B & B)
A way of packaging plants in which the roots are contained in a ball of soil held together in burlap.

Batter
The distance that each course or layer of a segmental retaining wall is set back from the underlying layer or course.

Benchmark (BM)
A fixed point with a known elevation. Used when surveying.

Best management practices (BMPs)
A group of design, installation, maintenance and management practices that conserve resources and protect the quality of the environment while being economically feasible and widely applicable. For example, the Irrigation Association has published "Turf and Landscape Irrigation Best Management Practices."

Biennial
A plant that completes its life cycle in two years.

Branch collar
Trunk tissue that forms around the base of a branch where it attaches to the main stem or a lateral. As a branch decreases in vigor or begins to die, the branch collar becomes more pronounced.

Branch ridges
The raised area of bark in the branch crotch that marks the junction of the branch wood and trunk wood.

Broadcast
To scatter seed, fertilizer or other material over the ground.

Caliper
The diameter of a tree trunk measured 6" (15 cm) above ground level for trees up to 4" (100 mm) caliper and 12" (30 cm) above the ground for larger sizes.

Cane
A stem of a shrub. Multi-caned shrubs are preferred because of their fuller form.

Clay
Very fine soil particles. Clay soils (soils containing a high percentage of clay particles) are often called heavy soils and are characterized by slow movement of water through the soil. Clay soils can be improved with soil amendments, such as manure, peat or mulch.

Conifer
A group of plants, mostly evergreen, that produces its seeds in cones.

Container stock
Trees or shrubs packaged with their roots and a growing medium in a plastic or peat-fiber container.

Course
Each layer or row of a segmental retaining wall. Each course is usually set back (called the batter) from the underlying course. It is important that the base course be placed on a properly compacted base because the base course determines the alignment of all succeeding courses.

Datum
A level surface used as a reference for elevations when surveying for grading and drainage.

Deciduous
A tree or shrub that loses all of its leaves at once, usually in the fall.

Disease
A pathogen that impairs the normal function or development of a plant.

Evapotranspiration (ET)
The combination of evaporation (water loss from land and water surfaces) and transpiration (water loss from plants).

Evergreen
Plants that do not lose all of their leaves at once. Evergreens can be conifers or broad-leaved.

Field capacity
The point at which soil becomes saturated and cannot absorb any more water.

Fertilization
The application of nutrients to promote plant vitality.

Girdling
To cut or constrict bark so that growth is slowed or stopped by inhibiting the movement of nutrients. Girdling can harm or kill plants. Root girdling occurs when roots begin to grow around the main stem of the tree and cut off or restrict the movement of water, plant nutrients and stored food reserves. Tree straps, initially installed for support, can also cause girdling if not removed.

Gradient
A measure of the change in elevation in relation to the change in distance. Gradient is expressed as a decimal and is always a positive number.

Guy
A rope or wire used as a tree support.

Hardpan
A layer of hard or compacted soil impenetrable to plant roots, water and nutrients.

Hardscape
"Hard" areas, such as patios, decks, driveways, paths and sidewalks or walls, that do not require irrigation.

Herbaceous
Plants with soft, non-woody stems. Generally refers to plants that die back to the ground each year.

Herbicide
A substance used to kill plants. An herbicide can be selective (designed to kill a narrow range of plants) or non-selective (designed to kill any plant it contacts). Herbicides can also be pre-emergent or post-emergent.

Hybrid
A cross between two plants of different variety, species or genus. Hybrids are usually created to produce plants with specific characteristics, such as disease resistance, unique flower color, etc.

Hydrozone
A distinct grouping of plants with similar water and climatic needs.

Infiltration rate
The rate at which water is absorbed into the soil. Clay soils have low infiltration rates; sandy soils have high infiltration rates.

Insecticide
A substance used to kill insects.

Instrument
Also known as a level or builder's level. A builder's level is a tripod-mounted telescope and spirit level used to sight markings on a leveling rod in order to determine elevations on a site. See also, Transit.

Integrated pest management (IPM)
EPA definition: The coordinated use of pest and environmental information with available pest control methods to prevent unacceptable levels of pest damage by the most economical means and with the least possible hazard to people, property and the environment.

Irrigation
The application of water to the soil to nourish plants.

Lateral branch
A branch growing out of a main trunk or stem.

Lateral line
An irrigation pipe that goes from a control valve to sprinkler heads, emitters, etc.

Leader
The dominant vertical branch that extends above the other branches.

Loam
A soil type composed of clay, silt and sand particles in relatively equal amounts. Loam is considered ideal for plants because it drains well but does not dry out quickly.

Macronutrient
One of the three major plant nutrients—nitrogen, phosphorus and potassium—required by plants in large amounts.

Mainline
An irrigation line that receives water from the source and distributes it to the control valves.

Management Allowable Depletion (MAD)
Also known as maximum allowable depletion, allowable depletion or allowable soil water depletion. The portion of plant available water that is allowed to be depleted for plant use prior to irrigation based on plant and management considerations. Expressed as a percent of the available water capacity. A medium-value turf is typically managed at 50% MAD, whereas a low-value turf may be managed at 75% MAD.

Microclimate
The climate of a specific area in the landscape that has substantially differing sun exposure, temperature or wind than surrounding areas or the area as a whole.

Micronutrient
A nutrient required by plants in small or trace quantities. There are several essential micronutrients, which do not include the plant macronutrients.

Organic matter (OM)
Naturally occurring material, such as manure, sewage sludge, peat, grass clippings, etc. Organic matter is often used as a soil amendment.

Perennial
A plant that lives for more than two years.

Permanent wilting point
The point at which plant roots can no longer extract water from the soil.

Pest
Something that can negatively impact plants. Weeds, undesirable insects and diseases are all considered pests.

Pesticide
Any substance or mixture of substances intended to prevent, destroy or control any pest, including unwanted species of plants or animals causing harm

and vectors of human or animal disease. The term includes substances intended for use as a plant growth regulator, defoliant, desiccant or agent for thinning fruit or preventing the premature fall of fruit. (Definition adapted from the Food and Agriculture Organization of the United Nations).

pH
The measure of a soil's acidity or alkalinity on a scale of 0 to 14. A pH of 7 is considered neutral. A pH under 7 designates acidic soil, while a pH over 7 designates alkaline or basic soil.

Phloem
Complex tissue that conducts food in woody plants.

Photosynthesis
The process by which plants produce their food using water, carbon dioxide and energy derived from sunlight.

Pitot tubes
A device for measuring the speed of fluid flow. A recommended tool for water audits.

Plant available water (PAW)
The available water located in the root zone. Expressed in inches or millimetres and is calculated by multiplying the root zone depth by available water.

Pore space
Spaces within soil that contain air and water.

Post-emergent herbicide
A chemical that kills plants after they have emerged from soil.

Pre-emergent herbicide
A chemical that kills plants after seeds have germinated but before plants have emerged from soil.

Root bound
The condition in which a plant's roots have become tangled and matted from growing in a container too long. This can lead to girdling of the roots. If planted without relieving this condition, a root bound plant will not grow well or anchor normally. Tall plants are in danger of toppling in high winds.

Runoff
The portion of rain or irrigation water on an area that is lost without entering the soil.

Sand
Large soil particles. Sandy soils (soils containing a high percentage of sand particles) are characterized by rapid water movement through the soil. Sandy soils can be improved with soil amendments such as manure, peat or mulch.

Scarify
To cut, scratch or loosen roots or soil before planting to prevent plants from being root bound.

Silt
Soil particles that are larger than clay and smaller than sand.

Soil salinity
The measure of soluble salts contained in soil. A high soil salinity can impair plant growth.

Soil structure
The combination of various soil particles (sand, silt, clay) that create a distinctive shape or arrangement. Single particles when naturally assembled into aggregates define the characteristics of pore spaces.

Soil texture
The coarseness or fineness of a soil, determined by the proportion of sand, silt and clay particles in its composition.

Specimen
The highest quality of the species available.

Stress
Any condition that can cause a plant to function abnormally or sub-optimally. Some causes of plant stress are disease and other pests, lack of water, sunlight or nutrients and poor soil.

Sunscald
Injury to plant tissue resulting from exposure to intense sunlight. Sunscald can cause bark to crack or split.

Surveying
The mathematical science that deals with measuring the earth's surface. Survey data and techniques are used to produce maps, create site designs and lay out landscape projects.

Sustainable landscape management
Practices for designing, creating and maintaining healthy and attractive landscapes that require fewer natural resources and low energy requirements, and are beneficial to the environment. Practices are numerous and include plant selection, water management, selection of materials, reuse and recycling, IPM programs and energy conservation.

Topping
Cutting a currently growing or one-year-old shoot back to a bud. Also refers to cutting an older branch or stem back to a lateral branch that is not large enough to assume the terminal role.

Translocation
The process by which water and nutrients move through a plant's vascular system (xylem and phloem).

Transpiration
The process by which plants emit water vapor through their leaves.

Water basin
A circular ridge of soil formed under a tree or shrub to contain water by preventing runoff during irrigation or rain.

Weed
An unwanted plant, often having an aggressive growth habit that can choke out more desirable plants.

Winter hardy
A plant's ability to withstand winter conditions.

Wound wood
The callus tissue produced by the cambium (the layer under the bark) that initially forms a thick ring around the wound. This ring is the wound wood. Eventually it may completely cover the exposed wood. Avoid wound dressings since they may prevent wound wood formation, which is the tree's natural healing response.

Xylem
Complex tissue that conducts water in woody plants.

Landscape Irrigation

Notes: